ADVANCE PRAISE FOR

TEACHING PETER McLAREN

"*Teaching Peter McLaren* is provocative, thorough, timely, engaging, challenging, reflective, critical, outstanding, unique, witty, and above all, a superb and needed contribution to the understanding of one of the most influential pedagogues of our times. In this book, Marc Pruyn and Luis Huerta-Charles put together the most comprehensive collection of articles addressing the contributions, changes, contradictions, influences, background, and potential of the ideas and praxis of a revolutionary scholar who has been a very creative, forceful, and brave voice for more than 30 years—Peter McLaren. This is the book that those who are passionate and committed to the creation of a better society and the urgent need to re-invent schooling as a space for social change and meaningful learning are waiting to read."

—*Gustavo Enrique Fischman, Arizona State University*

"*Teaching Peter McLaren* not only engages the work of one of the most formidable political sociologists in the field of education, it also sounds a challenge to educators and researchers worldwide that the purpose of educational research is not to explain the world, but to transform it. In a field that most often marginalizes its voices of dissent, it is heartening to see a book that honors one of our most outspoken and influential intellectuals and activists."

—*Kris Gutierrez, University of California, Los Angeles*

"*Teaching Peter McLaren* offers a wide-ranging critical analysis of one of education's most vibrant writers. The book itself provides an important historical overview of Peter McLaren's scholarly work across two decades, and the scholars brought together by Marc Pruyn and Luis Huerta-Charles present a rich polyvocal account of McLaren's significant contributions to critical pedagogy and social theory. Undergraduate, graduate, and academic readers alike will find this text an invaluable reference resource."

—*Michele Knobel, Montclair State University*

"Using his own rich experience as a teacher-activist, and with the inspiration of Paulo Freire and Ché Guevara, Peter McLaren has amazingly re-shaped Western pedagogy into a liberatory weapon for all oppressed people. This collection of essays on his work is an eloquent testimony to McLaren's powerful contribution to the discipline of education as a transformative critique and emancipatory praxis."

—*E. San Juan, Jr., Director of the Philippines Cultural Studies Center, Connecticut; Author of* Racism and Cultural Studies *and* Beyond Postcolonial Theory

"For more than three decades, Peter McLaren's provocative and passionate contributions to educational, social, and political thought have influenced and inspired pedagogues and activists the world over. Through both words and deeds, McLaren has unrelentingly challenged the myriad forms of injustice that exist in the world and has tirelessly committed his energies to the struggle for transformative social change. *Teaching Peter McLaren* is at once a remarkable testament to his formidable career and a critical engagement with his unique theoretical formulations. This welcome, overdue, and comprehensive book is a powerful tribute to the rich tapestry of McLaren's life work, and a must-read for all those who still believe that another world is indeed possible."

—Valerie Scatamburlo-D'Annibale, University of Windsor, Ontario, Canada

"Marc Pruyn and Luis Huerta-Charles have excelled by inviting scholars to submit powerful accounts of Peter McLaren's work for *Teaching Peter McLaren.* The narratives offered in this book capture the soul of McLaren's lifetime struggle to shift teaching and teachers beyond the confines of classroom management and schooling authoritarianism. Pruyn and Huerta-Charles bring together an unparalleled group of scholars whose work outside the canons make Peter McLaren's work praiseworthy. The reformation of teacher education does not lie in the production of more tests and accountability schemes as promoted by the misguided and under-funded *No Child Left Behind* initiative; it is located closer to an on-going discussion regarding the contextual pedagogical needs of learners. *Teaching Peter McLaren* points us in that direction."

—Hermán S. García, New Mexico State University

"*Teaching Peter McLaren* is a poignant and powerful testament to one of the greatest educational scholars of our time. The authors do not simply venerate McLaren, but rather provide critical and reflective insights to the mind and impact of McLaren as a teacher, scholar, and mentor. As students of McLaren, they have clearly all learned their lessons well: to be unflinchingly honest, engaging, passionate, critical, and creative in their writing while always remaining true to 'the project' of dismantling the structures of inequality and injustice. The fact that the text itself emerges as a transformative treatise, a revolutionary entreaty about a revolutionary scholar, is perhaps the greatest tribute one could make to the life and work of Peter McLaren. This book is a must read for students and educators everywhere as it manifests what real teaching and learning is all about."

—Sandy Grande, Associate Professor, Connecticut College;
Author of Red Pedagogy: Native American Social & Political Thought

TEACHING

PETER McLAREN

TEACHING
CONTEMPORARY
SCHOLARS

Shirley R. Steinberg & Joe L. Kincheloe
General Editors

Vol. 1

PETER LANG
New York • Washington, D.C./Baltimore • Bern
Frankfurt am Main • Berlin • Brussels • Vienna • Oxford

TEACHING PETER McLAREN

PATHS OF DISSENT

MARC PRUYN &
LUIS M. HUERTA-CHARLES | Editors

PETER LANG
New York • Washington, D.C./Baltimore • Bern
Frankfurt am Main • Berlin • Brussels • Vienna • Oxford

Library of Congress Cataloging-in-Publication Data

Teaching Peter McLaren / edited by Marc Pruyn, Luis M. Huerta-Charles.
p. cm. — (Teaching contemporary scholars; vol. 1)
Includes bibliographical references and index.
1. McLaren, Peter, 1948– —Influence.
2. Critical pedagogy. I. Pruyn, Marc.
II. Huerta Charles, Luis M. III. Series.
LB880.M393T43 370.11'5—dc22 2004006757
ISBN 0-8204-6145-8
ISSN 1533-4082

Bibliographic information published by **Die Deutsche Bibliothek**.
Die Deutsche Bibliothek lists this publication in the "Deutsche Nationalbibliografie"; detailed bibliographic data is available on the Internet at http://dnb.ddb.de/.

Cover art by Roy Carter
Cover design by Lisa Barfield

The paper in this book meets the guidelines for permanence and durability of the Committee on Production Guidelines for Book Longevity of the Council of Library Resources.

275 Seventh Avenue, 28th Floor, New York, NY 10001
www.peterlangusa.com

Printed in the United States of America

This book is dedicated to the working class; our sisters and brothers, the world over, who produce the planet's wealth, yet see so little of it. May this change. May we change it. Together. Hasta un mundo con justicia social, justicia económica y dignidad para todas. M.P.

To all the teachers who work hard in their classrooms to make a better world. And to those who make it possible to find hope within hopelessness and who fight for justice in an unjust world. L.H.-Ch.

Table of Contents

Acknowledgments

There are many wonderful, beautiful and special coleg@s, compañer@s, luchadoras/es and amig@s that have professionally and personally enriched our lives; people that bring us inspiration, joy, intellectual challenge, compañerism@ y quietud—que nos han mostrado el vacío fértil. We would like to thank these folks. Please also understand that any weaknesses in this volume (and there are most likely more than a few) are entirely la culpa nuestra. Any strengths in this text are the result of the high quality scholarship of the contributors and the following lovely people that have helped to make us who we are.

Marc would like to thank Chris Adams, Betsy Cahill, Joseph Carroll-Miranda, Silvia Chávez Baray, Rudolfo Chávez Chávez, Stacey Duncan, Gustavo Fischman, Roberto Leví Gallegos, Hermán García, Jeannie Gonsier-Gerdin, Rob Haworth, Amy M. Lam Wai Man, Kaitlin Alaím Langston, Mostafa MahieEddine, Curry Malott, Grace Martínez, Tallulah Moore, Jim O'Donnell and Jacquie Valencia.

Luis would like to thank Karen Huerta-García, Rudolfo Chávez Chávez, Jim O'Donnell, Hermán García, Irma Alanís-Cantú, Loui Reyes, Betsy Cahill, Grace Martínez, Juan Sánchez-García, María Mercado, Myriam Torres, Roberto Rentería-Espinoza and Ángel Alvarado.

And together, we'd like to thank a few other people as well. First, we'd like to express our appreciation to Shirley Steinberg and Joe Kincheloe; not only for being the dear, inclusive people that they are, but also for contributing so much to the progressive educational literature (as editors and as authors), including this new series. Second, we'd like to thank the supportive and hard working folks at Peter Lang Publishing; namely, Sophie Appel, Lisa Dillon, Stephanie Heuler, Patricia Mulrane, Chris Myers, Bernadette Shade and all the other people who work behind the scenes. It has been a pleasure as editors to work with this talented team. Third, we'd like to thank Roymieco Carter, who produced the original artwork that Lang turned into what the two of us think is an unique and striking cover. Check out Roy's other work at www.cartermedia.com.

Fourth, and finally, we would like to thank Peter McLaren himself. Peter's consistent calls for, and philosophical organizing efforts around, a critique of the ugliness and inhumanity that is capitalism, and its replacement with a revolutionary, loving socialism, over that past three decades, has been his constant message. This Marxist- and praxis-driven clarion call has been unfailing, poetic, far reaching and inspirational, the world over. Peter McLaren is our brother in the struggle for a more just world.

PART ONE

INTRODUCTIONS AND CONTEXTS

Foreword

Shirley R. Steinberg

This is a preface to a body of work in which I do not claim to praise, nor to bury, Peter McLaren. Rather, my humble words attempt to embrace him. Peter McLaren is a unique character placed in the script of an oh-so-bland three-act play located in the cultural and educational bowels of our absurdist realities. His multi-dimensions of humor, style, commitment, intellect and humanness allow the other players to thrive as he prompts them to dig deeper into their pedagogical and political souls. Peter makes us look good as teachers, as Peter is a teacher of teachers. He has proudly declared his allegiance to education and has demanded that other disciplines take note of the depth and nature of critical pedagogy.

Marc and Luis, and the authors of this volume, have succeeded in capturing the pedagogical essence of Peter McLaren. Avoiding the slurpy, sycophantic syrup of a festschrift, each contributor has added to the script and invited the audience to become participants within the teaching act. We were all challenged as we wrote for this volume, for writing about a writer and teaching about a teacher are indeed difficult. I believe everyone between these covers has risen to the task.

As you read through these essays, pair them with Peter's own words. Visit or re-visit his earliest work, wandering the corridors from which he first heard the cries that drew him to his life work. Seek those rituals which perform, with or without our assistance. Remind yourself of his vast knowledge, from the trivial to the solemn. It will be easy to see why this book needed to be published, why these words needed to unite in solidarity. McLaren is not one of the matinee idol pedagogues who seek the converted to reify his own position. He is an essential player for our psyches.

I invite you to enter this play with a pen in one hand and the works of Freire, Marx, Dewey, Frida and the others at your side. See how these muses weave in and out of his words and how he creates new entrances, new exits, and new levels from which we view. And imagine, if you will, this accessible, hilariously funny and angry participant negotiating the universe. Try to evoke the fullness of the educational left, eschewing the ridiculously stupid whining of past voices who have attempted to devalue Peter's words as they accuse him for being white and a male. Use Peter, add to his voice, argue with him, and share him—and never underestimate his loyalty and devotion to students, colleagues, social justice and to making this stage larger and just a bit more tolerable.

Preface

Reading Peter McLaren

Antonia Darder

I want to say words that flame.

Rumi

In the midst of enormous chaos and transition in my life, I was asked to write a few words about Peter McLaren for this book. I hesitated, not knowing how I might do justice to the task at hand. Then one morning, while reading the poet Rumi, I was struck by the passage above—for to say "words that flame" seems to have been one of the rare passions I saw in Peter McLaren from the day we first met.

In the late 1980s, I attended a conference on the work of Paulo Freire at the University of California, Irvine. Little did I know at the time that the event was to mark both my initiation into what is now commonly known as the field of critical pedagogy and the beginning of a lifelong friendship with my comrade, Peter McLaren. But in all honesty, I must confess that although I appreciated his rhetorical gift, unusual language and powerful writings, I did not easily warm up to the man. In fact, it took years for me to recognize the biases and prejudices that sharply colored my impressions. Yet despite my aloofness, Peter persisted in his efforts to engage me whenever the opportunity arose.

Today I'm grateful for his patience and perseverance. For what I learned over time was that Peter McLaren is one of the kindest and most generous souls that I have ever met in the world of academia. Yes, like so many of us pitiful humans, he forever struggles with personal questions of insecurity and self-doubt—but like few, he is ever willing to extend a hand and create opportunities for comrades and struggling young scholars who seek his support. I mention this because there are often those who are simply content to write radical discourses of solidarity without considering what these might mean in the real world. Peter, on the other hand, has been truly concerned with constructing relationships of solidarity in the living, whether it is with high-powered international scholars or the graduate students who engage him in the lecture halls and the university classrooms.

So, having revealed the more obscure and seldom-spoken impressions about this formidable scholar, I'll turn briefly to Peter McLaren's outstanding contributions to the field of critical educational theory. McLaren is, by far, one of the most prolific writers in the academy today. Published in journals around the world, with books and articles translated into various languages, he has extended widely a critical vision of what constitutes a revolutionary pedagogy in the midst of an internationalized economy and its ravaging violence upon the poor and disenfranchised.

Toward this end, Peter McLaren has courageously struggled to retrieve from his own work, as well as the work of other critical education theorists, a forthright critique of capitalism and its obstruction of a vision and practice of democratic schooling in this country. Despite the seductive nature of the postmodern twist, which took hold of many left scholars in the last decade, Peter McLaren forged out of the fog and returned to the most basic and central question begging address: How does the structure of capitalism and class formation, bolstered by such powerful ideologies as racism, sexism and heterosexism, continue to structure and perpetuate the tenacious inequalities at work in American schools and society today? The use of his fiery writing prowess and extensive influence in the field to grapple deeply with questions of capital marked a significant shift in the discourse of critical educators everywhere.

In the preface to *Ché Guevara, Paulo Freire and the Pedagogy of Revolution*, Joe Kincheloe dubbed Peter McLaren "the poet laureate of the educational Left." There is no question in my mind that Peter, whose passion is truly to say "words that flame," is well deserving of this honor, given his highly imaginative use of language and the eloquence of his rhetorical style, which cannot easily be matched today. What is even more significant here is the manner in which this man has committed and dedicated his intellectual vitality and brilliance toward championing a politics of social justice, human rights and economic democracy—an extraordinary feat that merits recognition whenever one teaches Peter McLaren.

Introduction

Teaching Peter McLaren: The Scholar and This Volume

Marc Pruyn and Luis Huerta-Charles

This introduction both sets the stage for the chapters that follow and provides the editors with an opportunity to share individually their knowledge of Peter McLaren and his intellectual endeavors over the past thirty years. Separate essays by Marc Pruyn and Luis Huerta-Charles contextualize their understanding of McLaren in a way that reflects their readings of, interactions with and teaching of the scholar. These will serve to introduce and outline the three major sections of the book: "The Arc and Impact of McLaren's Work," "McLaren Across Contexts" and "McLaren the Marxist." At the same time, the editors will consider how they, and others teaching McLaren, have encouraged students to travel the metaphorical and actual "paths of dissent" that have been the result of Peter's theoretical cartographic labor power.

1. Peter McLaren: Enfleshing a Praxis of Karlos

by Marc Pruyn

The Man with the Ché Tattoo

I've been fortunate enough to know two Ché nuts personally. Well, "Ché nuts" may be a little harshly put, so let's say Ché *aficionados*, Ché *celebrants*. The first can best be described as a male European North American doctoral student, Vietnam veteran and Hoosier enthusiast in his early fifties who wandered the halls of New México State University's Department of Curriculum & Instruction, here in the Chihuahuan Borderlands. And he wandered in a most interesting costume (we all, of course, wear costumes), one that included items (t-shirts, bags, buttons, baseball caps, coffee mugs) honoring and celebrating his support for the ideas of Ernesto "Ché" Guevara, his boosterism for a certain Iowa college sports team and his military service in Southeast Asia thirty years ago. The second can best be described as a male European North American professor and criticalist who regularly sported black Levis, hipster vests and black combat boots and wandered the halls of UCLA's Graduate School of Education & Information Science when it was temporarily relocated (just after one of LA's frequent—although this one a bit more destructive than most—earthquakes) on an entire floor in a sterile office building in downtown Westwood. He had long blond hair that half-hid his face, John Lennon glasses that didn't seem to quite fit the mid-1990s, a hammer-and-sickle ring and a set of unassuming shoulders that would soon boast two tattoo portraits: one of Emiliano Zapata and another of Ernesto Guevara.

Like I said, Ché nuts.

The first fellow was Randy. He died not long ago at the young age of 53. He worked as my graduate assistant. I chaired his doctoral committee. Randy was a sweet, kind, interesting, enthusiastic, bright, hard working and enigmatic guy who was really excited to be pursuing advanced graduate work in our department. He had only recently joined us in education after a stint in the History Department, where his thesis focused on the Cuban revolution. And even though Randy only knew Ernesto for a short time, he sure loved him! I had been really looking forward to exploring his (and my own!) contradictions and complex positionalities over many cups of rich, darkly roasted coffee here in our town of 100,000 souls at Milagro's coffee house.

The second fellow is Peter McLaren. He is alive and well and living off of Sunset Boulevard in the belly of the beast, in the gut of capital's dream factory (where I grew up).

Why do I bring up Randy's and Peter's mutual admiration for Ché Guevara? For several reasons. First, Ché speaks to us. He speaks to us through his writings and speeches, but he especially speaks to us through his living revolutionary example of solidarity, internationalism, optimism, populism and activism; through his living radical praxis. Ché did not only espouse the socialist ideal of the "new person," he embodied it; like Paulo Freire, Sojourner Truth, Miles Horton, Emma Goldman and Peter McLaren. Ché is a beacon on the left, a rallying Marxist fog horn, especially in these times of neo-liberalism, structural adjustment and super-exploitation. Peter serves the same function on the educational left.

Second, it was Ché who helped me, as a pedagogue, lead Randy to Peter. Ché was Randy's introduction to left theory and practice. Then he came over to education. During our first meeting, Randy asked, "Who should I read in education on the left? Who is advancing the ideas of Ché within education?" Well, for me, and for so many others, that's Peter McLaren. I reached over to my bookshelf—three feet from where I'm writing this right now—and pulled out Peter's *Ché Guevara, Paulo Freire and the Pedagogy of Revolution* (2000a) and photocopied (sorry, Peter, and copyright lawyers!) section one: "The Man in the Black Beret." I told Randy, "Read this." And although Randy's first reading of this text was not unproblematic—more below—I was able to nudge him into intellectually strolling through the fascinating and varied terrain of left educationalists. Of course, for those seriously interested in left pedagogy, McLaren is a must-read. Some begin this philosophical foray with Freire (I did; 1970, 1985) or Bigelow (1985, 1991) or Weiler (1988, 1991) or Loewen (1995) or Kincheloe (1998; Kincheloe, Steinberg & Chennault, 1998) or Steinberg (Steinberg, Kincheloe & Hinchey, 1999) or Slattery (1995). Randy began with Peter. And Peter began with Ché (and Paulo). But today, any serious engagement with left theory, politics, philosophy, ideology or research in education has to include McLaren. For many, it starts with McLaren. It did for Randy.

Readers, I would like to be completely frank with you. While this essay will certainly attempt to expound upon and critique the central ideas put forth in the work of Peter McLaren, it is largely a personal accounting of how McLaren's work has affected me, first as a teacher, then as a graduate student and finally as a professor.

Reading Peter McLaren

How, when, where and why did I first read McLaren? How did I first engage with his revolutionary ideas? Well, this requires a little back-story. So please bear with me.

I was a bilingual elementary school teacher for nine years in the 1980s and 1990s in Los Angeles' Pico Union District—where working-class Central Americans and Mexicans (fleeing Reagan and capital's wars of terror and economic domination) made their North American homes. I was born in LA, in Gotham-West; attended Hollywood High School; earned my BA from UCLA in political science (although, really, in political activism, Bob Marley & the Wailers, red wine and the study of Marxism); became an emergency credentialed bilingual teacher (I was bilingual and wanted to work with the Central American community I had become an activist within years before); earned a teaching credential and MA in bilingual/multicultural education from Cal State Dominguez Hills (a wonderful university that serves its Latina/o, African American and working-class communities well); and began a doctorate—back at my old alma mater, UCLA—in the early 1990s. I began to pursue PhD work at "la ucla" because of the encouragement of Max, Sylvina and Philip at Dominguez Hills; and because—thanks to our strong teachers' union, United Teachers-Los Angeles—we had a good contract at the time with the school district that would give us extra pay for completed post-graduate work. It wasn't until I began taking classes with Carl, Kris, Jeannie, Carlos, Harold and Peter, though, that I began to consider professorin' seriously as a job.

I became politically active in the 1980s as an undergraduate at UCLA, around issues first of divestment/anti-apartheid in South Africa, then against war and imperialism in Central and South America and in Palestine. That's when I became a leftie. As an undergraduate I read Marx—a lot of Marx—and Ché and Mao and Fidel and Braverman and Tucker and Goldman and X. In my master's work in education, I first sought out the leftie freaks, of course. That led me to Freire (1970, 1985) and Horton (Adams, 1972, 1975) and Bowles and Gintis (1976) and Apple (1979, 1982) and Giroux (1988) and McLaren (1986, 1989). But, as is the case with many of our students (including Randy, who after reading Peter's engrossing and important *Ché & Paulo* book [2000a] was a little befuddled), I had a hard time. I was into the progressive ideas that linked dominant educational practices with capital, exploitation and oppression (through systems of socialization), but the discursive practices of these new authors (some of whom I was reading in translation), and the new, specialized vocabulary they employed, was a bit daunting to me. But I got as much as I could out of these texts at the time, reflected upon them and continued being a mostly "liberal" pedagogue striving to understand and birth my inner criticalist.

It wasn't until several years later, in Carl Weinberg's educational foundations class, during my first semester as a UCLA doctoral student, that I reengaged with the educational left. For a read-critique-and-report-back assignment for Carl, I drew McLaren. I went to town: *Schooling as a Ritual Performance* (1986), *Life in Schools* (1989), *Cries from the Corridor* (1980). I also re-read Freire (1970, 1985). And I discovered Weiler (1988) and Aronowitz (1991) and Fine (Fine, Powell, Weis & Mun Wong, 1996) and Sleeter (1996). And as I journeyed through these texts (some afresh), I experienced a discursive and intellectual breakthrough: I *got* it! I was in the groove. I understood these folks, or at least began to. But two texts in particular were pivotal, and I happened to be reading them together: Freire's *Pedagogy of the Oppressed* (1970) and McLaren's *Life in Schools* (1989). In *Pedagogy*, I began to feel Freire's words and experiences and vision for emancipatory education. I felt his passion, caring and revolutionary love. In *Schools*, I felt all the same things, and—because of Peter's amazing command of language (and who, as Antonia mentioned above, has been dubbed the "poet laureate of the educational left" by Kincheloe) and his ability to combine classroom data and highbrow, sophisticated forms of philosophical analyses (see *Performance* and *Schools*! Hijola!)—I understood how the educational left situated itself and viewed struggle within pedagogical and other contexts.

Later, from the Chair of my dissertation committee, Kris Gutierrez—an amazing and inspirational sociocultural/sociolinguistic theorist and researcher—I learned that Peter was actually seeking a position at UCLA, that he was thinking of leaving the University of Miami in Oxford, Ohio, where he had worked for years with Henry Giroux—another important and foundational member of the criticalist community, some would venture an *original gangsta* (or is that, "*pranksta*"? A tip of the hat to The Offspring) of critical pedagogy, along with Freire, Bowles and Gintis, McLaren and Apple—to come and work with us. And Peter did indeed come and join our intellectual community in the privileged hills of Westwood/Brentwood, Los Angeles, to help us understand, theorize and advance a critical pedagogy for social justice. But he didn't stay in the hills, and neither did we; nor were we *from* those hills. We returned to East-Los to Pico Union to South-Central to Venice to Glendale to Culver City to the Valley to Hollywood. And we took Peter with us. And we did research together. And we wrote together. And we learned together. It was really something.

That's how I first read Peter McLaren: in privileged UCLA seminar rooms; in my Hollywood neighborhood late at night with LAPD helicopter spotlights and loudspeakers booming out, invading and harassing the Latinas/os and Armenians of my working-class neighborhood; on and in the East LA elementary playgrounds and classrooms where we conducted our team research; over conversations at coffee houses in one of the world's Queer Meccas, West Hollywood; working as his research assistant. That is how I first (successfully) began to read and understand McLaren, and critical pedagogy.

Now I live in the Chihuahuan Borderlands that surround the Las Cruces, El Paso and Ciudad Juárez corridor. And McLaren's work is as relevant and inspiring as ever. Some, myself included, would even argue that his current theorizing and writing is even more relevant today than it was in the 1980s, with his return (con ganas!) to analyses of political economy in the face of that ugly juggernaut that is global capitalism and the reign of Baby Bush.

What are McLaren's central ideas? What has been the arc of his intellectual endeavors over the past thirty years? Where has he made "errors"? What should he be doing that he is not? Or has not? What are his strengths? His weaknesses? Although I feel that others could probably address this much more thoroughly and eloquently than I ever could (including Luis, below), I will give it a try.

I have known three theoretical Peters: (1) populist Marxist Peter, (2) Marxist postmodernist Peter and (3) full-on Marxist Peter. And I think all three of these men have always existed, and still exist, in this Irish/Catholic/Canadian/North American radical white boy. I also believe each of these Peters is defensible, and has made important contributions, given how and when they existed. They have been helpful to us as theorists, scholars and pedagogues. Of course, each is also worthy of critique.

When I began reading Peter at UCLA, then when he came to live, work and theorize with us, what spoke to me was his radicalism. What drew me, and draws so many today, is what drew Randy and Peter to Ché. It is an unflinching and populist commitment to accurately and intensely scrutinize and critique the economic system under which most of us in the world live, the system that is at the heart of so much of humanity's suffering: capitalism, an economic and ontological system—a way of knowing and acting—that praises greed, individualistic accumulation and selfishness, over sharing, compassion and the collective good. Direct, honest and no-holds-barred analyses of these types speak to us. We know capitalism is wrong. We know that global economies driven by the profit imperative will lead to falsely created "scarcity," perpetual war (who will be *next* to join W's axis of evil, Malta?), mass starvation (can 30,000 children starving to death every day in a capitalist world that produces enough food to feed us all be right?) and meaningless (and dehumanizing and dangerous) forms of laboring and schooling. This is something most of us in the world experience, intuit or observe regularly (some much more than others). Of course, we're hegemonized to think that economic, gender, ethnic, cultural and sexual oppression is natural. But, amazingly, and despite the frustratingly effective and obfuscating cloak of hegemony, most of us know it's not.

And the populist Marxist Peter of the early and mid-1980s spoke to us—those of us within, but also those of us outside of, academia—in a way that made analyses of political economy resonate among broad sectors. That is why his work has become so popular worldwide and translated into so many languages. The work of this Peter (1986, 1989), along with that of Giroux

The work of this Peter (1986, 1989), along with that of Giroux (1988), began to extend Bowles and Gintis (1976), Apple (1979) and the Frankfurt School (Adorno, 1950, 1966/1973; Horkheimer, 1940, 1947; Marcuse, 1964, 1932/1987). It began to explain the daily goings-on within what Marx had described as the superstructure and Gramsci even more helpfully theorized as the social hegemonic order.

The populist Marxist Peter of the 1980s—whose radical, Marxist and accessible work began to focus on understanding and explaining the finer cultural and day-to-day machinations of capitalist re/production—led naturally to the Marxist postmodernist Peter of the late 1980s and early 1990s. Beginning with his work of this period, McLaren has consistently taken seriously the claims, challenges and insights raised by theorists and researchers working in the field of postmodernist/poststructuralist social theory. He has taken from this intellectual tradition what has been shown to be helpful in understanding social/economic/cultural conditions and the role discourse plays in creating, maintaining and/or restructuring relations of power between human beings. Critics claim that, for a time during this period in his scholarship, Peter was over-infatuated with French postmodernism and poststructuralism à la Foucault (1973, 1977), Baudrillard (1992), Bourdieu (1997, 1998) and Derrida (1973, 1981, 1994). It should be noted that many within critical pedagogy flirted with and attempted to address postmodernism's and poststructuralism's important challenges and ideas revolving around power, discourse and agency. But most did so at the expense of their former Marxist analyses. I don't believe McLaren did.

A more careful reading and analysis of his "postmodernist phase" reveals Peter's attempt to reconcile the important lessons of postmodernism with his firmly grounded Marxist roots and sympathies. McLaren never abandoned Marxism or historical materialist or political economic analyses. Indeed, he often successfully combined socialist-oriented educationalist activism with understandings of discursively and culturally constructed social relations, non-deterministic/non-orthodox understandings of Marxism *and* sensitivity to forms of oppression not based on—but still linked to—social class; such as sexism, racism, homophobia and linguisism. But even during this period, McLaren was always a cautious optimist regarding the full efficacy of postmodernist/poststructuralist thought. He rightfully insisted on maintaining strong connections to Marxian forms of analysis that seem to explain more adequately the current economic reality while remaining critical of postmodernist theory's tendency to de-centralize collective political struggle and agency. He cautions that "we should not forfeit the opportunity of theorizing both teachers and students as historical *agents* of resistance" (1995, p. 223; italics added), as strict postmodernist theory might have us do.

The McLaren of this period drew on the work of Gramsci (1971, 1981) and the Frankfurt School (Adorno, 1950, 1966/1973; Horkheimer, 1940, 1947; Marcuse, 1964, 1932/1987) and also carefully incorporated neo-Lyotardian poststructuralist perspectives (McLaren, 1995) into his work, while continually advocating for student agency. Synthesizing the work of these postmodernist/poststructural theorists, and the pedagogical theory of Paulo Freire, McLaren called for the development within students of subject positions as critical social agents, which he defined (1995) as "knowing how to live contingently and provisionally without the certainty of knowing the truth, yet at the same time, with the courage to take a stand on issues of human suffering, domination, and oppression" (p. 15).

In his more recent work (Hill, McLaren, Cole & Rikowski, 2002; McLaren, 1997, 2000a, 2000b, 2002; McLaren, Fischman, Serra & Antelo 1998), McLaren has called for a return to a Marxist- and Gramscian-inspired focus and re-emphasis on issues of working-class domination and oppression by bourgeois sectors—especially in this current climate of growing, diversifying and strengthening global capitalist/corporate power and control. If we lose sight of the central role class relations and exploitation play in educational contexts and elsewhere, he cautions, our analyses will be incomplete and our successes in struggling for social justice few and far between. This "full-on Marxist" Peter much more clearly and directly sees the importance of returning to a re-imagined, a re-read and a re-invigorated Marx. The following lengthy, but illustrative, quote from Peter is indicative of this newest period:

> While some postmodernists adventitiously assert that identities can be fluidly recomposed, rearranged, and reinvented…I maintain that this is a shortsighted and dangerous argument. It would take more than an army of Jacques Lacans to help us rearrange and suture the fusillade of interpolations and subject positions at play in our daily lives. My assertion that the contents of particular cultural differences and discourses are not as important as how such differences are embedded in and related to the large social totality of economic, social, and political differences may strike some readers as extreme. Yet I think it is fundamentally necessary to stress this point. It is true that…poststructuralist and postmodern theories have greatly expanded how we understand the relationship between identity, language, and schooling; but all too often these discourses collapse into a dehistoricizing and self-congratulatory emphasis on articulating the specifics of ethnographic methodologies and the ideological virtues of asserting the importance of naming one's location as a complex discursive site. As essen-

> tial as these theoretical forays have been, they often abuse their own insights by focusing on identity at the expense of power. (McLaren, 1997, p. 17)

In *Ché & Paulo* (2000a), Peter presents his most radically Marxist, theoretically developed and poetically articulate vision of education for social justice and change since he became one of North America's top educational criticalists in the mid-1980s. The thesis of this volume is that an analysis of global/late capitalism, and its socially, politically and hegemonically constructed *super*structure (and this superstructure's social, political and counter-hegemonic *de*constructability) needs to be re-centralized within educational (and other) struggles for social justice and change, but re-centralized without ignoring forms of oppression beyond classism. Rather, sexism, racism, homophobia, linguisism, nationalism, xenophobia, ageism and sizeism need to be understood within the logic and context of global/late capitalism. These forms of oppression would most probably have a life of their own even in capitalism's absence, but they are certain to be more highly exploited within the overall struggle of global capitalist expansion and competition for markets, market share and non-unionized/underpaid workers.

What McLaren does in *Ché & Paulo* is to explain clearly the connections between these "-isms" and global capitalism, using as a case study the Indigenous/worker struggle over land in Chiapas, México. Additionally, he successfully blends a Marxist analysis of our current economic and social condition with the nuanced understandings from postmodernism (hence, the "resonance") he developed through a decade-long study of the field, praising and critiquing where appropriate.

Ironically, and tellingly, Peter's current unequivocal call for a world society re-made and re-imagined through the Marxist lens of socialism, the collective good and radical democracy, is best summed up, in my estimation, in a quote that comes from his "critical postmodernist Marxist" period: "[What is needed is a] new socialist imaginary grounded not in specific forms of rationality, but in forms of detotalizing agency and the expansion of the sphere of radical democracy to new forms of social life" (McLaren, 1995, p. 24).

And, more recently, McLaren's edited volume with Hill, Cole and Rikowski, *Marxism Against Postmodernism in Educational Theory* (Hill et al., 2002), comes full circle, in some of his most succinct argumentation to date, by making the strongest possible case for a carefully contextualized and reasoned Marxist explanation for the current state of our educational system, society and world;

and, even more importantly, and heuristically, how and why we should collectively struggle to build a more just order.

2. Learning McLaren's Pedagogy of Revolution

by Luis Huerta-Charles

Learning is a socially and culturally constructed activity. It is shaped and determined by social, economic, cultural, political and historical factors that are interwoven with hegemonic discourses through social practices, institutional norms and rules used by dominant groups in molding people's subjectivity. In this way, people instill into their subconscious certain ideas and worldviews that are often not of their own creation and assume identities they believe are unchangeable and natural, as if things should happen just the way they do.

During learning processes, positioned subjects (Greene, 1995; Rosaldo, 1993) construct knowledge and bestow specific meaning to things, situations and events. Therefore, when learning occurs, individuals interpret anything they interact with from the perspectives and worldviews from which they are positioned; that is, people first use their previous knowledge to approach the learning of any fact or relation. However, learning does not just happen inside schools. It takes place in every situation where individuals interact with each other and with any object of knowledge. This could take place on the street, in homes, in factories, in churches or, obviously, in schools. For that reason, we say that learning is socially constructed.

In this essay, I will attempt to lead the reader through my own socially constructed knowledges and understandings of Peter McLaren (which began as a doctoral student). I will then move on to summarize and critique Peter's major contributions and notions.

About Peter's Personal Processes

I think Peter walks his talk. In other words, he is a coherent scholar because he lives his theory. As he says (1995), being an active social agent implies learning to live with and within contingency, uncertainty and tentativeness. I believe that through his intellectual-theoretical development, he has lived in that way. Frequently, McLaren has moved cautiously, combining his political educational activism with his understanding of the culturally and discursively constructed social relations within a global capitalist state (Huerta & Pruyn, 2001).

In some phases of his theoretical development, McLaren incorporated poststructuralist tools for analyzing oppressive forms of schooling and living based not just on social class analyses. However, he was cautious in this regard, and put under analytical scrutiny the poststructuralist thought he was using. Employing a Marxist-based analysis, he questioned poststructuralist perspectives and criticized their emphases on decentralizing the political struggle that misled critical analysis and channeled it into separate and isolated struggles (1997, 2000a, 2000b). He posits that some postmodern and poststructuralist theories have unwittingly helped to reduce the importance of significant elements of social critique that critical pedagogy had placed on the power/class relationship within the analysis of global capitalism. As he states:

> [T]hey view symbolic exchange as taking place outside the domain of value; privileging structures of diference over structures of exploitation and relations of exchange over relations of production;...encourag[ing] the coming to voice of the symbolically dispossessed over the transformation of existing social relations. Replac[ing] the idea that power is class-specific and historically bound with the idea that power is everywhere and nowhere. (2000a, p. 35)

In the same manner, Apple (1999) also criticizes these theories. He says that even though he does not want to widen the divide among critical groups at a time when it is important to forge alliances with them, it is necessary to point out some aspects of these postmodernist approaches that make them inappropriate for extending their influence over struggles for social justice. Apple notes that these strict postmodernist forms of analysis are misguided and inappropriate because:

> Their stylistic arrogance, the stereotyping of other approaches and their concomitant certainty that they've got "the" answer, their cynical lack of attachment to any action in real schools, [and] seeming equation of any serious focus on the economy as being somehow reductive. (p. 55)

As Peter is continuously aware of his own assumptions and the relationships they have with his own values, principles and commitment toward social justice and the construction of a democratic society, we have seen him move from critical theory to a poststructuralist framework. Now, we see him moving from critical pedagogy—a theoretical corpus he helped to construct—to what he calls a "pedagogy of revolution" (McLaren, 2000a, 2000b). For that reason, I say he walks his talk, because he is living with and within contingency and uncertainty while looking for perspectives that do not corrupt his principles.

McLaren's theoretical and intellectual development shows us that he is continuously constructing and elaborating explanations for understanding the world and trying to change it for the better. He has not been a static individual, because the static condition could make him take the world for granted, as if it were unchangeable and inevitable. If this happens, one runs the risk of becoming an ahistorical subject, paralyzed from acting to create change, because it is strange to us. There is a major risk in thinking this way. We could close the door to any hope that the world could be otherwise. If we do not take the risk of imagining that things could be different, we cannot begin the process of changing them, of seeking our utopian and social dreams (Greene, 1995).

During the course of his intellectual development, Peter has crossed borders as a cultural worker (Giroux, 1992). He challenges his own assumptions and asks us to engage in a reflexive analysis of our assumptions. He even asks critical pedagogy to engage in this kind of reflexive and critical process (McLaren, 1998, 2000a, 2000b). Peter's reading of the world and his consequent actions border on what Dewey (1993) calls "reflective action." In keeping with Dewey's ideas, Zeichner and Liston (1996) say that acting reflectively implies the application of three basic traits: an open mind, honesty and responsibility. I recognize McLaren as an open-minded intellectual acting reflectively, because he is the kind of scholar who listens to different points of view, pays attention to alternatives and considers the possibility of being wrong about his own rooted beliefs. I believe Peter is also responsible and honest in his actions, because he dares to examine and evaluate them periodically, holding the attitude that he can learn something new. To me, this kind of intellectual is one who is morally committed (Dewey, 1993; Zeichner & Liston, 1996).

About Globalization and Education

In his later works, McLaren (1997, 1998, 2000b; Allman, McLaren & Rikowski, 2002; Cole, Hill, Rikowski & McLaren, 2000; Fischman, 1999; Rizvi, 2002) has gone deeply into the analysis of global capitalist society. Along with other authors (Apple, 1998, 2000a, 2000b; Cornbleth & Waugh, 1995; Dijk, 1998; Giroux, 1992, 1997b, 1998), he has shown how powerful groups within certain contested terrains—in this case, the social relations of production and their influence on education—establish specific networks of power. Through these relationships, dominant groups use all available means for defeating or excluding voices of opposition in order to achieve public consent and create an hegemonic worldview that supports global capitalism.

Engineering public consent is a way of manipulating ideas and swaying public opinion in favor of government or dominant business groups (Chomsky, 1987, 1988; Chomsky, Leistyna & Sherblom, 1995; Herman & Chomsky, 1988). Hegemony is the process of maintaining domination through consensual social practices that take place in spaces such as church and schools, or through mass media, the political system and the family (Boggs, 1984; Brosio, 1994; Kincheloe, Slattery & Steinberg, 2000; McLaren, 1989). Those processes showcase the ability of the system to perpetuate itself (Boggs, 1984).

In the course of hegemonic struggle, powerful groups gain the consent of the oppressed, who usually are unaware that they are promoting their own domination by their acceptance of the values and social practices established by those groups. Dominant groups impose their worldview through given symbols, a structured body of knowledge, specific languages and social practices where unequal power relations and privileges are hidden (Chomsky, 1988; Herman & Chomsky, 1988; McLaren, 1989). In so doing, powerful groups establish alliances with like-minded groups (Apple, 1998, 1999) in order to silence adversarial voices. In this way, they achieve control of the means for deploying their worldviews.

McLaren has analyzed these processes considerably, and his contribution to our understanding of them has been significant. He has shown us how the discourses and social practices that derive from a global capitalist worldview have led people to take capitalist ideology as natural. As McLaren (1998; Rizvi, 2002) says, capitalism has been "naturalized" and integrated as part of nature itself (Cole et al., 2000; McLaren, 1998; Rizvi, 2002). During the 1980s and 1990s, "new capitalism" became a way of understanding the world. Neo-liberalism and the new capitalism controlled and subjugated individuals and society as a whole, through organizing social practices. Neo-liberalism, new capitalism's theoretical underpinning, became the guiding ideology of our current times (Apple, 2000a, 2000b; Burbules & Torres, 2000; Freire, 1970/1998; Gee, Hull & Lankshear, 1996; McLaren, 1997, 1998, 2000a).

As McLaren says, neo-liberalism "...has become the lodestar of the new world's order" (2000a, p. 20). This new world/work order shapes our society through specific hegemonic practices and ideological discourses. The result is an acceptance of working conditions in which human beings are dehumanized and considered valuable for exploitation alone (Forrester, 1996). People are literally considered "disposable" (Bales, 1999).

Within this neo-liberalist perspective, the state is considered weak, an institution that gives up its social functions. Thus, the new capitalist landscape is characterized by fierce competition for markets, reduced wages, more temporary jobs, destruction or weakening of labor unions around the world, increasing unemployment, less protective labor contracts and a reduction—if not destruction—of the welfare state (Apple, 1998, 2000a; Burbules & Torres, 2000; Forrester, 1996; Gee et al., 1996; McLaren, 1998, 2000a). The new capitalism promotes the maximization, by any and all means, of profit (Bourdieu, 1998). In other words, new capitalism, globalization and neo-liberalism have combined to cannibalize social and political economies (Adda, 1996; as quoted in McLaren, 1998).

McLaren and other critical educators (e.g., Giroux, 1997a), have shown that during the last decade, neo-liberalism and the new capitalism have more than ever influenced all aspects of our lives. Consequently, they have had a clear influence on education. Neo-liberal strategies for converting public schools into private spaces organized by the dynamics of management and efficiency have been quite effective; the ultimate return and triumph of Fordism! Parents' discretion to "choose" public or private schooling for their children, expressed through vouchers and "choice programs," is an example of this neo-liberal strategy for "improving" the quality of schools under a free market ideology (Apple, 1998, 2000a, 2000b; Cole, et al., 2000; McLaren, 1998, 1999, 2000a; Rizvi, 2002).

About Revolutionary Pedagogy

As global capitalism has brought "great wealth for a few and misery for the vast majority" (Rizvi, 2002, p. 6) and has generated inhuman living conditions for most people on the planet, McLaren has refocused his analyses toward the construction of alternative spaces where people can liberate themselves from hegemonic oppression (McLaren, 2002; Rizvi, 2002). As a part of his strategy for facing the conditions generated by the savage intensification of capitalism, Peter has shifted his alternative educational actions from the previous notion of "critical pedagogy" to what he calls "revolutionary pedagogy" (McLaren, 1999, 2000a, 2000b, 2002; Cole et al., 2000; Farahmandpur, Chapter 8 of this volume.)

McLaren (Rizvi, 2002) introduces the concept of revolutionary pedagogy based on Allman's (1999, 2001) notion of revolutionary critical education. This is not just an attempt at changing a theory's name. This has happened as a response to the continuous and generally successful process of domesticating critical pedagogy. As McLaren argues, "the United States has a seductive way of incorporating anything that it can't defeat and transforming that 'thing' into a weaker version of itself" (2000a, p. xxii). By extension, he says that critical pedagogy has become a caricature of the initial idea that gave birth to it: the struggle for a more just society that empowers the powerless to engage in struggles for liberation. For example, the same transformation has occurred with the ideas of Paulo Freire, which have now been domesticated and reduced to "student-directed learning approaches" that avoid discussing or rethinking "social critique and a revolutionary agenda" (McLaren, 2000a, p. 35).

Elsewhere, McLaren (1998, 1999, 2000a; Allman et al., 2002; Cole et al., 2000; Rizvi, 2002) has established differences between critical pedagogy and revolutionary pedagogy. He notes that critical pedagogy:

> …constitutes a dialectical and dialogical process that instantiates a reciprocal exchange between teachers and students—an exchange that engages in the task of reframing, refunctioning, and reposing the question of understanding itself, bringing into dialectical relief the structural and relational dimensions of knowledge and its hydra-headed power/knowledge dimensions. *Revolutionary pedagogy* goes further still. It puts power/knowledge relations on a collision course with their own internal contradictions; such a powerful and often unbearable collision gives birth not to an epistemological resolution at a higher level but rather to a provisional glimpse of a new society freed from the bondage of the past. (McLaren, 2000a, p. 185; italics in original)

Educators who hold a revolutionary pedagogical perspective must face the negative effects of global capitalism. McLaren (2002; Rizvi, 2002) says that revolutionary educators ought to support collective struggles for social change. Using a Marxist-based framework, revolutionary pedagogy could help educators understand, or sometimes overcome, forms of oppression, specifically those related to the process of schooling (McLaren, 2000b). As Allman et al. (2002, p. 13) note, teachers have the capacity to work with "red chalk" in order to open up alternative visions of capitalism in the classroom. McLaren (2000b) states that from this perspective, teachers now have the opportunity, and also the responsibility, to produce new forms of pedagogy within which they might incorporate social justice principles in order to counter the disease of global capitalism and its pervasive, negative effects. Within this context, it could be said that the creation of an authentic egalitarian and participatory socialist movement is one of the main aims of revolutionary pedagogy (Rizvi, 2002). Moreover, as McLaren (2000a) indicates, another important goal of this approach is to change the conditions that generate human suffering and to bring about the conditions necessary for liberation.

Criticisms from Students and the Academy

McLaren's ideas have had wide application in university classes, especially in teacher education programs. When I was a doctoral student in Las Cruces, New Mexico, McLaren's books were used in several of my classes, because critical pedagogy is one of the pillars upon which the department in which I studied (and now work) constructed its conceptual framework. And, as might be expected, Peter's critical constructions provoked diverse reactions from my classmates. As a doctoral student, I took a course that focused on critical pedagogy. And central within our readings, of course, was the work of McLaren. As I took this specific course, I noted that my classmates had diverse, and usually passionate, reactions to McLaren's work; across the spectrum of like to dislike. As I saw these reactions unfolding in this class, I chose to document this process empirically, taking field notes, making journal entries and even informally interviewing several of my classmates. My colleagues rejected, poked fun at, accepted and mocked Peter's ideas (I will briefly share some of these data below). Taking this class was a learning experience for me in another way. I found it quite personally instructive to reflect on my situatedness as a Latin American history student in relation to McLaren's framework and several students' resistance to the intellectual demands that critical theory required of them.

I must assume, first of all, that Peter's oeuvre is both challenging and difficult. As a matter of fact, some scholars (Apple, 1999; Huerta, Horton & Scott, 2001) have pointed out that the language elaborated by critical theorists such as Peter is too abstract and confusing. Moreover, McLaren's oeuvre demands special faith and a commitment to constructing a better, more human and just world. In the following analysis—again, drawn from my analyses of the data I collected in this critical pedagogy doctoral class—I try to illustrate that the nature of McLaren's work provokes different actions and reactions, depending upon where and how individuals are positioned as subjects, and how they interact with Peter's thoughts.

In one class, we were analyzing McLaren's *Revolutionary Multiculturalism* (1997). Some chapters of the book generated angry reactions from several students. Other classmates were confused but apparently more tolerant of Peter's essays. The former group's comments ran along the following lines:

> I can understand his criticisms but, how is it that rap music is a way of criticizing discrimination? That's crazy! Rap music does not say anything good at all!

This reaction was prompted by the chapter "Gangsta Pedagogy and Ghettocentricity: The Hip-Hop Nation as Counterpublic Sphere." However, without noticing, the student in question was bringing into the discussion her own prejudices about what she called "Black music." That class included some students who were Latina/o teachers and principals, and others who were white principals working in public schools where the student population was basically Latina/o.

Those classmates were refusing to accept something that McLaren (2002) says is constantly necessary: to rethink and reflect on their situatedness, or, in other words, to rethink their own situation as a part of the society. That implies a kind of critical elaboration, what Gramsci (1971; Said, 1979) calls the creation of our "self-inventory." This is a hard task to perform, because it implies the negation of ourselves, the recognition of what events and situations marked and led us to be the kind of individuals we are at this moment. When an individual begins the process of conducting this inventory, she or he must understand that they will need to scrutinize their own values and beliefs. That is the hardest part, because most of the time our beliefs are constructed and shaped during our childhood, and they represent our family traditions and socializations. Thus, questioning them is like questioning and rejecting the principles we are imbued with by our families. For that reason, it is easier for many of us to doubt critical elaborations and assume—or take for granted—that things are really working well for all in our global society.

In this context, it is often easy to criticize McLaren by denying his theories, because they are painful for us. It is easier to say "McLaren got stuck in the '60s" than to rethink our situatedness. It is also easier to say "He is an old-fashioned Marxist who is out of place" than to analyze the ideas he uses to relentlessly and unflinchingly challenge us. McLaren is aware of those superficial criticisms. I say "superficial" not as a way of discounting them or marginalizing people who do not accept critical positions, but because students did not offer an elaborate and reflective set of arguments in response to the issues Peter was addressing in his book.

McLaren's work has faced a number of incisive and pejorative criticisms. Some readers accuse him of being totalitarian for using old-style Marxist language (Rizvi, 2002); others identify him negatively as a "hippie from the 1960s." Some students in the aforementioned class tried to be "tolerant" of McLaren's ideas when he criticized U.S. discriminatory politics and social practices, as well as the logic of the capitalist system that controls social interactions. For instance, because the university was located in a "Borderlands" region, the chapter "Ethnographer as Postmodern Flâneur" provoked annoyed and mocking comments when McLaren (1997, p. 103) stated that he was "eating *menudo* at Sanborns"—which is a well-known restaurant in Juárez that is not normally accessible to poor people. My classmates made comments such as:

> This is not a restaurant for a revolutionary like he says he is.
>
> Why was he not eating menudo in the popular market, like the poor people in Juárez?
>
> If he wants to be a revolutionary, he should go like in Cuba with Fidel.

As I said before, students thought they were being "tolerant" of Peter's ideas, because in the United States "everybody is allowed to think the way they want." Nonetheless, if we reflect on these expressions, students' tolerance is a kind of superficial tolerance, one that states, "McLaren can say anything he wants, as long as he does not affect my own positionality." I would strip bare and analyze this comment, then extend it to its logical conclusion, restating it thus (and more honestly): "McLaren can say anything he wants, as long as he does not affect my *privileges* as a white citizen."

I believe McLaren is cognizant of this, because he clearly and consistently advances the notion that people live in the world, not outside of it. He even asks this question: "Does anybody need to live in a very small apartment with a small desk, in the worst depressed situation if, she/he wants to be revolutionary?" (McLaren, 2002; translation mine). He knows people have to live with dignity, and to live simply. This is something that hooks (2000, pp. 43–46) carefully explores as a part of the strategy used by the advanced capitalist system to lure people into the acceptance of conspicuous consumption, as if all people could have the same access to commodities, or as if our society were classless. McLaren (2002) says that this is a process of being sensible in your own principles, and that process requires that critical and Marxist intellectuals package their principles in a living praxis, walking their talks.

It is interesting to note that McLaren (1999, 2002; Rizvi, 2002) and other intellectuals (e.g., Giroux, 1992, 2002), openly admit that many criticisms from the academy address the way in which institutions of higher education have become allies of business and supporters of neo-liberal proposals, instead of noting their role as the moral witness or the critical conscience of the social world in which they are situated. Even McLaren says that, "the Academy is a vicious and hypocritical place that breeds neo-liberals masquerading as leftist multiculturalists and opportunists trying to pass themselves as selfless 'solidarists' in the struggle for justice" (Fischman, 1999, p. 33).

About the Concept of "Revolutionary" in the Educational Debate

The concept of "revolutionary" in the educational debate could raise many questions and doubts within the Mexican community of critical educators. First of all, I believe educators in México, as well as in Latin America, are still struggling with the concept of critical pedagogy. We need to understand that theoretical and educational processes take place in different ways, depending on the contexts that define the place where they are occurring. For that reason, while we in México and Latin America are still trying to understand it, the recognized founders of the critical pedagogy perspective are now moving toward more advanced notions (such as revolutionary pedagogy, as elaborated above). For instance, Latin American educators still have doubts about the essence of the concept of critical pedagogy. There remain doubts about how it might be instantiated in schools. What does it look like in the practice of teaching? What is the ethical and political commitment critical pedagogy must promote among educators?

Our history as Mexicans and Latin Americans (see Casali & Araújo Freire, de Alba & González Arenas, and Moraes in this volume) somehow makes us rethink the meaning of the idea of "revolution" or "revolutionary" within the critical educational discourse. For, more so than our North American sisters and brothers, we have had to face antidemocratic and oftentimes oppressive military governments. And, as a consequence, we have had to periodically fight social revolutions to sweep out oppressive governmental structures (and even governments themselves) and impose newer ones that were in some ways also oppressive or discriminatory. They were new governments that were seen as the last utopia made real, but sadly—and for different reasons and under different circumstances—they more often than not neglected to fully answer people's calls for ending oppression and human suffering.

First we need to clarify that the meaning of "revolutionary," in the pedagogical sense, is not related to the revolutionary-anarchist approach that implies, necessarily, an overthrow and killing of authority. It should not make real the metaphor of the dialectic relationship between master and slave, because the slave killed the master to become the new master and subjugate new slaves. We have to deconstruct this kind of dualism. "Revolutionary," therefore, needs to be understood as the recognition of the other. McLaren (Rizvi, 2002) is clear about this issue when he says that the challenge is to create an egalitarian and participatory socialist movement, not just to impose another form of oppressive rule.

For that reason, it is important to point out that revolutionary pedagogy is not a methodology, nor is it a set of procedures to follow. It must be mainly a philosophy, a sensibility, a way of understanding the world in which we live. It is the comprehension of the relation of the subject—as an individual and member of a group—with her or his own place in a specific historical and cultural context. It is a specific way of understanding the role of teachers in relation to the social, cultural and productive forces that surround us (McLaren, 2002). Revolutionary pedagogy is, then, the philosophical orientation of teaching practices that help us to achieve social, cultural, gender and sexual justice.

The concept of revolutionary pedagogy seems to entail a revolution à la Gramsci, because it must be a cultural revolution that helps people understand their situatedness in order to provide them with the necessary critical spaces where they can reflect on their own situations and imagine other possibilities for changing their reality. Gramsci (1981) states that culture is not just the encyclopedic knowledge found in big, classical books. Rather, it comprises organization, discipline of the self, the process of taking positions in front of the world, the conquest of a higher consciousness through which we arrive through the comprehension of the historic value of our own lives, our rights and our obligations. Hence, people would achieve culture within educational processes, because through interactive learning people could take possession of their own transcendental selves. As Gramsci says, we cannot really know the other, if we do not know ourselves.

Revolutionary pedagogy, then, must aim to help people achieve culture in this sense, in order to make them capable of changing the conditions of their world. Gramsci hopes people and "organic intellectuals" can make ascendant a new culture, the culture of ordinary people. This culture would then become the new (and different) hegemony, one based on social justice, equity and sharing—one that is, in other words, *counter* to the prevailing hegemony. In that way, conditions of domination and oppression could be reduced or abolished. Revolutionary pedagogy again brings out the notion of transformative intellectuals that Giroux (1988) and McLaren (Giroux & McLaren, 1986) elaborated on at the close of the 1980s.

In a similar way, McLaren (2000b) lends sense to his idea of revolutionary pedagogy when he says that all revolutions are cultural. Following Amin's (1998) idea of underdetermination, McLaren states that the determinations of economics, politics and culture possess a specific logic and autonomy.

Therefore, revolutionary pedagogy tries to re-engage us in continuous reflection on the unjust social relations within global capitalism and invites us to stand against all the cruel living conditions that have been its result. If we engage ourselves in the struggle to promote teaching practices that hold a revolutionary pedagogical focus, we may start thinking that the world can be transformed into a better place. Revolutionary pedagogy is still a quest, a process-in-the-making that is permeated with the idea of releasing the imagination, because, as Greene (1995) notes:

> Imagination…is what enables us to cross empty spaces between ourselves and those we teachers have called "other" over the years… [It] is the one that permits us to give credence to alternative realities. It allows us to break with the taken for granted, to set aside familiar distinctions and definitions. (p. 3)

The challenge is in front of us. It is up to us to face it or not.

3. Organization of This Volume

In Part Two of this volume, "The Arc and Impact of McLaren's Work," the contributors strive to, using Luis' words, "face this challenge" by laying out the global, timeless themes that have been elaborated by Peter. Roberto Bahruth reflects on and analyzes his own development and growth as a scholar and intellectual over the span of his career, now viewed in retrospect through a McLarian lens. In so doing, he is able to elaborate and critique Peter's contributions. Alípio Casali and Ana Maria Araújo Freire poignantly and thoughtfully assess Peter's over-arching impact on the educational left—and progressive movements more generally—from their unique positionality not just as Brazilians but as central players within the Latin American criticalist movement, and paisanas and familiares of Paulo Freire himself. And Zeus Leonardo's chapter clearly and carefully takes us through the slow, steady and considered development of Peter's co-construction of the field of critical—and now "revolutionary"—pedagogy itself, as well as his development as a critical/revolutionary pedagogue.

In Part Three, "McLaren Across Contexts," the contributors both evaluate the impact of Peter's theorizing in different situated realities and for different groups of people, and critique the impact of his work across these different realities and ways of knowing and making sense of our worlds. Alicia de Alba and Marcela González Arenas situate and analyze McLaren's work in the Mexican and Latin American contexts, pointing out his strengths, weaknesses and paradoxes. Pepi Leistyna shares with us how he draws on Peter's notions of "critical multiculturalism" in trying to understand and make sense of the reality of a school district attempting to create and implement a program of "multicultural professional development." In her chapter, Marcia Moraes attempts to understand and critique McLaren by way of elaborations of critical pedagogy in two different contexts: rural areas within the state of Rio de Janeiro (where she works with K-12 teachers), and in the city of Rio de Janeiro, where she teaches MA students.

Finally, the authors whose work comprises Part Four, "McLaren the Marxist," bring us back to where Peter is now, offering a strong Marxist critique of our current global, economic state and situation, as well as our potential for the future. In the hopeful, "The 'Inevitability of Globalized Capital' Versus the 'Ordeal of the Undecidable,'" Mike Cole uses a Marxist critique and an analysis of the contributions of Peter to call into question the viability and survivability of global capitalism in the long term. In "The Revolutionary Critical Pedagogy of Peter McLaren," Ramin Farahmandpur thoroughly, and not uncritically, looks back at the educational left over the last 25 years, noting and criticizing how this intellectual community has largely—and, he argues, detrimentally—abandoned Marxism in favor of assorted "posts-" and "neos-." As part of this discussion, he situates and analyzes the work of McLaren as a central player in this community. Dave Hill, in "Critical Education for Economic and Social Justice: A Marxist Analysis and Manifesto," calls for nothing less than the title of his chapter/manifesto implies: a reinvention and reinvigoration of critical pedagogy through Marxian analyses and action. And he argues that the current work of McLaren is central and helpful in the refocusing he thinks is so important for critical/revolutionary pedagogy at this juncture. In "Karl Marx, Radical Education and Peter McLaren: Implications for the Social Studies,"

tion and Peter McLaren: Implications for the Social Studies," Curry Malott concludes the volume by guiding us through his conception of a re-created and radicalized social studies education as driven by a firm return to Marxist analyses, politics and praxis as informed by progressive social studies theorists and the current Marxian work of Peter McLaren.

We hope that you will find this volume on Peter McLaren and his body of important intellectual, philosophical and political work (and how we as pedagogues have understood and attempted to use that work) provocative, helpful and interesting, especially as the world's "leaders" (*shudder*) and power brokers continue to draw us into acts of perpetual war and ever-deepening and dehumanizing forms of economic, pedagogical, ethnic, gender, sexual, religious and nationalist oppression. All this takes place in the name of "freedom" but is actually in the service of the economically powerful and privileged.

We also invite you in advance to explore the forthcoming volumes in this *Teaching* series, edited by Shirley Steinberg and Joe Kincheloe and published by Peter Lang. These texts will endeavor to explore—as we have attempted to do here in the case of Peter McLaren—the important contributions of leading educational radicals and progressives on the left. We believe that it is indeed a time for stock-taking, reflection and re-invigoration on the educational left, and especially for action-taking. We hope this volume will assist in that work.

References

Adams, F. (1972). Highlander Folk School: "Getting information, going back, and teaching it." *Harvard Educational Review*, 42, 497–520.

———. (1975). *Unearthing seeds of fire.* Winston-Salem, NC: John F. Blair.

Adda, J. (1996). *La mondalisation de l'économie.* Paris: Découverte.

Adorno, T. (1973). *Negative dialectics.* New York: Seabury. (Original work published 1966)

Adorno, T. et al. (1950). *The authoritarian personality.* New York: Norton.

Allman, P. (1999). *Revolutionary social transformations: Democratic hopes, political possibilities and critical education.* Westport, CT: Bergin & Garvey.

———. (2001). *Critical education against global capitalism: Karl Marx and revolutionary critical education.* Westport, CT: Bergin & Garvey.

Allman, P., McLaren, P. & Rikowski, G. (2002). *After the box people: The labour-capital relation as class constitution and its consequences for Marxist educational theory and human resistance.* Retrieved September 3, 2002. On-line at http://www.ieps.org.ukcwc.net/afterbox.pdf.

Amin, S. (1998). *Specters of capitalism: A critique of current intellectual fashions.* New York: Monthly Review Press.

Apple, M. (1979). *Ideology and curriculum.* New York: Routledge.

———. (1982). *Education and power.* London: Routledge.

———. (1998). Knowledge, pedagogy, and the conservative alliance. *Studies in the Literary Imagination*, 31(1), 5–23.

———. (1999). Between neo and post: Critique and transformation in critical educational studies. In C.A. Grant (Ed.), *Multicultural research: A reflective engagement with race, class, gender and sexual orientation* (pp. 54–67). London and Philadelphia: Falmer Press.

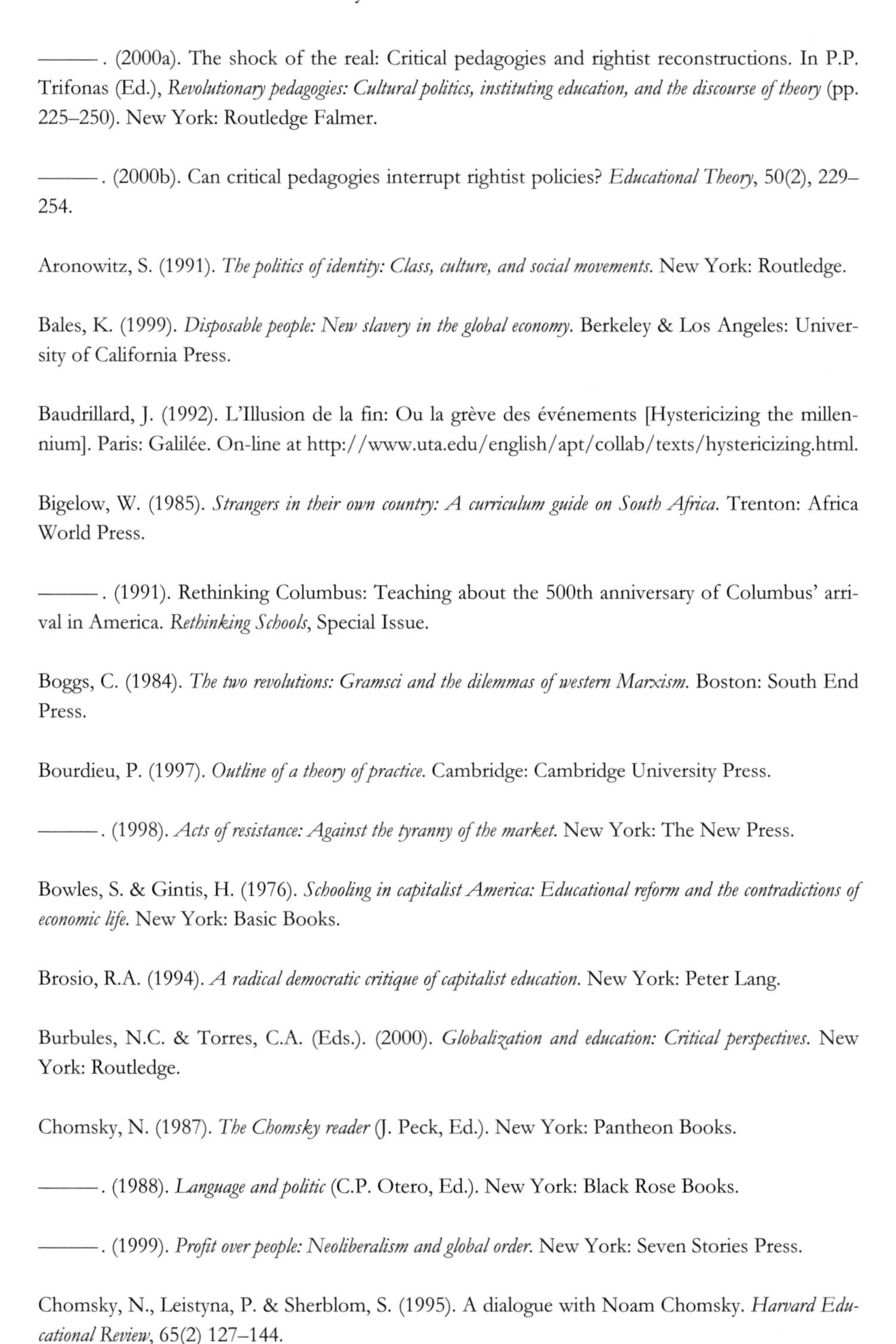

———. (2000a). The shock of the real: Critical pedagogies and rightist reconstructions. In P.P. Trifonas (Ed.), *Revolutionary pedagogies: Cultural politics, instituting education, and the discourse of theory* (pp. 225–250). New York: Routledge Falmer.

———. (2000b). Can critical pedagogies interrupt rightist policies? *Educational Theory*, 50(2), 229–254.

Aronowitz, S. (1991). *The politics of identity: Class, culture, and social movements.* New York: Routledge.

Bales, K. (1999). *Disposable people: New slavery in the global economy.* Berkeley & Los Angeles: University of California Press.

Baudrillard, J. (1992). L'Illusion de la fin: Ou la grève des événements [Hystericizing the millennium]. Paris: Galilée. On-line at http://www.uta.edu/english/apt/collab/texts/hystericizing.html.

Bigelow, W. (1985). *Strangers in their own country: A curriculum guide on South Africa.* Trenton: Africa World Press.

———. (1991). Rethinking Columbus: Teaching about the 500th anniversary of Columbus' arrival in America. *Rethinking Schools*, Special Issue.

Boggs, C. (1984). *The two revolutions: Gramsci and the dilemmas of western Marxism.* Boston: South End Press.

Bourdieu, P. (1997). *Outline of a theory of practice.* Cambridge: Cambridge University Press.

———. (1998). *Acts of resistance: Against the tyranny of the market.* New York: The New Press.

Bowles, S. & Gintis, H. (1976). *Schooling in capitalist America: Educational reform and the contradictions of economic life.* New York: Basic Books.

Brosio, R.A. (1994). *A radical democratic critique of capitalist education.* New York: Peter Lang.

Burbules, N.C. & Torres, C.A. (Eds.). (2000). *Globalization and education: Critical perspectives.* New York: Routledge.

Chomsky, N. (1987). *The Chomsky reader* (J. Peck, Ed.). New York: Pantheon Books.

———. (1988). *Language and politic* (C.P. Otero, Ed.). New York: Black Rose Books.

———. (1999). *Profit over people: Neoliberalism and global order.* New York: Seven Stories Press.

Chomsky, N., Leistyna, P. & Sherblom, S. (1995). A dialogue with Noam Chomsky. *Harvard Educational Review*, 65(2) 127–144.

Cole, M., Hill, D., Rikowski, G. & McLaren, P. (2000). *Red chalk: On schooling, capitalism and politics.* Brighton, UK: The Institute for Education Policy Studies.

Cornbleth, C. & Waugh, D. (1995). *The great speckled bird: Multicultural politics and education policy-making.* New York: St. Martin's Press.

Derrida, J. (1973). *Speech and phenomena, and other essays on Husserl's theory of signs.* Evanston, IL: Northwestern University Press.

———. (1981). *Positions.* Chicago: University of Chicago Press.

———. (1994). *Specters of Marx: The state of the debt, the work of mourning, and the New International.* London: Routledge.

Dewey, J. (1993). *How we think.* (Rev. ed.). Lexington, MA: D.C. Heath and Company.

Dijk, T.A. van. (1998). *Ideology: A multidisciplinary approach.* London: Sage.

Fine, M., Powell, L., Weis, L. & Mun Wong, L. (Eds.). (1996). *Off-white: Readings on race, power, and society.* New York: Routledge.

Fischman, G. (1999). Peter McLaren: A call for multicultural revolution. *Multicultural Education,* 6(4), 32–36.

Forrester, V. (1996). *El horror económico* [The economic horror]. México: Fondo de Cultura Económica.

Foucault, M. (1973). *The birth of the clinic: An archaeology of medical perception* (A. Smith, Trans.). New York: Pantheon.

———. (1977). *Discipline and punish: The birth of the prison* (A. Sheridan, Trans.). New York: Pantheon.

Freire, P. (1970). *Pedagogy of the oppressed* (M. Rámos, Trans.). New York: Continuum.

———. (1985). *Politics of education.* South Hadley, MA: Bergin & Garvey.

———. (1998). *Pedagogy of freedom: Ethics, democracy, and civic courage.* Lanham, MD: Rowman & Littlefield.

Gee, J.P., Hull, G. & Lankshear, C. (1996). *The new work order: Behind the language of the new capitalism.* Boulder, CO: Westview.

Giroux, H.A. (1988). *Teachers as intellectuals: Toward a critical pedagogy of learning.* Westport, CT: Bergin & Garvey.

———. (1992). *Border crossings: Cultural workers and the politics of education.* New York: Routledge.

———. (1997a). Is there a place for cultural studies in colleges of education? In H.A. Giroux & P. Shannon (Eds.), *Education and cultural studies: Toward a performative practice* (pp. 231–247). New York: Routledge.

———. (1997b). *Pedagogy and the politics of hope: Theory, culture, and schooling: A critical reader.* Boulder, CO: Westview.

———. (1998). *Channel surfing: Racism, the media, and the destruction of today's youth.* New York: St. Martin's Griffin.

———. (2002). Neoliberalism, corporate culture, and the promise of higher education: The university as a democratic public sphere. *Harvard Educational Review*, 72(4), 425–463.

Gramsci, A. (1971). *The prison notebooks: Selections* (Q. Hoare & G. Smith, Eds. and Trans.). New York: International Publishers.

———. (1981). *La alternativa pedagógica* [*The pedagogical alternative*]. Barcelona: Fontamara.

Greene, M. (1995). *Releasing the imagination: Essays on education, the arts, and social change.* San Francisco: Jossey-Bass.

Herman, E.S. & Chomsky, N. (1988). *Manufacturing consent: The political economy of the mass media.* New York: Pantheon Books.

Hill, D., McLaren, P., Cole, M. & Rikowski, G. (Eds.). (2002). *Marxism against postmodernism in educational theory.* New York: Lexington Books.

hooks, b. (2000). *Where we stand: Class matters.* New York & London: Routledge.

Horkheimer, M. (1940). The authoritarian state. *TELOS*, 27.

———. (1947). *Eclipse of reason.* New York: Oxford University Press.

Huerta, L., Horton, J. & Scott, D. (2001). *How do we know preservice teachers are comprehending, willing, and able to apply critical pedagogy in their classrooms?* Paper presented in a round table at the American Educational Research Association. Annual Meeting 2001: *What we know and how we know it.* Seattle, WA.

Huerta, L. & Pruyn, M. (2001). Compromiso moral, utopía y justicia social: Revisión del libro de Peter McLaren, *Ché Guevara, Paulo Freire, and the pedagogy of revolution.* In *Cuadernos de Formación Docente, 1, de la Escuela Normal "Miguel F. Martínez."* Monterrey, México.

Kincheloe, J. (1998). *Who will tell the workers? The socioeconomic foundations of work and vocational education.* Boulder, CO: Westview Press.

Kincheloe, J., Slattery, P. & Steinberg, S.R. (2000). *Contextualizing teaching: Introduction to education and educational foundations*. New York: Addison Wesley Longman.

Kincheloe, J., Steinberg, S. & Chennault, R. (Eds.). (1998) *White reign: Deploying whiteness in America*. New York: Palgrave Macmillan.

Loewen, J. (1995). *Lies my teacher told me: Everything your American history textbook got wrong*. New York: Touchstone.

Marcuse, H. (1964). *One dimensional man*. Boston: Beacon.

———. (1987). *Ontology and the theory of historicity* (S. Benhabib, Trans.). Cambridge: MIT Press. (Original work published 1932)

McLaren, P. (1980). *Cries from the corridor*. Toronto: Methuen.

———. (1986). *Schooling as a ritual performance: Toward a political economy of educational symbols and gestures*. London: Routledge.

———. (1989). *Life in schools: An introduction to critical pedagogy in the foundations of education*. White Plains, NY: Longman.

———. (1995). *Critical pedagogy and predatory culture: Oppositional politics in a postmodern era*. London and New York: Routledge.

———. (1997). *Revolutionary multiculturalism: Pedagogies of dissent for the new millennium*. Boulder, CO: Westview.

———. (1998). Revolutionary pedagogy in post-revolutionary times: Rethinking the political economy of critical education. *Educational Theory*, 48(4), 431–462.

———. (1999). Contesting capital: Critical pedagogy and globalism. A response to Michael Apple. *Current Issues in Comparative Education*, 1(2). Retrieved and available on-line at http://www.tc.columbia.edu/cice/vol01nr2/pmart1.htm.

———. (2000a). *Ché Guevara, Paulo Freire and the pedagogy of revolution*. Lanham, MD: Rowman & Littlefield.

———. (2000b). Gang of five. In M. Cole, D. Hill, G. Rikowski & P. McLaren (Eds.), *Red chalk: On schooling, capitalism & politics*. Brighton, UK: The Institute for Education Policy Studies.

———. (2002). *Si de ofrecer espacios se trata. Entrevista a Peter McLaren* [On offering spaces: Interview with Peter McLaren]. Retrieved August 10, 2002. Retrieved and available on-line at http://www.pedagogia.netfirms.com/cuaderno/amclaren.html.

McLaren, P., Fischman, G., Serra, S. & Antelo, E. (1998). The specters of Gramsci: Revolutionary praxis and the committed intellectual. Original manuscript. *Journal of Thought.*

Rizvi, M. (2002). Educating for social justice and liberation: An interview with Peter McLaren. *Znet.* Retrieved and available on-line at http://www.zmag.org.

Rosaldo, R. (1993). *Culture and truth: The remaking of social analysis.* Boston: Beacon Press.

Said, E. (1979). *Orientalism.* New York: Vintage.

Slattery, P. (1995). *Curriculum development in the postmodern era.* New York: Garland.

Sleeter, C. (1996). *Multicultural education as social activism.* Albany: State University of New York Press.

Steinberg, S., Kincheloe, K. & Hinchey, P. (Eds.). (1999). *The Post-formal reader: Cognition and education.* New York: Garland.

Weiler, K. (1988). *Women teaching for change: Gender, class and power.* South Hadley, MA: Bergin & Garvey.

———. (1991). Freire and a feminist pedagogy of difference. *Harvard Educational Review*, 61, 449–474.

Zeichner, K.M. & Liston, D.P. (1996). *Reflective teaching: An introduction.* Mahwah, NJ: Lawrence Erlbaum.

PART TWO

THE ARC AND IMPACT OF McLAREN'S WORK

Chapter 1

Peter McLaren: A Scholar's Scholar

Roberto Bahruth

> The basic pattern of critique, outrage, exhortation, hope, possibility and vision (what has been called the prophetic voice) recurs in other biblical narratives and social texts as well as in history across time and space. (David Purpel in *Moral Outrage in Education*, 1999, p. 117)

The nature of the questions originally sent to us by the editors of this book as prompts for reflection upon the ways in which Peter McLaren has influenced our pedagogy has led me to an almost autobiographical account of both my epistemological and ontological development as a scholar. This has been a helpful process and experience for me as I contemplate a career that began in technicism and is now charged with and revitalized by more critical understandings of teaching, learning and literacy. Peter has undoubtedly contributed greatly to my emerging criticity and determination to demand more of myself and of my students since I began my professional transformation that is described below.

My Political, Ideological and Theoretical Orientation Before McLaren

In 1983 I first read Paulo Freire's article "The Importance of the Act of Reading" (1983). It was the beginning of my own transformation from well-intentioned technicist operating within a system that only hinted at being unsuitable for learning because of the obvious frustrations and failures of non-traditional students. What was to follow, sparked by reading more of Paulo's work, was a growing awareness of the politics of an educational system that had previously been convincingly neutral to my acritcal eye, an eye that had been blinded by my own subjection to traditional schooling.

As I became more political, first through my refusal to accept the language of deficit—a language created by the status quo that protects traditional educational practices from critical examination by placing the blame on the victims—as an explanation for the failure of the migrant children in my fifth-grade classroom (Hayes, Bahruth & Kessler, 1998). Transcending the language of deficit is one path whereby, sooner or later, we are going to have to face "the embarrassing connections between not learning and not teaching" (Bahruth, 2000a). Later, after seeing the success of my students upon my change in praxis, I became driven to arrive at deeper understandings of critical theory in education. In 1984, I was accepted in the doctoral program at the University of Texas at Austin, and in the very first semester there I was assigned to read an article by Peter McLaren (1982). In our discussions, he became associated with the school of neo-Marxists, which also included Michael Apple, another author I had been assigned to read.

Although I grew up in the 1960s and participated in a cultural revolution—a decade that still stands as a shining example of democracy in action—the term Marxism had been thoroughly vilified as a result of the Cold War. (It is interesting to note that Aronowitz [2000, p. 172] asserts that current trends in the corporatization of institutions of higher education are "to make sure the 1960s never happen again.") At first, because of my received culture, I was alarmed by the term "neo-Marxist," yet I was intrigued by the skillful deconstructions of traditional schooling articulated by McLaren, Apple and others. As a teacher of ten years, what I was reading through their work was a description that named, and thereby made more perceptible, many of the mechanisms which I had encountered as a teacher of underclass students. One of my professors, Doug Foley, had written a book about the same town in which I had been teaching. The findings of his qualitative research also followed a class structural analysis, problematizing capitalism along the way (Foley, 1977, 1990). Revelations abounded as I read his work and connected it to my personal experiences with the local politics of "North Town."

I continued to read, developing a fetish for certain authors because of the boldness of their discourse and the utility of their descriptions and deconstructions in helping me to see the oppressive nature of "schooling as a ritual performance" (McLaren, 1986). Freire, McLaren and Apple became standard fare in my pursuit of critical theory. I was also assigned to read *Learning to Labour* by Paul Willis (1977), who later wrote the introduction to Foley's book (1990). In addition, I read articles by Bordieux and Labov, and I recall reading Freire's call for the neo-Marxists to offer viable alternatives to traditional schooling, since he felt it was immoral to deconstruct without offering a vision. As the years have passed, I have witnessed through their academic writing how McLaren, Apple and others have taken Paulo's criticism into consideration.

Perhaps the greatest development in my understanding began when I attended a meeting in 1989, in Albuquerque, New Mexico, where I met and spent several days with Donaldo Macedo and Hermán García. It was the beginning of a friendship and alliance that has lasted for years. They suggested I read Giroux's *Theory and Resistance in Education* (1983), which I did. The following year at a gathering of the same group, now joined by one more of my teachers, Rudolfo Chávez Chávez, our conversations went much further into the politics of education and the pedagogical implications for professors who did not want to domesticate their students.

Reflecting on these memories, I am filled with hope as I trace my own emergence into criticity thanks to a balance of personal scholarship, ongoing self-critique of my pedagogy, the discourse provided by critical theorists and the patient investments of my colleagues. Their efforts and direction enabled me to grow in ways that made it easy to discuss critical issues in education when I was fortunate enough to meet later on with Donaldo Macedo and Lilia Bartolomé in Boston, Henry Giroux and Shirley Steinberg at State College, Pennsylvania, and with Peter McLaren, Donaldo Macedo, Haggith Gor-Ziv and David Gabbard in Jackson Hole, Wyoming. Through these ruminations, I have come to appreciate more fully Paulo's deeper appreciation of the meaning of literacy displayed in his own personal reflections in *Letters to Cristina* (1996).

McLaren's Influence on My Pedagogy

I constantly push the thinking of my students, but I need Peter's scholarship because he pushes my own. Through Peter's writing I have evolved to a higher level of ontological clarity and purpose. His boldness has given me permission, perhaps even demanded me, to be bolder in my pedagogy (McLaren, 2000b). I remember reading his introduction to *Teachers as Intellectuals* (1988), where he turned Henry Giroux from a scholar into a person, humanizing him by sharing Henry's history. It was the first time I began to identify with a scholar because of shared working-class roots. I enjoyed the candid intimacy of Peter's voice, which began to reveal the human behind the discourse, sometimes seemingly angry, but now showing a side which academic discourse rarely allows the reader to come to know. Eventually, I have come to associate the strength of Peter's writing with what David Purpel has termed "moral outrage" rather than anger, and I have been affected by Peter to the extent that the boldness of my pedagogy is now informed by a moral outrage of my own. It is interesting to note that, years later, I noticed similar qualities in the autobiographical introductions to Macedo (1994) and Giroux (1996), and throughout the texts of bell hooks, but especially in *Teaching to Transgress* (1994). And there was more.

Macedo (1994) coined the term "stupidification" to describe the effects of shallow technicist "teaching," a term which Chomsky (2000) expresses as "the social construction of not seeing." Both describe the blindness through which I tried to teach without knowing that the system had no intention or concern that minority students really learn or succeed. In fact, the only time my performance was ever called into question by the administration was when I was effective in working with minority students. McLaren's early deconstructions of education using class structural analysis made the politics of education crystal clear for me. While it is clear to most critical pedagogues that many "-isms" intersect in the politics of oppression and exploitation, the overwhelming common denominator identifying students who are academically assassinated through traditional schooling, "culture of poverty," is undeniable. Student performance need not be documented through standardized testing when a simple survey of zip codes would serve just as well to predict how a student would fare in a one-size-fits-all educational system centered on privileged-class knowledge and cultural capital.

Over the course of twenty years of ruminations on education, I find myself returning to two variables that explain and help me to identify sources of injustice: power and class. Joel Spring (1991) defines power as "the ability to control the actions of other people and the ability to escape from the control of others." Power and how it is used reveals praxis. It can be used in either humane or anti-humane ways. People in positions of power who are unaware of their own privilege often perceive the powerless and poor as undeserving, less human. When the first President George Bush was in power, a joke circulated across America that he was born on third base and lived his whole life thinking he had hit a triple. Unfortunately, it is also often the case that people who are born into poverty and rise to positions of power do so by acting white and identifying with privileged ideologies. Of course, hegemony would attempt to prevent their success if they displayed signs of treason along the way. Education that turns on privileged-class epistemologies and cultural capital often serves the role of colonizing outsiders to the ideology of the ruling class. Acting as neocolonialists, they serve hegemony by becoming mini-oppressors themselves (Fanon, 1965; Said, 1978; Freire & Macedo, 1987; Bahruth, 2000b).

Power also defines powerlessness or at least perceived powerlessness that can be disturbed as people awaken to social consciousness. The oppressed do not need to be informed that they are oppressed. However, part of the cultural work of critical pedagogues is to help them to throw off their internalized oppression and to recognize the mechanisms of hegemony that function to exploit and dehumanize them. To this end, I quote from Eduardo Galeano (1989):

> El colonialismo visible te mutila sin disimulo: te prohibe decir, te prohibe hacer, te prohibe ser. El colonialismo invisible, en cambio, te convence de que la servidumbre es tu destino y la impotencia tu naturaleza: te convence de que no se puede decir, no se puede hacer, no se puede ser.
>
> Author's Translation: Visible colonialism mutilates you without trying to hide it: it prohibits you from saying, from doing, from being. Invisible colonialism, on the other hand, convinces you that servitude is your destiny and impotence is your nature: it convinces you that you are unable to say, unable to do, unable to be.

For all of the effort to avoid the "c" word—class—which Chomsky (2000) has called a four-letter word in America, and the initial class-structural analysis I learned about through the first works I read by McLaren and others, it has become clear that poverty is a common denominator among those whom schools are failing.

This is not to say that privileged-class children are receiving a critical education, either. By avoiding the social, historical, political and economic contexts of education under the pretense of neutrality, and by labeling children with a language of deficit, privileged-class students are allowed to graduate with little or no social consciousness as well. This is why another aspect of the cultural work of critical pedagogues is to help the privileged to discover their privilege. It is also important to note that class is not the only bias, and to recognize other aspects such as gender, race, ideology, religion and sexual orientation as part of the dynamics of oppression.

In his book *The Night Is Dark and I Am Far from Home* (1975), Jonathan Kozol tells the story of a student at Harvard, how her education had ensured that she would not discover her own privilege, and the devastating effect it had on her when she accidentally did. I have found that commitment and convictions to do cultural work stem from deep theoretical and philosophical foundations.

Domestification of teachers and students is often achieved through an emphasis on methodology over pedagogy.

Current trends in education threaten democracy by ensuring domestification of teachers and students in the name of accountability (Gabbard, 2000; Aronowitz, 2000). Kohn (2002) states that the recent movement in standards, alignment and accountability is the most "undemocratic" in the history of education in America. Now, more than ever, I find myself in need of a strong voice, and I look to Peter. Recently, I read Gustavo Fischman's interview with him on the subject of *Revolutionary Multiculturalism* (2000). It came into my hands serendipitously in the sense that I was beginning to question my own boldness and considerable investment in my pedagogy. I was tired, feeling worn down by the "non-engagement" (Chávez Chávez & O' Donnell, 1998) I knew I would have to face at the beginning of each semester. I began to question whether my efforts would result in any significant pedagogical/ideological shifts by my students and whether they would have the commitment to do the cultural work necessary to democratize education. After all, if I were beginning to feel fatigue, after so many years of strong convictions, how could I be sure my students would stay the course? Once again, long-distance, Peter's words gave me renewed strength, and I began to share them with my students:

> We cannot—we must not—think that equality can occur in our schools or society in general without at once and the same time demanding and participating in political and economic revolution. No sphere of domination must remain unassailed by the project of liberation. We need to remain steadfast, we cannot embark in a flight from being, that is, a flight towards the world of commodities that can only objectify being. We need to remember that we do not own ourselves; we don't belong only to ourselves. We belong to being. Because we belong to being, we need not covet the fruits of capital, for they are also the fruits of exploitation. Exploitation violates being. To find our multicultural soul is always an exercise of praxis, not ownership. It is an act conjugated with love in the interests of social justice. I am not trying to be metaphysical here since I connect objectified being with labor, with the laboring and toiling body, with the alienated worker, with the commodification of labor, with the exploited and the oppressed. (Fischman, 2000, p. 212)

I began to expand my cultural work in the communities surrounding the university.

McLaren's work has also helped me to make direct linkages between capitalism and exploitation to the extent that I have become much more critical of popular culture and how it works to shape our lives as males and females, as members of groups and as consumers. I encourage my students to explore the agendas of popular culture, advertising and symbolism (Giroux & Simon, 1989) to discover the strong influences on shaping identities in a culture of superficial subjectivities defined through their possession of objects. I also encourage them to explore ways to teach counter-hegemonically so their students will be more critical and less likely to be shaped or exploited by codes of popular culture. Peter's work is reaffirming and helps to center my efforts as a critical educator. Elsewhere, he cautions readers about threats to critical pedagogy and what must be understood if it is not to be watered down and co-opted at the buzzword level of shallow understandings. According to McLaren (2000b):

> The struggle that occupies and exercises us as school activists and educational researchers needs to entertain global and local perspectives in terms of the way in which capitalist relations and the international division of labor are produced and reproduced. (p. 352)

Trickle-down, but Not Watered-down, McLaren

Opening moves in my pedagogy attempt to prepare students for the discomfort they will feel as they confront their own privilege. Using their own voices and personal narratives to articulate injustices they have witnessed during the course of their education, they begin to learn from each other about anti-humane practices in schools. Even if not affected directly, they begin to see what was always there but was obscured by the status quo. Freire stated that we must have faith in human goodness, and I have found that once students begin to learn about a wider scope of reality than their deliberately myopic traditional schooling has allowed for, they respond to critical pedagogy in positive ways. They also become more critical of their traditional schooling and eventually come to know of their own victimization for having been kept ignorant and narrowly educated. My goal aims to place my students in a moral dilemma where they must decide whether they want to be teachers acting as cultural workers who teach to transform society, or factory workers who maintain the status quo.

When new students ask me why they have to read "articles that are so political" for my class, I respond by asking them why no one has ever asked them to read dangerous discourse before. What can they conclude about the politics of their entire educational experience if they have never heard counter-hegemonic arguments? Isn't this also political? I ask them if they would prefer to hear diverse views on education and be given an opportunity to make up their own minds, or instead have their professors decide what is the correct position without ever telling them that alternative views exist. I ask them what conclusions have been drawn about their own intelligence as teachers when they are only exposed to the master narrative of traditional education, replete with the language of deficit. I also share with them how my initial explorations into critical pedagogy came because of curiosity and scholarship and not because the reading was assigned in one of my education classes; in fact, even my eventual readings of McLaren were for courses in anthropology and sociolinguistics.

It intrigues me how students will turn a critical eye on humanizing education once they learn that their voices will be respected without fear of punishment. To reveal the politics of hegemony, I ask them whether they ever dare to question professors who are patriarchal in their praxis, and to consider what they know would happen should they dare to do so. We all know what happens and how grades are often assigned more as a reward for conformity than for intelligence. I also explain that I want to encourage open participation, and if I were to silence any one of my students who differs with me, I would be silencing all of them vicariously.

I have found that teachers who have been domesticated by their teacher-preparation programs will fold and teach against their better instincts. This is why there is such a strong call for deep structural changes in teacher preparation from critical pedagogues. I believe teachers who have been involved in an intellectualization of their profession, systems theory and the mechanisms of both oppression and resistance, can become transformative intellectuals who will have strong commitments to the well-being of every student, will refuse to practice discriminatory technicism and will work to democratize classrooms. They will know intuitively that what they are being asked to do will not produce the results promised by those who prescribe, yet they will be the ones held accountable when poor results come in. This is the practice of counter-hegemony that needs to be understood if we are to democratize society through education.

One of my graduate students recently wrote:

> In my clarifying of purpose and with a growing criticity, I have examined my own personal and professional identity and philosophy of life as a basis for a developing philosophy of education which in fact relates to the cultural work of critical educators, that which I am becoming in my own process.

Peter McLaren's statement that "I belong to being," as contrasted to "I belong to me," was a seed planted in my consciousness. The importance of moving from "ego" to a deeper or more authentic self, an examination of the ontological questions posed by Purpel, are the foundation for a life-long transformational process (Knapp, 2001).

Another student reflects on her emerging understanding of the political nature of education:

> Personally, I need to continue to be vigilant about how and when my own silence is complicity. Part of the detriment of my early schooling was that I was conditioned to be agreeable, polite and to perform to expectation without rocking the boat. It is uncomfortable for me to go against the grain of that early conditioning. I have to guard against slipping into silent complicity in order to be a true advocate for my students and their families. If we want social change and true empowering education for all our students regardless of race, gender, ethnicity or social class, then teaching must be constantly self-critical, thereby becoming consciously political. (Diepenbrock, 2000, p. 7)

In Farsi there is a saying: "A wolf does not give birth to a lamb." Kathleen's reflections above remind me of my own emerging awareness of the politics of education as I studied Bartolomé, Chávez Chávez, Paulo and 'Nita Freire, Giroux, Gor-Ziv, McLaren, Macedo and Steinberg, among others. In his call for the intellectualization of teachers, Giroux (1988) suggests that those teachers who respond with scholarship arrive at new insights that enable them to more effectively create the pedagogical spaces necessary for democratic education.

Yet Freire's "patient-impatience" (1998, p. 44) serves as a reminder that it is a slow and generative process for learners who find it uncomfortable "to go against the grain of that earlier conditioning." Students often respond to critical pedagogical spaces with "non-engagement" (Bahruth & Steiner, 1998) and a disbelief that schools could be sites of oppression for teachers and students. I introduce the following metaphor when well-behaved teachers question the deconstructions of hegemony: a dog is totally unaware of the chain around its neck until it chases a squirrel. What these teachers interpret as freedom in their classrooms is rarely understood as a narrow spectrum that gives a false sense of liberty. I ask them what squirrels they have ever chased. Have they ever challenged the social injustices of daily educational practice? Do they ask why teacher aides teach poor children, while this would be totally unacceptable in a "gifted and talented" class? Do they ever ponder why culturally different learners are warehoused and marginalized in portable buildings, storage rooms, closets? What would happen if children from privileged households were handled this way? What response would teachers be likely to expect if they became aware of these political issues in schools and began to question these practices in faculty meetings? These questions serve to promote reflections and to provide the "metaphysical assist" toward an emerging criticity. According to Bruner (1994):

> I believe that the ways of telling and the ways of conceptualizing that go with them become so habitual that they finally become recipes for structuring experience itself, for laying down routes into memory, for not only guiding the life narrative up to the present, but for directing it into the future. I have argued that a life as led is inseparable from a life as told—or more bluntly, a life is not "how it was" but how it is interpreted and reinterpreted, told and retold: Freud's psychic reality. Certain basic formal properties of the life narrative do not change easily. Our excursion into experimental autobiography suggests that these formal structures may get laid down early in the discourse of family life and persist stubbornly in spite of changed conditions… [A] special, historically conditioned, metaphysical condition was needed to bring autobiography into existence as a literary form, so perhaps metaphysical change is required to alter the narratives we have settled upon as "being" our lives. The fish will, indeed, be the last to discover water—unless it gets a metaphysical assist. (p. 36)

I invite my students to consider their "preparation" more critically. I have them read Schmidt's (2000) reminder:

> Remember also that professional training is preceded by at least sixteen years of preparatory socialization in the schools. Students who go on to professional training tend to be the "best" students—those who, among other things, excel at playing by the rules. Over time, playing by the rules becomes part of their personal identity, a feature of who they are. Engaging in an act of resistance is a frightening step for such people, and therefore many never try. Taking a stand would break with the long-rewarded behavior that got them into graduate school in the first place.…It is not easy to maintain a non-conforming outlook within an institution.…Such oppositional activity does involve personal risk.…The lesson here is that the greatest threat to the survival of the individual as a potential source for change comes, ironically, from *not* taking this risk. Those who act are those who will survive as independent thinkers. They fight without demanding guarantees of victory or immunity from attempts at retribution. They know that the individual is obliterated not by confronting the system, but by conforming to it. (pp. 250–252)

Obviously, not all of my students take to heart the moral dilemma I try to put before them. Some insist upon adhering to the shallow literacy which has conditioned them to avoid ontological explorations. I have long since given up on trying to reach all of them, since hegemony and received culture run deeply and invisibly through their lives. I have found that when I water down my discourse for those who are least likely to accept the challenge, I shortchange those who are hungry for more meaningful educational experiences. Just as many of my fellow students in the doctoral program at UT were unable to shake off their comfort with doing the minimum to get by, I also recognize these groomed dispositions of many students who have been rewarded for being well behaved. However, I have seen the value of my own investment in scholarship and know that there will always be students in my classes who appreciate the critical pedagogical spaces I create with them. Similar to the two students cited above, I believe many of my students develop strong convictions which allow them to stay the course as cultural workers, while resisting the pressures to do factory work.

What is the source of convictions that allow critical educators to persist counter-hegemonically while knowing hegemony holds out no rewards or recognition to them, indeed will distract, discourage and punish (Schmidt, 2000), will even attempt to bribe them—as John Silber attempted with Henry Giroux (Giroux, 1996)—to be well-behaved servants of an empire where the emperor wears no clothes?

When I first began to read McLaren, I was still relatively comfortable with capitalism as a way of life. Members of the privileged class seem to feel a sense of well-being in a system whose inherent biases favor them consistently. Education in such a system works to ensure that the privileged are sheltered from making any connections between wealth and poverty. The greatest influence Peter has had on my pedagogy has been to give focus to a need to help my students discover their own privilege as I work counter-hegemonically to awaken their social consciousness. Using minority voices in the literature, where victimization at the hands of an unjust system is well articulated through poems and short stories, students become exposed to a discourse on human conditions they have been kept unaware of through a curriculum designed in a vacuum, which avoids social, political, historical and economic contexts in the distribution of knowledge.

In 1997, David Gabbard informed me that Peter had just had a dispute with a mainstream educational journal about the content of his article on Ché Guevara. The editors were comfortable with the pedagogical aspects of Ché, but they had asked Peter to remove sections referring to current conflicts between the oppressor and the oppressed: specifically, Peter's sections on the Chiapas conflict in Mexico led by the Zapatistas. Leaving critical discourse and corrections in the historical footnotes of the official version of history at a safe historical distance of thirty years serves as a mechanism of hegemony. Peter's attempt to link the historical with history as it was being made in Chiapas seemed too dangerous a discourse for the editors. Critical scholars (Chomsky, 2000; Schmidt, 2000) have mentioned how professionalization ideologically prepares professionals to practice a form of self-censorship away from dangerous discourse. David's own dissertation resulted in a book dedicated to an historical analysis of what he refers to as "Silencing Ivan Illich" (1993).

David and I were serving on the editorial board of *Cultural Circles*, and he suggested contacting Peter to solicit the article for our journal, since his outrage had caused him to retract the article rather than compromise the integrity of his work. The timing worked perfectly, and the piece was eventually printed in *Cultural Circles* (McLaren, 1998) in its entirety. The article prompted numerous kudos for its boldness and the meaningful linkages it made with contemporary struggles against exploitation visited upon the third, fourth and fifth worlds under the guise of "development."

Working directly with Peter on this article revealed to me aspects of him I had never gleaned from his writing. I discovered the depth of his investment in scholarship and his meticulous attention to detail. I also met the human being behind the scholar, as he would request changes or modifications with humility and a gentleness not reflected in the bold voice of his writing. We chuckled like a couple of schoolboys when he suggested we add some red to color the star on Ché's beret in the photos, a touch which cost very little, but received numerous amused comments from those who read the piece. He would apologize when requesting a last-minute change or two that he considered critical to polish the piece. He agreed with the logic of preceding his featured article with a piece by Gabbard (1998), his former student, as the lead article, which framed his discourse historically. Eventually, the article was expanded to become a book (McLaren, 2000a). Although I wasn't expecting it, he acknowledged my efforts in the book and was thus the first to recognize my investment, though I had done the same for many others. All of these small considerations showed me a "walk the talk" praxis. I discovered that Peter had evolved beyond the trap in academia of career building. He writes because he has something to say, and he takes risks when "speaking truth to power" (Said, 1996; Chomsky, 2000).

I finally got to meet Peter at a conference (NRMERA, 1998) on critical pedagogy in Jackson Hole. I asked him to participate in the conference along with Donaldo Macedo, David Gabbard and others, and he cancelled another, much more lucrative engagement to join us. The conference broke from traditional structure in many ways. Several critical scholars—men, women, Anglo and Latino—were seated in a circle within a circle of the participants and were asked to address critical questions in education (Macedo, 1994). In the spirit of what Donaldo calls "the politics of representation with the representation of politics"—rather than the hegemonic ploy of only having a token politics of representation without diversity of voices beyond a "well-behaved" discourse (Chomsky, 2000)—participants got to hear how different critical educators negotiated for meaning, sharing diverse views and learning from each other. Participants were also invited to direct their own questions to all or specific speakers. It was during this session that Peter interjected a chilling quote from Parenti (1998), which caused a long pause: "What is it that those in power want? Just one thing, really. They want it ALL!"

The circle of scholars was employed at the opening and closing of the conference and received favorable acknowledgment from participants as a refreshing departure from a paper read by one person. Of course, we arranged for the invited scholars to present their individual work during the conference as well, and this led to an interesting anecdote. A conservative professor from a local university, who had attended this conference many times in its more traditional venues, approached Peter, David, Donaldo and me as we were discussing Peter's paper. Peter sincerely wanted our observations and critical comments. The professor complimented Donaldo and David on their presentations, but then turned and informed Peter that his paper stretched his comfort zone just a little too much for his liking. Before the rest of us could say anything, Donaldo responded by saying, "There are millions of humans in the world who are born, live their entire lives and die without ever knowing the luxury of a comfort zone!" Having lived in Africa, Donaldo knew the difference between perceived oppression in the world of ideas and the brutal realities of colonization. There was a long pause in the conversation, and the professor walked away scratching his head, at least in the proverbial sense. The rest of us were wishing we had thought to respond in such a succinct way, knowing that nothing more needed to be said. It was a powerful moment.

Militarism and Armed Conflict: How Far Do We Take Revolution?

The most problematic of McLaren's work is his eulogizing of Ché and his work on the situation in Chiapas and the armed struggle of the Zapatistas. While it is undeniable that militarism is the coercive force of hegemony, responding to militarism with more of the same provides a conundrum that needs to be sorted out. A dimension of critical pedagogy is the development of self-critique so as to be vigilant that we are not inadvertently reinforcing the hegemony we are attempting to challenge. Obviously, Peter (2000b) cautions his readers of the perils of a liberal humanism as well. I am still wrestling with the question of balance between cultural work in classrooms and violent revolution. I am sympathetic to the armed struggle in Chiapas and Oaxaca, since these first-people nations have long been exploited and abused by "los recién llegados" (the recently arrived ones), a term used by native Mayan ancestors in Guatemala in reference to those who have only five hundred years of history since their arrival. I also admire the pedagogy of Ché, who taught his soldiers how to read and write, and insisted upon cultural classes as part of the formation of critical citizenship. My next conversation with Peter will be along the lines of militarism.

However, I am also aware that traditional schooling is arranged along military models (Gor-Ziv, 2001), with teachers working like drill sergeants, keeping their students in lines to drink, to sit, to go to the cafeteria, to leave school, and so forth. Lessons are linear and sequential, and everyone is required to be on the same page at the same time. Behaviorist paradigms in school and the military promote training so that predictable behaviors will occur in given situations. Conclusions are made about the intelligence of students based upon their performance, yet the content or developmental appropriateness of the curriculum is rarely questioned. Homogeneity in the classroom prepares students for more of the same in the military and the workplace.

Humanizing the educational experience of all learners holds great promise, and we must be careful that our practices in the classroom do not reinforce the hegemony we are attempting to change. In the words of Loren Eiseley: "The teacher is genuinely the creator of humanity, the molder of its most precious possession, the mind. There should be no greater honor given by society than permission to teach, just as there can be no greater disaster than to fail at that task" (1987, p. 118). Humanity would benefit from more educators like Peter, who with ontological clarity and the resulting strong convictions could wrest their pedagogy away from the greedy.

References

Aronowitz, S. (2000). *The knowledge factory.* Boston, MA: Beacon Press.

Bahruth, R. (2000a). Changes and challenges in teaching the word and the world for the benefit of all of humanity. Invited paper: Ninth Annual International Symposium on English Teaching. Taipei, Republic of China: Crane Publishing Company.

———. (2000b). Bilingual education. In D. Gabbard (Ed.), *Knowledge and power in the global economy: Politics and the rhetoric of school reform* (pp. 203-209). Mahwah, NJ: Lawrence Erlbaum Associates, Publishers.

Bahruth, R. & Steiner, S. (1998). Upstream in the mainstream: Pedagogy against the current. In R. Chávez Chávez & J. O'Donnell. *Speaking the Unpleasant: The politics of (non)engagement in the multicultural education terrain.* New York: SUNY Press.

Bruner, J. (1994). Life as Narrative, In Dyson and Genishi (Eds.), *The need for story.* NCTE Press.

Chávez Chávez, R. & O'Donnell, J. (1998). *Speaking the unpleasant: The politics of (non)engagement in the multicultural education terrain.* New York: SUNY Press.

Chomsky, N. (2000). *Chomsky on miseducation.* Ed. D. Macedo. Lanham, MD: Rowman and Littlefield.

Diepenbrock, K. (2000). Teaching as a political act: A reflection paper for the Whole Language Spanish Course. Paper submitted to author.

Eiseley, L. (1959). The sorcerer in the wood: For Joe Willets. *The Lost Notebooks of Loren Eiseley.* Ed. K. Heuer. 1987. New York: Little, Brown & Co.

Fanon, F. (1965). *The wretched of the earth.* New York: Grove Press.

Fischman, G. (2000). Challenges & hopes: Multiculturalism as revolutionary praxis: An interview with Peter McLaren. In F. Schultz (Ed.), *Annual Editions - Multicultural Education 00/01.* Guilford, CT: Dushkin/McGraw-Hill.

Foley, D. (1977). *From peones to políticos.* Austin, TX: The University of Texas Press.

———. (1990). Learning capitalist culture: Deep in the heart of tejas. Philadelphia, PA: University of Pennsylvania Press.

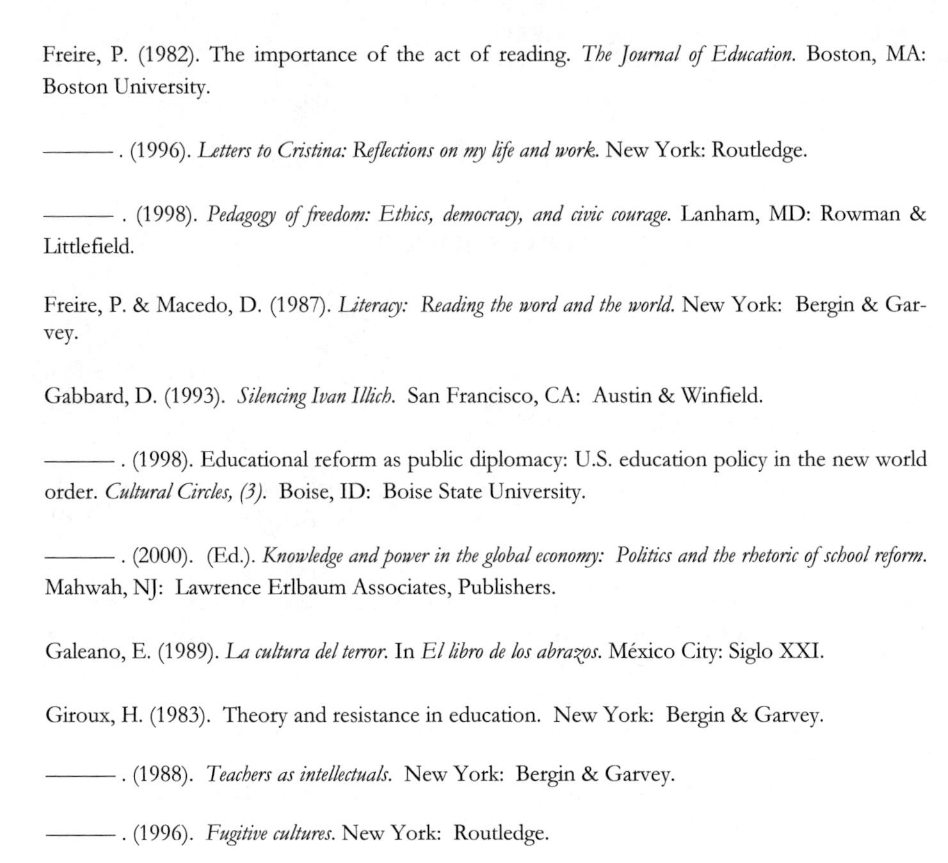

Freire, P. (1982). The importance of the act of reading. *The Journal of Education.* Boston, MA: Boston University.

———. (1996). *Letters to Cristina: Reflections on my life and work.* New York: Routledge.

——— . (1998). *Pedagogy of freedom: Ethics, democracy, and civic courage.* Lanham, MD: Rowman & Littlefield.

Freire, P. & Macedo, D. (1987). *Literacy: Reading the word and the world.* New York: Bergin & Garvey.

Gabbard, D. (1993). *Silencing Ivan Illich.* San Francisco, CA: Austin & Winfield.

———. (1998). Educational reform as public diplomacy: U.S. education policy in the new world order. *Cultural Circles, (3).* Boise, ID: Boise State University.

———. (2000). (Ed.). *Knowledge and power in the global economy: Politics and the rhetoric of school reform.* Mahwah, NJ: Lawrence Erlbaum Associates, Publishers.

Galeano, E. (1989). *La cultura del terror.* In *El libro de los abrazos.* México City: Siglo XXI.

Giroux, H. (1983). Theory and resistance in education. New York: Bergin & Garvey.

———. (1988). *Teachers as intellectuals.* New York: Bergin & Garvey.

———. (1996). *Fugitive cultures.* New York: Routledge.

Giroux, H.A. & Simon, R.I. (1989). (Eds.) *Popular culture, schooling and every day life.* New York: Bergin & Garvey.

Gor-Ziv, H. (2001). Personal communication. Tel Aviv, Israel.

Hayes, C., Bahruth, R. & Kessler, C. (1998). *Literacy con Cariño.* Portsmouth, NH: Heinemann Educational Books.

hooks, b. (1994). *Teaching to transgress.* New York: Routledge.

Knapp, J. (2001). Written response to Comprehensive Exam Question for MA program. Boise State University, College of Education.

Kohn, A. (2002). Keynote address. AACTE Annual Conference. New York.

Kozol, J. (1975). *The night is dark and I am far from home.* New York: Simon & Schuster.

Macedo, D. (1994). *Literacies of power.* Boulder, CO: Westview Press.

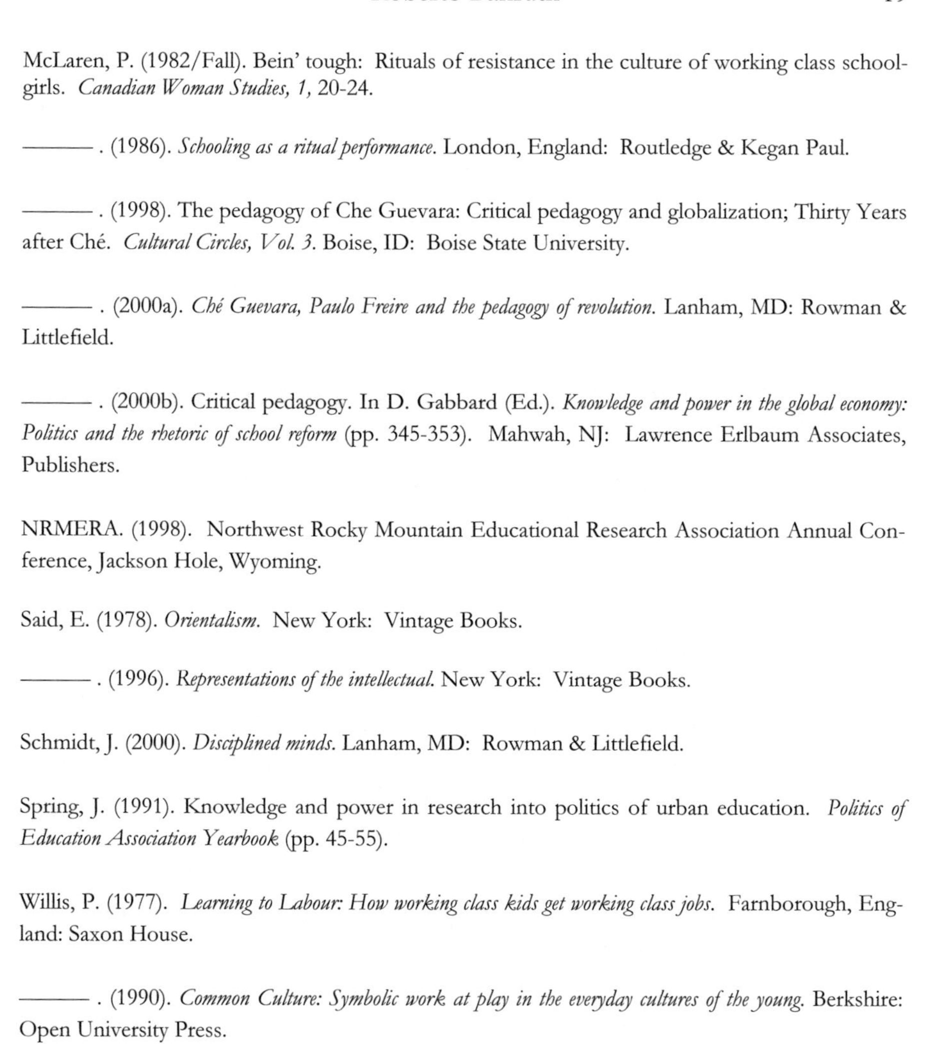

McLaren, P. (1982/Fall). Bein' tough: Rituals of resistance in the culture of working class schoolgirls. *Canadian Woman Studies, 1,* 20-24.

———. (1986). *Schooling as a ritual performance.* London, England: Routledge & Kegan Paul.

———. (1998). The pedagogy of Che Guevara: Critical pedagogy and globalization; Thirty Years after Ché. *Cultural Circles, Vol. 3.* Boise, ID: Boise State University.

———. (2000a). *Ché Guevara, Paulo Freire and the pedagogy of revolution.* Lanham, MD: Rowman & Littlefield.

———. (2000b). Critical pedagogy. In D. Gabbard (Ed.). *Knowledge and power in the global economy: Politics and the rhetoric of school reform* (pp. 345-353). Mahwah, NJ: Lawrence Erlbaum Associates, Publishers.

NRMERA. (1998). Northwest Rocky Mountain Educational Research Association Annual Conference, Jackson Hole, Wyoming.

Said, E. (1978). *Orientalism.* New York: Vintage Books.

———. (1996). *Representations of the intellectual.* New York: Vintage Books.

Schmidt, J. (2000). *Disciplined minds.* Lanham, MD: Rowman & Littlefield.

Spring, J. (1991). Knowledge and power in research into politics of urban education. *Politics of Education Association Yearbook* (pp. 45-55).

Willis, P. (1977). *Learning to Labour: How working class kids get working class jobs.* Farnborough, England: Saxon House.

———. (1990). *Common Culture: Symbolic work at play in the everyday cultures of the young.* Berkshire: Open University Press.

Chapter 2

Peter McLaren: Creative Dissent

Alípio Casali and Ana Maria Araújo Freire
Translated by Fernanda Fernandes

We are living the hallucinatory wakefulness of nightmare reason. (McLaren, *Revolutionary Multiculturalism*, p. 52)

Writing about Peter McLaren is not an easy task. Peter conveys complex, profound and uneasy ways of thinking and writing. He often chooses to write about things that may disturb or incite in today's world, a world in which established powers try to categorize people, societies, nations, religions and life options as "good" or "evil." Peter often seeks paths that are difficult to follow, paths that he forges with a deft and heightened awareness that reflect his deep and wide-ranging intellectual makeup.

It is also difficult for those unfamiliar with dialectic reasoning to follow McLaren's theoretical comings and goings and his profusion of ideas. It is a challenge for those who lack a background of certain philosophers, sociologists and educators, because Peter refers to many of them in his writings—through corroboration or refutation—as he takes us through the complex analyses of a man deeply concerned and engaged with the destiny of humanity. It is certainly something very complex and not easily understood by students who begin reading his writings. And because of the nuances of his movements of time and place, cases and facts, denunciations and announcements, which always strongly and intensively—sometimes dramatically—infiltrate his writings, it is simply not easy to read Peter McLaren.

Peter's language is at once concrete and symbolic. The adjectives he uses are frequent and very powerful. While this is common in much of North American writing, in McLaren's work these adjectives assume a peculiar character that enriches and beautifies everything he says, and that possesses the power to emphasize and clarify his thoughts. It is also part of his character not to be afraid of naming North American men and women who "are making the world ugly," as Paulo Freire used to say. He denounces those who are creating and perpetuating all manner of oppressive and repressive ideologies and imposing imperialist policies and practices that demand the submission of the world's most vulnerable populations, including sectors of the oppressed within the United States, the country that he has adopted or—perhaps more accurately—that has adopted him.

Peter McLaren is a unique thinker, educator, writer and activist. This sentence is admittedly a truism, but it is difficult to resist mentioning those traits. In the current era of speedy technology and image blitzes, we are accustomed to looking at people in a very superficial way, since we are constantly bombarded with so many images, so much of the time. But it is impossible not to notice Peter in the middle of the crowd, much as it is impossible not to be completely drawn in by his image: the extravagance of his mode of dress, his disheveled hair, his tattoos, his quick, sudden gestures, his attentive manner and luminous aura. At first he seems a caricature, a remnant of the counterculture of the 1960s. More than a few who are motivated by casual prejudice refuse to read his books or listen to him. They categorize him as a writer to be avoided, lest one be disturbed by the uneasiness that sometimes comes with his way of thinking and acting.

Peter's talk is full of movement. His texts are a spectacle of colors, sounds, tastes, images, gestures and actions. At first his speech seems to betray a "postmodern language," the same sort that reduces meanings to contents, and which may be seen and appreciated in the speech of politicians or media celebrities. "Appreciated" is the correct word, because such "postmodern" procedure certainly has this intention: to divert the interlocutor's consciousness, hypnotize him or her, and, like the illusionists, make reality disappear and reappear, as if its existence depended exclusively on language. But Peter denounces these empty practices and the deceptive inconsistency of these performative narratives.

After a close examination of what Peter says and writes, the cliché of a verbose activist melts away, and the image emerges of an acute and perceptive thinker, an inexorable analyst, a creative critic, swathed in conceptual subtleties, metaphors and representations that betray a sharpness and truth. Peter seems to mimic some of the style of those he excoriates, but he does it to humiliate them. He chooses some of their very same weapons in order to make them feel ridiculous. His choice of language expresses Peter's own way of being. As he himself says: "I do not have the words to express what such boundary identity means. Everything I have is what George Bataille (1988) refers to as *mots glissants* (slippery words)" (2000, p 23–24).

There may not be a more accurate way to describe McLaren than as one who possesses a "boundary identity." He inhabits boundaries: economic, political, cultural, aesthetic and ethic. Limits are suggested by his gaze, his attentiveness, his gestures, his comprehension. As a reporter from the "frontier," he is always at the place where the decisive event occurs, in order to reveal it in all its complexity, in its trivial cruelty.

In Peter's speech, his complete soul emerges. The historic examples with which he illustrates his talks and texts are not mere collections of bits that are clipped from newspapers and magazines. They are rather expressions of his own experiences, of a daily life that has always reflected a close commitment to students from ghettoes, to poor people who wander the streets, to artists who live on the fringes of society. His analyses are dense, permitting him to produce great ethnographic studies, and through such studies he is able to recreate the complexity of our shared humanity. It is not a case of trying to "interpret" or "discover" a person's hidden sense, but rather to talk about its inexhaustible completeness of meaning within the limits of language. Peter creates real anthropology.

Peter is neither neutral nor amorphous. He is not a thinker providing exploitation and manipulation services for the bourgeoisie. He is a man who knows why the issues he deals with and the facts he analyzes are the way they are. And he knows how to choose courageously the side he wishes to be on: the side of life, close to those who are oppressed by racism and deprived of justice.

A close reading of Peter's texts makes us aware of the special way in which he approaches the subjects he treats. As he gets close to them in a deep and loving manner, they in turn get close to his humanist pulsations. We also perceive the way in which they become more "formal," more distanced from the "romanticism" McLaren is accused of. But that healthy romanticism—the way Paulo Freire used to write—is also a form of reading and writing about the world, one which reestablishes a belief in women and men. It is a way of interpreting what is essential in the world, so that we are forced to acknowledge that we require true utopias in order to exist as human beings, much in the same way as we need oxygen to survive.

In his writings, Peter says that the world is a work in progress, and that as men and women we cannot fail to engage with it in order to prevent it from becoming an ungovernable force that enables neo-liberalism to deprive us of our capacity to make decisions and choices. On the contrary, we can and must act in order to transform our societies. We have to fight against being turned into subjects of history and to resist becoming robots in preparation for a "brave new world," as if history were not a product of freedom, and as if humanity were genetically programmed for barbarousness. Peter asks himself and forces us to ask: What kind of world are we creating? One that rejects human abilities and believes in the inevitability of capital linked to certain "market ethics"? In reality, talking about "market ethics" is nonsense, an oxymoron; it denies the fundamental contradiction embodied in this term and blurs the real meaning of ethics.

Peter argues successfully that in a cruel world full of atrocities and selfish acts of every kind, we can find men and women who think and act honorably, people who believe in the human ability to build a better and more just world. These are men and women who are ready to dismantle established concepts and destroy the elitist and criminal prejudice and discrimination of white supremacists. Such acts of prejudice and discrimination are among the many characteristics of industrial capitalism and Eurocentrism, characteristics that have now been become typically "American."

To read Peter and to take in his critiques is to be devoured by the ethical maelstrom into which globalized, mass societies have been propelled: a condition in which the State is reduced to dust and in which the Market has been elevated to the status of an idol to be worshipped by both Wall Street and the drug dealers in the Brazilian slums. Peter takes us to the places where structural unemployment and hunger kill more people than wars, to places where diverse cultures, genders, ethnic groups, sexualities and religions are being illuminated by new epistemological, political and ethical discourses.

Peter's writing forces us to direct our attention to the sad spectacle of economic injustices and the cultural exclusion of those who are considered different. Reading him does not lead to being able to apologize for ignorance, but rather to losing the excuse for non-commitment. He beckons us to a new mission: the refusal of simply being voices in assent of the opinions put forward by the media, and of not agreeing with the "evidence" of official policies. He calls us to disagree, to oppose, to dissent, to resist.

Peter has, above all, an acute sensibility concerning differences and transformations. He gives us systematic and dense reflections: Who is the Other? What constitutes such "otherness"? What are the principles of this otherness? What does the presence or absence of otherness ethically obligate me to do? How do we function as strangers for Others? What ethical imperatives does this place on us? This is a theme whose understanding is urgently demanded by both the multicultural point of view and ethnography, and about which we cannot be satisfied with incomplete explanations. Peter has an immense collection of personal, political and cultural experiences to enrich and "thicken" the necessary and compelling debate about these subjects.

Peter has been living at otherness' boundaries. Very few thinkers have demonstrated such a profound ability to understand the subtleties of protest that are conveyed as "cries from the corridor" (*Life in Schools*, 1997, p. 48). Very few would have the courage to exist in an environment and to identify themselves in such a way as to allow themselves be violently excluded in certain situations. He identifies himself as white, Anglo-Saxon, Christian and male, and announces his unrestricted solidarity with those who suffer from exclusion and discrimination. This is the characteristic courageous, political-cultural posture of Peter that informs both his pedagogical practice and thought process. It is through such concrete political-cultural ways of facing things as an activist that Peter reveals the best of his pedagogy. His students are now not only the suburban boys from the Jane Finch Corridor on the outskirts of Toronto but include men and women from everywhere. They are scattered throughout the continents and hail from different cultures, ethnic groups, religions, age groups, genders and sexualities. His talks and texts provoke everyone, calling for dialogue, commitment and re-creative action. This is a fundamental aspect in the linking of his convictions with those of Paulo Freire. In Freire, it is dialogue that defines pedagogical action and that leads to a fundamental ethics in which the other person, working from the principle of his or her unlimited capacity to alter them self, expresses their word and world, in a critical and transformative exercise.

In the preface to McLaren's book on Paulo Freire and Ché Guevara, such a sensitive quality is evident. The identification of Peter with these two men who, much more than others, have undertaken to seek and find solutions to Latin American problems through a similar capacity to love, is totally understandable. Both the Brazilian educator and the Argentinean-Cuban politician have embodied such love toward human beings and have conveyed it in all their thoughts and actions. Peter, a culturally and economically "privileged" man because he was born white and had the chance to study in a First World country, did not take advantage of the social conditions of his birth. He did not regard them as a privilege to be retained, but he used them to try to understand exactly the nature of the privileges afforded to those born white and middle-class. He drew from the perspective of his status to better understand the mistaken ideology of the "inner superiority of the white man," created precisely to favor the hidden interests of the white, European, ruling-class male. He channeled such advantage into an expression of love toward all of humanity, particularly those who are excluded from the benefits of society.

In his book *Revolutionary Multiculturalism* (2000), Peter once more explicitly recognized the influence of Paulo Freire and his critical way of thinking and acting. We see clearly, especially in chapters seven and eight of that volume, that his sensitive, understanding view of the world is firmly grounded in the lovingness found in Freire's literature (a fact that has been pointed out by Ana Maria Araújo Freire in the preface to *Revolutionary Multiculturalism*). Peter McLaren is not a "follower" of Paulo Freire. Paulo vehemently rejected any such desire on the part of those who wanted to join him as simple followers or disciples of a "model and example." But the fact is that Peter did receive inspiration from Paulo, agreed with many of his ideas and broadened them while developing others. Peter creates his own interpretations about what he feels, sees, observes, researches and analyzes. And the major ones are exactly those that are essential to someone who wants to establish his existence in the world as a thinker and humanist activist: sensibility and tolerance in standing in solidarity with others. This, too, was true of Paulo Freire and remains true for all those who, like Peter, worry about the condition of humanity (although this is unfortunately seen by some today as a retrograde, outdated and condemnable trait). In this way, Peter is able to create his own theory while maintaining deep roots in the matrix of Paulo Freire, and we believe that this is the bond that best links the thoughts of the Canadian to those of the Brazilian: the sensibility, the tolerance and the solidarity toward the oppressed.

Such virtues, together with Peter's capacity for astonishment, fright and emotional curiosity (the latter an uncommon trait in women and men from the North Atlantic), which has more and more been turned into an epistemological one, explains the profusion of subjects that he deals with and that he shares with us via his books. These are perhaps the main affinities between Peter and Paulo. Within the historical contexts in which they have lived and made themselves "heard" by the world, each of them has made his own mark: one with compassion toward the miserable people of one of the poorest regions of the planet (the northeastern part of Brazil) and the other taking his experiences from the relatively "wealthy" (at least in comparison) Canadian proletarian class. And because of their respective life experiences and work, grounded in the distinct theoretical sources that incited and fed their curiosity, each of them lent certain peculiarities to their works. This is also what happened to the ideas of democracy and multiculturalism.

Freire's message aims to create worldwide citizenship by respecting the needs and the personal characteristics—as well as the cultural differences—of each group of people. When multiculturalism is understood as a sociality of difference that allows the oppressed to fight against social antagonisms in an uninterrupted movement of dissent and consensus, we will then be making a contribution to democratic tolerance. In the multiculturalism that preserves the genuine identity of each group of people in a totality that has to be fraternal, diverse and in solidarity, and with a true dialogical basis, there is no place for any kind of violence. There must be coherence within difference, tolerance in unlikeness, humility in diversity, solidarity in the face of injustice. This is what the process of freedom demands. We see multiculturalism in accordance with Paulo's understanding of it: something that makes an attempt to redeem our degraded humanity, that tries to imbue people with our most important human characteristics—searching incessantly for all of us to become more important beings by means of an authentic communication as well as an effort to overcome oppression and injustice.

Paulo Freire's vision of the world—his communication theory—has as its fundamental pillar the ME-YOU relation. For him there is no sense in having a ME and a YOU; what is important is the ME-YOU relation, which necessarily implies acceptance of difference. As such, it requires dialogue: a dialogue of loving subjects who are curious about the object to be discovered. It is a conscious, intentional dialogue that assists men and women in discovering and naming their ontology, their ideal human experience, because we take possession of knowledge to transform the world and make it better, something that only men and women can do. According to Paulo Freire's pedagogy, difference is the starting point for the dialogue between the ME and the YOU, so that knowledge interferes in the world. Thus, from Freire's point of view, the ability to have dialogue dialectically overlaps the epistemological, political, ethical, aesthetic, cognitive and psychosocial-historical dimensions.

In Freire's pedagogy there is a paradoxical element. Cultural and pedagogical consensus becomes the starting point and the initial reason for the act of educating, and it is predicated on a consensus between the educator and the student in the sense of them both being citizens. Such forms of consensus, however, tend to be altered during the pedagogical experience. The objective of the educator is to have the student grow and mature to a point at which he or she becomes able, from the cognitive and cultural point of view, to feel things differently from his or her teacher. Such a dissension is actually what permits the development of critical consciousness in the student. At the same time, the civic-political equality that originated in the consensus necessary to start the pedagogical process will tend to be manifested in a different way—as dissension—as the student grows and matures. Such a dialectic between dissension and consensus constitutes the essential part of the pedagogical process for Paulo Freire. So, pedagogically speaking, consensus has to be found through dissension; conversely, dissension derives from a prior consensus. Only by adopting this dialectical relationship can the practice of dissension become fertile and liberating. The "pedagogy of dissent for the new millennium" espoused by McLaren (*Revolutionary Multiculturalism*) is built precisely on such a dialectical conception of dissent and consensus.

It is hoped that this discursive explanation and development of the idea of consensus and dissensus between Peter McLaren and Paulo Freire may, as does every pedagogic action, become an agent of change in pedagogical practices and educational policies, in the sense of creating a dignified human life for all.

But access to such fundamental and conceptual building blocks from McLaren is not always easy. The experience of Brazilian students reading Peter's texts reveals the validity of one of the main themes with which he occupies himself, that is, the experience of cultural boundaries. What our Brazilian students who read Peter identify with immediately is the object to which he points: the existence of cruel injustice all over the world, which ritualizes itself in the daily violence of institutions everywhere that operate through exclusion and discrimination. Our students do not doubt that Peter is "one of us" and that he is on the side of the oppressed in such a struggle. Peter's position is one of radical solidarity that we have come to expect from critical activists and thinkers of the North Atlantic.

His limitation is naturally one that faces any thinker who speaks from another cultural location and who speaks in a language linked to his own culture. But in the South, the hardships of life are more violent: poverty and hunger hurt and take more lives, and the injustices are doubled. Such circumstances spark commentary that is more heated, more direct, more immediate. Radical exclusions demand radical solutions in the short term. It is not by chance that the social structure is fragmented here at a much faster rate, nor is it by chance that the chaos here seems to be more immediate and threatening.

Peter's critical thought has no limits as an ethical example of radical commitment in favor of life, justice and freedom. His ideal reminds us of that of Paulo: the capacity to be unique, but also to be the expression of a particular culture, of a particular gender, of a particular skin color, of a particular aesthetic position; and at the same time to be human. This is expression in its more universal sense. Because of this, Peter must go on being exactly who he is: a human being who is always in motion. We want him to continue talking, in a vigorous language, about the great challenges of the North Atlantic culture and hemisphere, the great challenges of other cultures and the great challenges of humanity. And we hope such dissension will be, for us and for him, a bridge from the present to a future where all human differences will shine in such a way that—with them and because of them—we build a peaceful, just, always-in-tension and shifting sociality, one that is constantly steeped in learning and the creative process.

References

McLaren, P. (1997). *A vida nas escolas: Uma introdução à pedagogia crítica nos fundamentos da educação* (L.P. Zimmer et al., Trans.). Porto Alegre: Artes Médicas.

———. (1999). *Utopias provisórias: as pedagogias críticas num cenário pós-colonial* (H.B.M. Souza, Trans.). Petrópolis: Vozes.

———. (2000). *Multiculturalismo revolucionário: Pedagogia do dissenso para o novo milênio* (M. Moraes & R.C. Costa, Trans.). Porto Alegre: Artes Médicas Sul, 2000.

———. (2001). *Ché Guevara, Paulo Freire, and the pedagogy of revolution.* Boulder, CO: Rowan & Littlefield, 2000; *El Che Guevara, Paulo Freire y la pedagogia de la revolución.* México: Siglo XXI.

Chapter 3

Peter McLaren's Politics and Ethics of Solidarity: Notes on Critical Pedagogy and Radical Education

Zeus Leonardo

As a young man growing up in Toronto, Canada, during the turbulent years of the 1960s counterculture, Peter McLaren studied theater arts and Elizabethan drama before leaving the university to work for five years as a classroom teacher in the Jane Finch Corridor, an area in which Canada's largest public housing projects are located. His struggle for better teaching and learning conditions in the schools, as well as his political activism on behalf of new immigrant populations from the West Indies and Southeast Asia, prompted McLaren to publish his first book, *Cries from the Corridor: The New Suburban Ghettos*, a diary of his teaching experiences. The book soon became a bestseller in Canada, sparking a national controversy on the state of Canadian schools and the changing demographics of the Canadian population.

Following the book's publication, McLaren had taken a leave of absence from his school board to pursue doctoral studies at the Ontario Institute for Studies in Education at the University of Toronto, when he learned that he was barred by the board from ever teaching again in an inner-city school. McLaren then decided to concentrate on theoretical writing, inspired by the work of the late Brazilian philosopher Paulo Freire and by a seminar he attended at a semiotics summer institute that was conducted by Michel Foucault. When McLaren found it virtually impossible to find full-time employment in Canadian universities, Henry Giroux invited him in 1985 to leave Canada and to join him at the Center for Education and Cultural Studies based in Miami University of Ohio's School of Education and Allied Professions, where McLaren also served as associate director of the Center. After a lengthy and prolific collaboration with Giroux, McLaren left the Center in 1993 to join the faculty of the Graduate School of Education and Information Studies at the University of California, Los Angeles, where he currently teaches.

One could approach writing about Peter McLaren's oeuvre from a variety of positions. In fact, one may conclude that writing about McLaren is an impossible task, in the Derridean sense of the word. On one hand, his scholarship travels and travails within the problematique of historical materialism. Indeed, it would be inaccurate to conclude that McLaren's recent publications signal his *return* to Marxism (see McLaren, 2000). In multiple editions of *Schooling as a Ritual Performance* (1993) and *Life in Schools* (1989), McLaren's analysis of education has been informed by critiques of the political economy of gestures and rituals, of desire, and more recently of global capitalism (see McLaren, 2000). In short, Marxism was never a pen away. On the other hand, his engagement of theory (and he is foremost a theorist) spans over a decade of Freirean influence, confrontations with postmodernism, whiteness studies and cultural studies. With this in mind, representing McLaren is an intimate part of teaching McLaren.

In the field of critical pedagogy, McLaren's influence is clearly felt. In the company of Freire and Giroux, McLaren's contributions toward the creation of a new subdiscipline is perhaps his greatest academic achievement. Through his writings, we learn that critical educational theory is an indispensable part of social solidarity and emancipation. By representing McLaren's work in this manner, we are able to assess his influence on the intellectual development of the educational field as a whole. As a result, McLaren's programmatic suggestions come to the surface and allow educators to grasp his unique insights rather than learning about any singular influence on the development of his thought. This move also avoids any reduction of McLaren's work as the endorsement of one narrative or author. This chapter will outline McLaren's eclectic contributions to critical pedagogy, assess his conceptualization of radical education and analyze his general framework for revolutionizing social life.

In a chapter from *Critical Pedagogy and Predatory Culture* (1995), titled "Critical Pedagogy and the Pragmatics of Justice," Peter McLaren outlines the tenets he perceives to be common to critical pedagogy. His theses on critical pedagogy include eleven points:

1. Pedagogies should constitute a form of social and cultural criticism.
2. All knowledge is fundamentally mediated by linguistic relations that inescapably are socially and historically constituted.

3. Individuals are synechdochically related to the wider society through traditions of mediation (family, friends, religion, formal schooling, popular culture, etc.).
4. Social facts can never be isolated from the domain of values or removed from forms of ideological production as inscription.
5. Relationship between concept and object and signifier and signified are neither inherently stable nor transcendentally fixed and are often mediated by circuits of capitalist production, consumption and social relations.
6. Language is central to the formation of subjectivity (unconscious and conscious awareness).
7. Certain groups in any society are unnecessarily and often unjustly privileged over others and while the reason for this privileging may vary widely, the oppression which characterizes contemporary societies is most forcefully secured when subordinates accept their social status as natural, necessary, inevitable or bequeathed to them as an exercise of historical chance.
8. Oppression has many faces and focusing on only one at the expense of others (e.g., class oppression vs. racism) often elides or occults the interconnection among them.
9. An unforeseen world of social relations awaits us in which power and oppression cannot be understood simply in terms of an irrefutable calculus of meaning linked to cause-and-effect conditions.
10. Domination and oppression are implicated in the radical contingency of social development and our responses to it.
11. Mainstream research practices are generally and unwittingly implicated in the reproduction of systems of class, race and gender oppression.

Throughout this essay, McLaren's eleven theses will inform the organization of my synthesis. En route, however, I will not give them equal attention but instead will highlight the points that are central to his philosophy, such as the productive tension between materialism and representation, or their analytic equivalents in ideology critique and discourse analysis.

McLaren's critical pedagogy asserts that schooling is a social and cultural practice. It is inherently a socialization process, an introduction to a way of life and a cultural politics of learning. As such, as a social phenomenon, schooling involves the inculcation of values, which is reminiscent of Freire's (1994) insistence that teaching is always directive. McLaren locates the sociality of "life in schools" as a site of struggle over material organization and regimes of representation. Some of his leading questions are: On what grounds do you justify your pedagogy? How inclusive of other voices is your discourse, and whose interests do your methods serve? Is your discourse flexible or rigid to change? To transformations? How central are issues of social justice and human rights to your approach?

With a socialist politics in mind, McLaren encourages teachers to assume the role of Giroux's (1988) "transformative intellectuals." Using a Gramscian sense of the "organic intellectual," McLaren's intellectual links knowledge to the practice of liberation. This position is different from its common usage of intellectual as a professional position. Likewise, teaching is not only a professional but a praxiological vocation. McLaren's intellectual is a mediator of social and cultural life, not a functionary of educational institutions. McLaren (1991a) clarifies:

> Transformative intellectuals are mobile subjects sensitive to the shifting contexts of contemporary social life. The transformative intellectual is engaged in the act of struggle—a cultural politics, if you will—in which new forms of identity and subjectivity are sought. They are sought in the context of a deepening of democracy. (p. 149)

A teacher working to dismantle oppression is an example of McLaren's intellectual, though not the only one. An intellectual must practice "phronesis," or strategical common sense, in order to arrive at the essence of social and cultural formations (McLaren, 1992, p. 17). However, McLaren is also mindful of the imposing nature of meta-narratives that intellectuals mobilize when they speak for the oppressed.

Critical, but far from dismissive, of modernist teleologies of scientific progress, determinisms and reductivisms (of which Marxist orthodoxy is an example), McLaren seriously engages postmodern innovations, coming up with his own brand of "critical postmodernism." In an article with Giroux, McLaren (1986) engages Foucault's notion of the "specific intellectual," or educators whose expertise is socially specific and culturally effective for the conditions in which they find themselves. McLaren finds the specific intellectual wanting because it cannot account for the shifting terrain of subjectivity within the development of late capitalism, a subjectivity that is produced within the antagonisms determined by the economy. For McLaren (1998b), the dialectic between an organic and specific intellectual represents the tension of radical work that a "border intellectual" (p. 369) tries to resolve. Globally, an educator pieces together the apparent fragmentation of social life. Capital, world racism, and patriarchy that know no nation mobilize cultural workers to link high and popular culture, the academy and the bazaar, the opera and Oprah. McLaren's quixotic intellectual is at home with quotidian forces, understanding that there is no neat separation between mass and elite knowledge. At the same time, McLaren is also mindful that the global finds its provisional rest in local places. It is the work of radical critique to trace the inflow of global forces into particular places, the amalgamation of which outflows to construct our notion of the totality we refer to as "society."

Furthermore, a cultural critic realizes that cultures are in a constant state of struggle for meaning. Or, more specifically, culture assumes the structures of a discourse wherein the signifying powers of language render it intelligible, or in some cases, distorted. Stuart Hall (1997) agrees with this sentiment when he describes discourse as a general "politics of representation," a regime of meaning that slips final closure and is often characterized as a field of contestation for supremacy. Unlike Foucault, Deleuze and other "self-abnegating intellectuals" (Spivak, 1988), McLaren still believes in the intervening role of the educator. Rejecting a ludic approach to culture as simply a site of pleasure, or jouissance, McLaren works from a conflict theory of culture. McLaren (1991a) explains: "Within the critical perspective, culture is a site of disjuncture, rupture, and contradiction—a terrain of contestation for multivalent practical-discursive structures of power" (p. 144). Siding more with the sociological, less with the anthropological, notion of culture, McLaren constructs a definition of culture as a discursive field that closely resembles the structure of language without severing it from relations of production.

Culture is less a collection of artifacts than a representational apparatus for constructing the subjects and objects of linguistic statements: who speaks and who is spoken to. Stated another way, McLaren finds the ludic definition of culture lacking, for it levels power differentials to a common denominator that is measureless, as if the power of the oppressed were equitable with the power of the oppressor, in terms of a relation of force. This law of equivalency denies the production of cultural politics, or the struggle over meaning that often takes place in the context of asymmetrical material relations. It is the privilege and burden of the intellectual to piece together disparate elements of a social formation in order to intervene in the face of uncertainty. Linda Alcoff (1995) says as much when she writes, "To say that location *bears* on meaning and truth is not the same as saying that location *determines* meaning and truth. Location is not a fixed essence absolutely authorizing an individual's speech in the way that God's favor absolutely authorized speech of Moses" (p. 106; italics in original). The struggle over meaning is a political site that McLaren does not hesitate to negotiate despite the fact that his voice may be a privileged medium for such an occasion. Not unlike Alcoff, he understands that there is too much at stake to abdicate his role as an intellectual simply because it is his privileged and institutional location. To Foucault's chagrin, McLaren leaves an imprint, an undeniable stamp on his meaning without determining it (see Foucault, 1991; cf. Said, 1979).

According to McLaren, culture is a field wherein practices are neither innocent nor unmediated by the struggle for power. Here he agrees with Foucault (1978, 1980), who reminds us that the outcome of the struggle against regimes of power begets power; it does not escape the circuits of power. For example, when Civil Rights activists rose up against the U.S. establishments of the 1960s, they were not getting "outside" of power relations. Rather, they were redirecting, appropriating or harnessing them for their own radical purposes. Locating himself in a Freirean framework, McLaren emphasizes that "culture is never depoliticized; it always remains tied to the social and class relationships that inform it" (1994a, p. 200). McLaren understands all too well the asymmetrical relationship between, for example, the culture of poverty and the culture of privilege. Culture is inscribed by the mode of production that supplies its materials and makes its objectification possible, as well as the linguistic relations from which class subjects gain their sense of self as workers or owners of the economy. In terms of schooling, working-class culture bears the traces of the contradictions that limit its own horizon of understanding (Willis, 1977).

For McLaren, all knowledge is fundamentally mediated by linguistic relations that inescapably are socially and historically constituted. In a Bourdieuan sense, the differential status between students' linguistic capitals distorts the stories they tell through their language. Whereas people's narratives represent specific ways of knowing the world, linguistic relations deem some knowledge of the world unpresentable, therefore silenced or represented for. The subaltern narrative is saturated with regimes of knowledge that make it problematic to assert an authentic subaltern representation uninflected by the distorting effects of the dominant culture (Spivak, 1988). Using a Foucauldian lens, McLaren appropriates the power/knowledge nexus to explain that since language is a crucial mediating structure that people use to make sense of their world, the knowledge resulting from the process of signification is implicated in the conflict over power.

Engaging deconstruction, McLaren also locates the way language constitutes voices that are carriers of contradictions. As such, different people take up different subject positions that are embedded ideologically in social grammars. Traditionally, dominant histories have subsumed the colonized voice, but could never escape their radical alterity, their ability to supplement the colonizer's identity (cf. Memmi, 1965). Recent developments in postcolonial discourses have ruptured colonial domination to reveal the voices of the colonized, their ability to subvert the colonial subject. McLaren joins the movement to privilege what Foucault calls "subjugated knowledges" while maintaining the differences between and within colonized voices. As a result, such a project is conducive to de-colonizing the narratives students live and tell one another. That said, McLaren is also critical of postcolonial discourse for its unbridled belief in the autonomy of the cultural field, independent of the determining imprint of political economy, as if signification stood outside production.

McLaren's contention is that individuals are synechdochically related to the wider society through traditions of mediation (e.g., family, friends, religion, formal schooling and popular culture). The social and discursive nature of experience is an ecosystemic instance McLaren consistently discusses in his work. Whereas he agrees with the feminist focus on experience as a starting point for a political project, he adds that experience never speaks for itself and must be mediated through ideologies, theories or problematics. Social subjects must go beyond experience as personal and innocent, and interpret it in the arena of power through critical discourses. Mediating institutions like family, religion and education filter experience in such a manner that creates dispositions in students, some of which remain unquestioned or unanalyzed. Appropriating theories by Bourdieu, Willis and Giroux, McLaren accords experience only relative autonomy, reminding us of the truth in Raymond Williams' (1977) concept of the "structure of feeling." That said, experience is not reduced merely to ideological status. Rather, Giroux and McLaren (1992) insist that experience is actively constructed with value systems and codes embedded in what we refer to as "reality" (p. 12). Experience never speaks for itself but is inscribed, for example, within the constitutive discourses we bring to bear on it; indeed, we must speak for it. McLaren qualifies the idea of unbridled agency, or a completely autonomous experience of history, with an intersubjective, materially enfleshed body/subject (McLaren, 1986; see also Biesta, 1995).

Hence, McLaren posits that social facts can never be isolated from the domain of values or removed from forms of ideological production as inscription. Ideology seeps into every decision we make, from the words we choose to mobilize to make sense of our world (see Freire & Macedo, 1987) to the policies with which we govern our schools. In diametric opposition to objectivists, McLaren (1989) wholeheartedly makes the effort to demystify politics by admitting his own. In his writings, he recognizes that his whiteness, as a racial construction, has anointed him powers not doled out to marginalized people of color. McLaren disabuses himself of the privilege he did not seek but was given.

He rejects the authority society has bequeathed onto whiteness and maleness. He even poses the possibility of whiteness as an ethnicity, since whiteness, as the center, has relegated ethnicity to status of the Other, less pure than white and exotic in comparison. To the extent that McLaren positions himself against whiteness, he disidentifies with its colonizing form of subjectivity, while admitting the reality of whiteness' structural position of advantage and the unearned privileges that come with it (McLaren, 1997; see also Leonardo, 2002).

McLaren's whiteness is a "fact" of social construction, but he maintains that one's ethnicity, gender and class do not guarantee one's politics. Social subjects possess relative autonomy to choose the values that serve justice and humanity. McLaren insists that solidarity with concrete people of history serves as a prerequisite to an ethics grounded in universal justice. We can liberate ourselves only through a critical dialectical engagement with others. Thus, he locates values in a state of constant negotiation and not a tattoo we reveal branded on our white, brown or black skins. Questions like "What is it that society has made of me that I no longer wish to be?" liberate one's private identity from the walls of her social inscriptions and ascriptions. A critical recognition of others as constitutive of one's subjectivity enables us to form matrices of intersubjectivity with people, not dependence but interdependence (see Leonardo, 2000). Within the invocation of the "I" is a trace of the other. Social "facts," like ascriptions, can be redirected for the project of emancipation but only after full understanding and disclosure of the social forces that condition our identity development. Indeed, McLaren uses his identities as part of, not separate from, his alliances with oppressed people. In short, solidarity does not require one to ask the other for identity papers (McLaren, 1998b).

Because discourse, like meaning itself, is in a state of constant negotiation, McLaren privileges the formation of subjectivity over identity. Reacting to formal logic's emphasis on the law of identity, Giroux and McLaren (1992) substitute subjectivity for identity to emphasize the contingency in our social positions. Whereas identity traditionally has been constructed as fixed and stable, subjectivity is constantly shaped and reshaped through discourse. Giroux and McLaren's distinctions are important and deserve to be quoted at length:

> We use the term "subjectivity" here as distinct from identity because subjectivity permits us to acknowledge and address the ways in which individuals make sense of their experiences, including their conscious and unconscious understandings, and the cultural forms available through which such understandings are either constrained or enabled. The term "identity" on the other hand implies that there is a fixed essence that

> exists independently of the range of discourses made available to individuals. That is, the term identity suggests a unitary, self-constituting sovereign subject whose autonomous, primordial characteristics are pre-discursive in nature, allegedly constituted outside of language, history or power. (p. 14)

The passage does not suggest that McLaren rejects the notion of identity formation. Identity politics is still very important for self-actualization in the face of recognizing how groups of people have been oppressed on the basis of their identity. Rather, McLaren urges us to find a common ground wherein we can negotiate a liberatory politics, which includes the discourse of identity, but moving beyond it as well. In fact, McLaren appropriates Kearney's ideas on the politics of location. Solidarity predicates itself on ethics as having priority over epistemology and ontology. Rather than asking "Who are you?," solidarity demands "Where are you?" Locating yourself beside marginalized peoples in the midst of struggle, you answer, "I am here and here for you." This is a subtle turn in language but one which McLaren hopes will contribute to building solidarity (McLaren, 1998b).

McLaren accentuates the role of language in forming subjectivity. His strategic use of Joan Scott's incisive finding illuminates the issue: "Experience is a subject's history. Language is the site of history's enactment" (cited in McLaren, 1994b, p. xxvi). McLaren considers language a major mediating factor in the formation of subjectivity. First, it creates meaning out of experience while simultaneously constituting part of that experience. Second, language is relational. It constructs the relationships speakers and receivers enter and negotiate with one another. The vernacular one uses to relate to another structures the symbolic interaction between participants in a heteroglossic "conversation." Third, language is implicated in the domain of power. The current debate between cultural literacists and critical literacists points to the truth in Macedo and Freire's maxim, "to read the word is to read the world." In his review of Freire and Macedo's work on social literacy we can hear McLaren (1991c) asking, "Whose world do we choose to participate in—the cultural literacists', based on the politics of sameness and domination, or the criticalists', based on difference and liberation?"

By building a mission with and not for the other, McLaren unfixes the false dichotomy between the object and subject of history. In one, he sees constitution of the other. Reacting to Saussurean structuralism, McLaren deals a crippling blow to the argument that meaning is fixed, aligning himself with critical poststructuralists who question the existence of modernist "transcendental" signifiers, without abdicating the responsibility to articulate a position against human exploitation and oppression. Consequently, McLaren rejects any notion of "canons" and "Great Works" hailed by the essentialists and perennialists as transcending the works' historical specificity. Foucault has already questioned the very notion of originary "authorship." However, McLaren takes to task both structuralism and poststructuralism for building theories of history without agents, the first through a scientizing of language and the second through a de-emphasis on the knowing subject. In particular, poststructuralists focus on textuality and the perpetual "play" of language at the expense of the material processes that provide the pre-conditions for our use of language. Scatamburlo-D'Annibale and McLaren (in press) strike a blow against the thesis that language maintains relative autonomy from relations of production. To McLaren, these avant-garde thinkers limit themselves from contributing radically to a liberatory politics because they assume, to Marx's chagrin, that they can fight phrases with phrases. They fall short of moving theory toward critical praxis, not the least of which is offered by Marxist theory.

Domination is a totality of relations. Traditionally, it has sufficed academic writing as an unproblematic, nondiscursive concept. With the rise in critical work on cultural politics and pedagogy, the discourse on hegemony has usurped the privileged seat of the discourse on domination. Systematically analyzed by Antonio Gramsci (1971), hegemony complexifies the notion of control by depicting it as a struggle to win and maintain the subordinate groups' consent. As such, domination ceases to be an accurate or complete assessment of the nature of control, which Giroux (1981) points out is both discursive and filled with internal contradictions. Gramsci's work on hegemonic struggle is infused into much of McLaren's writing, without stripping it of its Marxist origin, which as Hall (1996) reminds us, represents Gramsci's main problematic. Oppression in the era of the "cultural logic of late capitalism" (Jameson, 1991) does not assume only the guise of coercion (and we should not forget that Gramsci also analyzed coercion) but rather functions on the level of common sense. Hegemonic values of capital infiltrate every aspect of a postmodern culture fragmented into fields of contestation between production and consumption. The hegemonic culture in any given society wins consent through a complex set of apparatuses, one of which is school. In turn, the subordinate groups internalize (though never completely) these norms.

What Gramsci contributes to cultural revolution is an emphasis on the possibilities of agency. Domination is never complete, only partial and constantly negotiated. McLaren (1989) adds that educators must differentiate between forms of hegemony, some of which do not suggest the evil presence of oppression. Because a discourse achieves hegemonic status does not imply that it is dominating. A hegemony built around a radically contingent democracy does not merely invert the status quo and subsequently flip-flops oppression's directive flow, with a new set of oppressors and oppressed. McLaren emphasizes that the indexical nature of language regimes prevents radical and utopic ways of building a discourse around a "true" democracy. We are reminded of Bachelard's concept of the "epistemological break," suggesting that transformations occur through a shift in the problematic, rather than the inversion of poles, which maintains the previous logic intact.

McLaren's interpretation of hegemony projects the universality of common sense in a manner similar to Althusser's (1971) theory of ideology. To Althusser, like the unconscious, ideology persists in all societies, including communism. Ideology represents a subject's lived relation to the real relations, not a distortion of them. Likewise, to McLaren hegemony is a lived relation to common sense, not all examples of which are menacing. To the extent that common sense must always be questioned, we cannot escape it. Thus, like ideology, hegemony has no outside. The subject who thinks through common sense takes for granted certain features of modern social life. Faithful to Gramsci, McLaren suggests that counter-hegemonic struggles are revolutions without a conclusion, a perpetual movement of greater emancipation through critical self-reflection.

One consequence of the sophistication in today's oppression is its cloaking of reified forms. Whereas early feminism focused largely on sexual division of labor, radical feminists, most of whom were white middle-class women, did so at the expense of race and class disparities. As a result, "racist feminists" were ideological schizophrenics. In addition, feminist teachers affirming girls' experiences and ignoring both their class inscriptions may end up representing pedagogical correctness, yet ideological incorrectness (see Giroux & Simon, 1989). In an attempt to present a more complex portrait of oppression, McLaren implicates the oppressed as participants in their own oppression. By injecting the argument for complicity, he opens the pores for agency. If the oppressed are seen as active in their own oppression, then they also can redirect this activity toward liberation. McLaren encourages his readers to unpack critically the many ways oppression through racism, class exploitation and sexism dialectically reinitiate each other, something bell hooks refers to as "interlocking oppression" and which Weiler names in her writing as "triple oppression." While accepting the truth in hooks's and Weiler's insight, McLaren adds his own addendum to this triad.

McLaren (1994c) devotes attention to sexual politics in order to widen our view of oppression (see also McDonough & McLaren, 1996). McLaren's concept of "enfleshment," whereby certain epistemic and political codes are fixed onto the subject's body, is critically important in the discussion of sexuality. Ostensibly influenced by Foucault's genealogy of sexuality, McLaren is outraged at this socially stigmatizing and politically marginalized topic as "sexual apartheid." Heterosexual academics fail to encourage one another to research the politics of sexuality, fearing that any participation in the dialogue would instigate a degree of questioning about one's sexual stability or identity. The resulting predicament is what some may call "heterosexism." McLaren stresses that it is crucial to deal with our desires and pleasures as they contribute to our hopes and ideals. Yet he does not suggest that sexuality occupies only the realm of desire; with Ebert (1996) he argues that the logic of capital has colonized even our desires. Market analysis leads him to concur with Ebert that desire is implicated in commodified forms of sexuality.

Sensing that the struggle for control differentially affects people, McLaren recognizes the limitations of holding fast to Marxist objectivism. Rendering oppression to the observable or "verifiable" simplifies the complex nature of social suffering. McLaren realizes that despite the insights of Marxist science, different groups qualitatively experience exploitation. Thus, a science of history must be coupled with a depth hermeneutics of experience, of accounting for the dimensions of subjectivity that a more complete radical theory offers. Dealing with oppression within a calculaic singular cause-effect schema neglects the complex meaning people attach to their experience and how they decide to respond to their conditions. This fetishism of the empirical world is what leads positivists inevitably to fail to account for intentions, motivations and contradictions. They merely excuse as noise the data that do not fit the paradigm, in Kuhn's sense of the term as organizing community principles.

McLaren's research agenda reflects on the asymmetrical relationships between participants in any given interaction. As a social practice, research carries with it a dimension of violence. For example, mainstream research protocols and methods are often unwittingly implicated in the reproduction of systems of class, race and gender oppression. Uncritical and unreflexive authors who do not take into account power relationships between the researcher and participants augment social inequalities through social research. McLaren argues that our theoretical framework, ideological assumptions and latent prejudices mediate our representation of a given context. For what purposes and goals? On what discourse do you ground your research probes? As such, Kincheloe and McLaren (1994) reject traditional notions of "validity" and "reliability" on the basis that these standards hold qualitative researchers and critical ethnographers accountable to positivistic beliefs about an objective reporting of "facts" and events without attention to researcher subjectivity and personal accountability.

McLaren recognizes the importance of research in its efforts to transform academic work and the society to which it is accountable. Kincheloe and McLaren explain:

> As critical researchers transcend regressive and counterintuitive notions of validating the knowledge uncovered by research, they remind themselves of their critical project—the attempt to move beyond assimilated experience, the struggle to expose the way ideology constrains the desire for self-direction and the effort to confront the way power reproduces itself in the construction of human consciousness. (p. 152)

Research can move beyond practices of colonization and toward the possibility for radical self-actualization. Academic work possesses the power to contribute to a true dialogue, in Freire's sense of it. A materialist research program predicated on the politics of difference develops values of hope in place of anomie. Critical inquiry does not fear changing the context of its site, as its bourgeois opponents fear. It removes the scholars' apprehension of affecting its members, which it cannot avoid. Rather, critical intellectuals conduct research in hopes of changing, of transforming research sites and their constituents. Kincheloe and McLaren (1994) cite Lather on this point: "Catalytic validity points to the degree to which research moves those it studies to understand the world and the way it is shaped in order for them to transform it" (p. 152). McLaren's research agenda is an act of historical significance. He best expresses this in his comments on writing. Writing, for McLaren (1998b), is a "social practice, a political practice, a form of cultural criticism" (p. 371). It is a process of reflection on the possibilities for self-transformation in the context of a collective purpose. Writing, like research, is a reading of the world, a world located in the words we choose to describe the world as it might be.

McLaren's prolific writing career in critical pedagogy has made it possible for critical young scholars in education to appropriate a vernacular with which to name their experience in the most politicized way possible. In a post-Freirean era, educators can move forward with the confidence that the subdiscipline thrives under McLaren's leadership. In this essay, I have tried to map out the basic tension found in McLaren's work. The conflictual nature of critical writing suggests that this tension is productive because it shows that the social struggle becomes part of the way we represent the social itself. McLaren's engagement with discourse analysis and ideology critique negotiates the contradictions found in social relations of capital, world racism and transnational patriarchy. These contradictions create part of the structuring principles that inscribe McLaren's texts and through which readers navigate.

Engaging McLaren's eclectic work may initially appear to hold no center, since it holds no tradition untouched, no concept unturned. Marxism, postmodernism, structuralism, cultural studies, feminism, postcolonialism, symbolic anthropology, race and ethnic theory, Freirean pedagogy, Frankfurt critical theory, critical ethnography and critical media studies make up his elusive repertoire of influences. To fix the meaning of McLaren's contributions would represent a form of academic violence and only serves to domesticate him. However, one thread remains clear: McLaren's politics always puts material transformation as the ultimate test of his ideas. A materialist in the end, McLaren's brand of theory ultimately favors the body over the mind, the concrete over the abstract, and the real over the hyperreal. As critical pedagogy enters its fourth decade, a second generation of critical pedagogists tracks the grooves left by its founders, of which McLaren is decisively one. Not a bad position to be in.

References

Alcoff, L. (1995). The problem of speaking for others. In J. Roof & R. Wiegman (Eds.), *Who can speak? Authority and critical identity* (pp. 97–119). Urbana: University of Illinois Press.

Althusser, L. (1971). *Lenin and philosophy*. New York: Monthly Review Press.

Biesta, G. (1995). The identity of the body. In M. Katz (Ed.), *Philosophy of education 1994* (pp. 223–232). Urbana, IL: Philosophy of Education Society.

Ebert, T. (1996). *Ludic feminism and after*. Ann Arbor: University of Michigan Press.

Foucault, M. (1978). *The history of sexuality*. Volume 1. New York: Vintage Books.

———. (1980). *Power/Knowledge*. Colin Gordon (Ed.). New York: Pantheon Books.

———. (1991). What is an author? In C. Mukerji & M. Schudson (Eds.), *Rethinking popular culture* (pp. 446–464). Berkeley & Los Angeles: University of California Press.

Freire, P. (1994). *Pedagogy of hope*. New York: Continuum.

Freire, P. & Macedo, D. (1987). *Literacy*. South Hadley, MA: Bergin and Garvey.

Giroux, H. (1981). *Ideology, culture, and the process of schooling*. Philadelphia: Temple University Press.

———. (1988). *Teachers as intellectuals*. New York, Westport, CT, & London: Bergin and Garvey.

Giroux, H. & McLaren, P. (1986). Teacher education and the politics of engagement: The case for democratic schooling. *Harvard Educational Review*, 56(3), 10–35.

———. (1992). Writing from the margins: Geographies of identity, pedagogy, and power. *Journal of Education*, 174(1), 7–31.

Giroux, H. & Simon, R. (1989). Popular culture as a pedagogy of pleasure and meaning. In H. Giroux & R. Simon (Eds.), *Popular culture, schooling and everyday life* (pp. 1–29). New York, Westport, CT, & London: Bergin & Garvey.

Gramsci, A. (1971). *Selections from prison notebooks*. New York: International Publishers.

Hall, S. (1996). Gramsci's relevance for the study of race and ethnicity. In D. Morley & K. Chen (Eds.), *Stuart Hall* (pp. 411–440). London & New York: Routlege.

———. (1997). Introduction. In S. Hall (Ed.), *Representation: Cultural representations and signifying practices* (pp. 1–11). London, Thousand Oaks, CA, & New Delhi: SAGE.

Jameson, F. (1991). *Postmodernism, or, the cultural logic of late capitalism.* Durham: Duke University Press.

Kincheloe, J. & McLaren, P. (1994). Rethinking critical theory and qualitative research. In Y. Lincoln & N. Denzin (Eds.), *Handbook of qualitative research* (pp. 138–157). Thousand Oaks, CA, & London: SAGE Publications.

Leonardo, Z. (2000). Betwixt and between: Introduction to the politics of identity. In C. Tejeda, C. Martinez & Z. Leonardo (Eds.), *Charting new terrains of Chicana(o)/Latina(o) education* (pp. 107–129). Cresskill, NJ: Hampton Press.

———. (2002). The souls of white folk: Critical pedagogy, whiteness studies, and globalization discourse. *Race Ethnicity and Education*, 5(1), 29–50.

McDonough, P. & McLaren, P. (1996). Critical, postmodern studies of gay and lesbian lives in academia. *Harvard Educational Review*, 66(2), 1–14.

McLaren, P. (1986). Schooling the postmodern body: Critical pedagogy and the politics of enfleshment. In H. Giroux (Ed.), *Postmodernism, feminism, and cultural politics* (pp. 144–173). Albany: State University of New York Press.

———. (1991a). Critical pedagogy: Constructing an arch of social dreaming and a doorway to hope. *The Sociology of Education in Canada*, 173(1), 137–160.

———. (1991b). Introduction: Postmodernism, post-colonialism and pedagogy. *Education and Society*, 9(1), 3–22.

———. (1991c). Culture or canon? Critical pedagogy and the politics of literacy. *Harvard Educational Review*, 58(2), 213–234.

———. (1992). An interview with Peter McLaren (with Mary Leach). *Educational Foundations*, 6(4), 5–19.

———. (1993). *Schooling as a ritual performance: Toward a political economy of educational symbols and gestures.* New York & London: Routledge.

———. (1994a). Postmodernism and the death of politics: A Brazilian reprieve. In P. McLaren & C. Lankshear (Eds.), *Politics of liberation* (pp. 193–215). New York & London: Routledge.

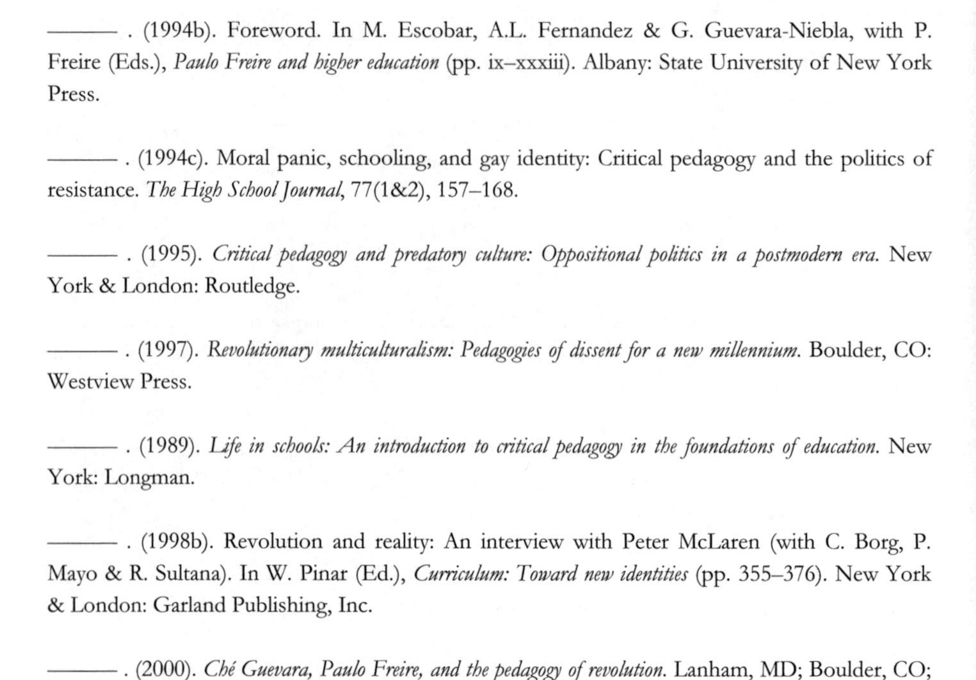

———. (1994b). Foreword. In M. Escobar, A.L. Fernandez & G. Guevara-Niebla, with P. Freire (Eds.), *Paulo Freire and higher education* (pp. ix–xxxiii). Albany: State University of New York Press.

———. (1994c). Moral panic, schooling, and gay identity: Critical pedagogy and the politics of resistance. *The High School Journal*, 77(1&2), 157–168.

———. (1995). *Critical pedagogy and predatory culture: Oppositional politics in a postmodern era.* New York & London: Routledge.

———. (1997). *Revolutionary multiculturalism: Pedagogies of dissent for a new millennium.* Boulder, CO: Westview Press.

———. (1989). *Life in schools: An introduction to critical pedagogy in the foundations of education.* New York: Longman.

———. (1998b). Revolution and reality: An interview with Peter McLaren (with C. Borg, P. Mayo & R. Sultana). In W. Pinar (Ed.), *Curriculum: Toward new identities* (pp. 355–376). New York & London: Garland Publishing, Inc.

———. (2000). *Ché Guevara, Paulo Freire, and the pedagogy of revolution.* Lanham, MD; Boulder, CO; New York & Oxford: Rowman & Littlefield.

Memmi, A. (1965). *The colonizer and the colonized.* Boston: Beacon Press.

Said, E. (1979). *Orientalism.* New York: Random House.

Scatamburlo-D'Annibale, V. & McLaren, P. (in press). The centrality of class in the politics of race and difference. *Journal of Educational Philosophy and Theory.*

Spivak, G. (1988). Can the subaltern speak? In C. Nelson & L. Grossberg (Eds.), *Marxism and the interpretation of culture* (pp. 271–313). Urbana & Chicago: University of Illinois Press.

Williams, R. (1977). *Marxism and literature.* Oxford: Oxford University Press.

Willis, P. (1977). *Learning to labor.* New York: Columbia University Press.

PART THREE

McLAREN ACROSS CONTEXTS

Chapter 4

McLaren: A Paradoxical and Outstanding Intellectual

Alicia de Alba and Marcela González Arenas

> It is important to acknowledge that identities are never completed but always in the process of negotiation; they are continually struggled over within a polyvalent assemblage of discourses....[They are] in fact the result of struggles over meaning by various groups in the larger society....We can, I believe, free ourselves from the dead weight of dominant corporate consumer narratives. We can do this, I am convinced, by crossing cultural boundaries and negotiating new, hybrid identities. We can help students bring to a halt the immutable constancy of imperial identities of the patriarchal family, the authoritarian state, and the narrative of the unthinking, obedient citizen of consumer society. (McLaren, 1994)

Because it has been difficult for us to write completely in English a chapter on Peter McLaren's ideas, we decided to write it as though we were having a written conversation with him, as if we were simply having a friendly talk. We would want to ask him to listen to what we have to say as Latin Americans, as Mexican women scholars, trying to understand ourselves as "split subjects" assuming different positions in the midst of this generalized structural crisis. At the same time, we want Peter to understand our positionality in relation to our country, Mexico, to our people, to our world and our historical time, in a deep, human, educational, cultural and political way.

For us Peter has an authentic, strong political and educational commitment. He shows his intensity and passion on every page of his work, and that has been good for us and for his many readers. We discover through Peter's work a controversial and outstanding individual who assumes multiple subject positions. For us, given our contextualities and specificities, an important thematic area of engagement we would like to have with Peter deals with cultural contact between him and his interlocutors, especially the impact of his ideas on Latin America. Thus, we would like to take advantage of this opportunity to engage him on this issue.

In this regard, the present chapter focuses mainly on the work of this paradoxical and outstanding critical pedagogue, whose influence on Latin American educative contexts has evoked different, and even contradictory, responses throughout the region, ranging from open rejection of his ideas to passionate defense of his work. In this chapter, we attempt to engage Peter in a critical dialogue that leads us to and through a thorough cultural contact with him that might, it is hoped, foster broader and more accurate readings of our realities (his and ours). This is a cultural contact that we believe has not taken place yet, in spite of the intense cultural dialogue that has occurred over the last three decades between U.S. and Latin American critical theorists.

In so doing, we feel it is necessary first to describe some of McLaren's central contributions to critical pedagogy within the context of the crisis of radical theories, utopias, politics and social projects, and from a critical postmodernist point of view. A brief discussion of the ideas of McLaren's interlocutors, mainly from Latin America, follows. We then attempt to describe the different ways in which U.S. critical pedagogues' proposals have been received in Mexico, where marginalization, underdevelopment, poverty and corruption are stark realities.

We conclude this chapter with a discussion of how and why cultural contact has not yet truly taken place, in spite of the controversial and diverse reception that McLaren's ideas have had in our country and the increasing (but not yet sufficient) cultural exchanges that have taken place among Mexican pedagogists regarding McLaren's ideas.

At this point, it is relevant to re-mention our identity as Latin American women, scholars and pedagogues engaged in the project of rethinking our reality from the postfundamentalist, postmodern logic, within this generalized structural crisis we are currently experiencing.

Understanding McLaren Through the Current General Structural Crises

To fully understand the nature and complexity of the twenty-first-century social crises, we need to explore them within the socio-historical settings that have produced them, in order to understand its potentialities and possibilities. This state of affairs, influenced by historical, economic, cultural and environmental factors, has been brought about by structural transformations in capitalism, wherein the working class of postindustrialized societies has suffered important negative transformations. Moreover, this juncture, as Laclau and Mouffe (1985) state, is marked by the deep, massive penetration of the capitalist modes of production into all areas of the social life, whose dislocatory effects—jointly with those that arise from bureaucratic forms that have characterized the welfare state—have generated new forms of social protest; crisis and the fall into disrepute of society models established by the so called "existing current socialism," that include the denunciation of new domination forms established in the name of the proletariat dictatorship. Additionally, during the last fifteen years, socialism has been discredited as a viable option to the oppressive realities of capitalism, mainly after the fall of the Soviet Union and the further expansion of capitalist oppression and hegemony. Our reality is to a great extent a reflection of those historical changes, further described by de Alba (2000) as a "general structural crisis," intimately linked with the international economy and the globalization of information. In revisiting Laclau and Mouffe's work (1985), de Alba defines this general structural crisis as:

> The generalized weakening of the relational system that constitutes, founds, reproduces and allows for the society's functioning; a relational system that defines the identities of its social and political spaces; a weakening that leads to the proliferation of floating elements. (p. 87)

The emergence of new social actors has also accompanied such changes. Simultaneously, the social myths and utopias of the Enlightenment and Romanticism have been strongly eroded (Althusser, 1967), to the extent that some even speak of the "end of history" or the "collapse of ideologies." Such a problematic context becomes even more acute in settings such as Mexico, a country that lies within the sphere of influence of the politically most important country of the neo-liberal and globalized era: the United States.

Even given the complexity and overwhelming nature of this state of affairs which can install within us a sense of despair and pessimism, it is important to stress what Gómez-Sollano (2000) calls the "productive character" of this general structural crisis, which "...places us as subjects [in relation to] knowledge and history...[where we are made to] face the challenge of assuming responsibility for the transformations that are taking place" (p. 166). This crisis, as de Alba (2000) notes, embraces a melting pot of unknown opportunities for contributing, in different ways, to the main task of transforming the reality of social ills by the creation of a better world. The challenge, then, lies in how we position ourselves in the face of this crisis.

As socialist utopias have failed in their ahistorical, essentialist and authoritarian versions, the capitalist utopia has also made painfully clear its own deficiencies and shortcomings. Capitalism's inability to find solutions to social and economic problems is more than evident; it is indeed scandalous. And the myriad deficiencies of neo-liberalism's social and political proposals are not only obvious but clearly outrageous. However, as Buenfil (2000) points out, "…as no project raises from nothing, it is our responsibility as a generation to formulate proposals and retrieve stones and bricks from those old ruinous buildings that can serve to construct a different framework" (p. 9).

With this in mind, any critical theory (or pedagogy) for furthering social justice faces many obstacles. Critical educators have to confront the problems that stem from the deterioration of their working conditions, despite the assurances that federal governments and states offer about the importance of education. And the skills and abilities of critical pedagogues are under suspicion, especially in the post-9/11 era. Teachers who are theoretically and ideologically aligned with projects for social justice face the unrelenting, shameless and increasingly authoritarian subordination of educational processes and goals to the power of the marketplace in a way that transforms an important sociocultural process into a "business like any other," driven by profit making goals and strategies.

Because education has been reduced to a "consumer good," more is needed than occasional "educational reforms." In fact, those reforms often increase rather than diminish educational malaise and contribute to the continuing loss of autonomy in the educational process, both within institutions and among educators. Yet to move from our present position in the direction of a critical social-political program for education will not be easy.

In this sense, Gómez-Sollano (2000) recognizes that the challenges we are confronting at this juncture also offer opportunities for learning, for organizing and for acting in the name of social justice. As she notes, taking advantage of this juncture, we can elaborate proposals that promote subjects' ability to situate themselves within their own historical contexts and we can also construct options with a historically viable future in order to (paraphrasing):

- *Learn or see* the connections among the daily projects and the big ideas men and women accept as truthful;
- *Stress and promote* men's and women's ability to recognize their own life contexts;

- *Question ourselves* about the implications of assuming and recognizing the presence of history, in what we think and know, that make it possible to transmute cultural heritage into present experience and future possibility; and,
- *Assume the challenges* this represents in terms of individuals' formation, in such a manner that we learn to see beyond accumulated knowledge, beyond the apparent reality

Gómez-Sollano (2000) demands a critical, reflexive introspection and examination of all of our social identities as we try to address our own histories as part of a larger attempt at social liberation. As Zemelman (1987) puts it, we need to take advantage of our abilities to understand critically and to reconstruct our realities toward viable utopias. A potential—and necessary—utopia could be defined as more human, hopeful, fair and natural.

As de Alba (2000) points out, we live in an ever-changing world that seems to lack direction. Here in Mexico, we are rethinking the curriculum in a context of generalized structural crisis in which we find social "irruptive traits" and "contours" rather than specific political and social projects. The irruptive traits refer to cases in which some new and unknown elements—or elements of the prevailing social configurations—appear in a significant way in social spaces. These elements can fulfill two functions. The first is to contribute to the dislocation and disruption of the current order. The emergence of the Zapatista National Liberation Army (EZLN) in the state of Chiapas, Mexico, at the beginning of 1994, is an example of such an irruptive event; the passage of the North American Free Trade Agreement (NAFTA) between Mexico, Canada and the United States, at the same time, was not.

The second function involves the display of features or elements that tend either to delineate the contours of new discursive social configurations, or to cause them to lose strength and significance. In other words, traits are elements that have a limited capacity for articulation, and their importance lies in the irruptive "significativity" they acquire in the context of a general structural crisis and in their potential to become elements that tend to become empty signifiers in the new discursive configurations. It is, however, also possible for them to disappear during a period of crisis (de Alba, González-Gaudiano, Lankshear & Peters, 2000, p. 159).

Contours are shaped by a group of emerging elements articulated by a society in the throes of general structural crisis. The contours' multiple elements are the traits that are apparent by their invasive significativity from the first moments of crisis through its different phases. Contours have superior articulation capacity than do traits and can be observed in the later stages of a general structural crisis. In fact, contours are configured as spaces of significance articulated in new and unknown ways in the genealogy of a social configuration. As such, they can remain in the moment of their constitution and the process of sedimentation or be excluded from it (de Alba et al., 2000).

These social irruptive traits and contours emerge as incipient moments of articulation among multiple and constant movements and floating elements. According to Laclau and Mouffe (1985), "articulation" refers to "any practice establishing a relation among elements such that their identity is modified as a result of such a practice." And floating elements refer to "any difference that is not discursively articulated" (p. 105).

In order to elucidate the notion of "generalized structural crisis," we will examine the case of Mexico in particular. The 1980s and 1990s brought a climate of increasing, globalized structural crisis. The fall of the Berlin Wall, the reunification of Germany and the disintegration of the Soviet Bloc signaled the beginning of a new order that has had repercussions throughout the world. On both the international and local levels, these new situations can be characterized—albeit in complex and varied ways—in terms of the generalized structural crisis and its impact on ideologies and hegemonies.

Until the 1980s these ideologies and hegemonies were capable of "speaking to" and constituting the social subjects of nation-states. They now find themselves in a process of dislocation and disarticulation, with an intensification of floating signifiers and new and incipient articulation processes. In the current generalized structural crisis, multiple movements can be observed in signification elements that were previously tied to, or sedimented (fossilized) into certain signifiers. In this situation the "status" of the "elements" are the floating signifiers that are not able to be articulated in a discursive chain (Laclau & Mouffe 1985, p. 113). Signification elements that in an earlier time made the structures appear to be strong and fixed are now in an accelerated process of dislocation and disarticulation.

In this context, we need to construct new utopian horizons from which sociopolitical projects might emerge and enable a new hegemonic rearticulation of societies. The global changes that have occurred so rapidly since 1989, combined with the erosion of the foundations of Western thought, have propelled the educational field—and, within it, curriculum—into a highly complex situation. This situation can be analyzed from a number of angles, such as: (a) academics' difficulty in constituting themselves as subjects in the process of curricular determination; (b) the complex "surface of inscription" or context that is characterized by "split subjects" and by what we will call "social irruptive traits and contours" rather than by sociopolitical projects of the type that have guided the processes of constituting the curriculum-society link in the past; (c) the recognition that theoretical tools that had allowed us to understand educational problems are no longer adequate; and, (d) the increment of cultural contact and its impact on social and educational spheres (de Alba et al., 2000, p. 149).

McLaren and His Interlocutors: Between Two or Many Worlds

It will always be challenging for us to interpret McLaren's work. He is undoubtedly an intellectual architect, a courageous scholar, a social fighter and a cultural worker theoretically grounded in historical materialism. He is engaged in the creation of revolutionary conditions (including the politics of identity and analyses of difference) within which the dispossessed might liberate themselves through praxis.

Educators today can stand with McLaren or against him, but not without him. They can agree or disagree with his interpretations of events taking place in the current capitalist social realities. They can agree or disagree with his works regarding the manner in which subjectivity is constituted through language; with his statements on the relationship between social action, discourse and historical memory; with his constructions on narratives and meta-narratives that possess subjects in the social configurations of meaning; and with his view on the way in which Ché and Freire "can be used as the wellspring for creating the type of critical agency necessary to contest and transform current global relations of exploitation and oppression" (McLaren, 2000, p. xxvi).

However, today's educators cannot be indifferent to McLaren's work. As a professor at the Graduate School of Education and Information Studies at the University of California, Los Angeles, this Canadian-American educational theorist is internationally recognized and associated with critical and interdisciplinary approaches to social action. He has played a significant role in shaping the educational-political landscape of our time.

As an intellectual, a writer and a teacher, his academic success in North and Latin American educative contexts has not led him to forget where he came from and where his loyalties lie.

Moreover, since his discussions are always written with intensity and passion, his readers never react to them calmly or quietly. Emotion and intensity inevitably envelop their response.

McLaren's extensive oeuvre includes insightful books such as *Life in Schools*; *Schooling as a Ritual Performance: Toward a Political Economy of Educational Symbols and Gestures*; *Critical Pedagogy and Predatory Culture: Oppositional Politics in a Postmodern Era*; *Revolutionary Multiculturalism: Pedagogies of Dissent for the New Millennium*; and, *Ché Guevara, Paulo Freire and the Pedagogy of Revolution*. These texts have enjoyed world wide readership and have had a particularly strong impact on the United States and Latin America. Through his books, essays and speeches, he has forged paths of liberating forms of education and revisited the themes, works and authors related to the main issues of critical pedagogy and its practice as developed in the United States. He has been engaged in this work for well over two decades now. His overarching goal, it seems to us, has been to provide students with self-empowering pedagogical conditions—including a language of social analysis and cultural critique—in order to inspire informed social activism.

Peter is one of the rare white, anti-colonial educators who throughout his work courageously calls for the abolition of whiteness and the abolition of capital. Like the works of other brilliant critical pedagogists including Apple, Giroux, Aronowitz and McCarthy, Peter's books, essays, papers and talks have been well received in Latin America. In order to gain a better understanding of the kind of relationship that exists between McLaren and his Latin American interlocutors, we think it is important to consider the research of Orozco (1998), who studied Mexican university teachers between 1992 and 1994, with a focus on the issue of critical educator formation and the different ways they embodied U.S. critical pedagogy.

Following Zemelman (1987)—and from the perspective of a critical thinking capable of developing an epistemology of historical consciousness (understood as the coming together of cognitive, gnoseological and axiological functions)—Orozco became interested in the relationship between critical thinking and education. This interest derived from her idea that her own formation process as an education professional should go beyond "training" in certain academic knowledges or routine skills that have nothing to do with sociopolitical daily life. In positing this thesis, she was seeking a formation space where teachers could construct the knowledge and theoretical tools necessary to question reality, to trace or state new problems.

Orozco's approach to U.S. critical pedagogy grew out of a problem that university scholars faced during the transition from the 1980s to the 1990s. That period saw the beginning of a strong critique from diverse social sectors (government, enterprises, professional colleges, unions, civil society, etc.) of the public university and the educational system in general. That critique pointed out the absence of links between school processes and national problems. In order to address this issue, she tried to determine the argumentative possibilities educators commanded once they accepted as principle the value of critical reason.

From this perspective, Orozco began her research with questions such as: What is a "critical posture"? How does, or can, a subject's critical posture develop as the subject critically faces her or his own reality? What does being a "critical subject" mean? What are the features of a configured "critical mind"? She also focused specifically on the field of education: How might a teacher education curriculum, with a focus on "critical formation," be developed?

In conducting this research, Orozco had to explore the theoretical contributions of critical intellectuals from multiple disciplines and theoretical social debates—debates that have been around since the 1970s, but which have only recently been included into the curriculum for preparing educators in Mexico. She used as her sources the works of Henry Giroux, Michael Apple, Stanley Aronowitz, Thomas Popkewitz and Peter McLaren. These intellectuals, from a non-dogmatic Marxian positionality, criticized the previous discourses of economic reproduction and questioned the assertion that schools are only spaces of reproduction and domination; they theorized the possibility of *agency*.

Orozco specifically targeted the work of Giroux and McLaren because of their focus on three basic issues: (1) their acknowledgment of and building on the thinking of Paulo Freire, especially in regard to his notion of education as a political and cultural practice for social consciousness; (2) the importance Giroux and McLaren lend to theory and the epistemological foundations in the construction of a new language of possibility in education; and (3) the emphasis they place on the relationship between subjectivity and the subjects' critical ability to understand reality.

Orozco found that there exists a homogeneous unproblematic reception of this pedagogical perspective in Mexico, and she classified the different readings of the U.S. critical pedagogy discourse into three large groups. The first is the "embelesamiento," or ecstasy, group. In this group, readers become trapped, fascinated with Giroux's and McLaren's ideas, as if their ideas are an absolute and essential way of viewing or conducting education. The feature of criticity, most valued by ecstasy readers, is the critique against the authoritarianism of the powerful. However, these readers do not allow themselves the necessary time for a careful study of the contents of the critical perspective. They do not situate the epistemological and theoretical borders or limits from which those authors write, let alone the reconstruction or construction of educative problems as situated within their own contexts. Orozco posits that ecstasy readers probably account for a good number of attendees at speeches given by Giroux and McLaren in Mexico. However, this reading cannot be critical of *the* critical discourse, because the receivers become trapped, subordinated, annulled as knowing subjects. Finally, this reading is a naive one, immediate and acritical (Orozco, 1998, p. 58). All this, of course, is antithetical to the central messages of Giroux and McLaren—and before them, of Freire—that a critical/liberatory approach to pedagogical and social action cannot, and should not, be mandated by any specific methodology or remain un-critiqued. Rather, it needs to be (re)created afresh, in each context.

The second group is the "rejection" group. Rejecters maintain that these North American scholars do not come to offer us something relevant for our educational contexts. We can see, according to Orozco, two kinds of rejection in this posture. In the first one, readers declare that these authors speak about critique and call themselves "revolutionaries," but since they come from a developed, powerful country like the United States, they cannot teach anything to countries like ours because they are unfamiliar with us. In the end, they continue to be "whites from the north." Moreover, suggest the rejecters, since these authors call themselves "neo-Marxists" and build on subjectivity and the value of culture and daily life, they cannot be considered authentic Marxists. The Mexican readers from this group believe that "neo-Marxism" does not maintain the essence of Marxism, which is class struggle. In this way, neo-Marxism it is a betrayal of Marxism (or at least reflects an ignorance of the original essence of Marxism). We believe that this reading of Giroux and McLaren, as representatives of North American critical pedagogy, is an acritical one; its defenders speak from a dogmatic position without a coherent conceptual argumentation.

The second kind of rejection cannot be considered an acritical one. Thinkers from this perspective advance a theoretical argumentation, for example, from the perspective of Durkheim. These rejection readers are specialists in educational theories and academically work on specific objects, they consider themselves as subjects, read attentively the "Other's" arguments, and write with an academic language. They think that Giroux and McLaren, for example, are dogmatic. However, as Orozco (1998, p 60) states, that this type of rejection reader make just a literal analysis of Giroux and McLaren's discourse, which limits their possibilities for exploring critical pedagogy works in a deeper form.

The third group is the "interlocution reading" group. Orozco posits that this is the smallest group, made up of only a few Latin American scholars, including Edgar González, Alicia de Alba, Adriana Puiggrós, Ángel Díaz-Barriga, Dora Elena Marín and Roberto Follari. Members of this group enter into conceptual dialogue with North American criticalist theorists and debate and discuss common problems (as well as continually attempting to understand and negotiate their differences). The interlocutors are also authors with their own theoretical work, and for this reason they can be defined as possessing discursive identities.

Cultural Contact: The Unsettled Agenda Between McLaren and His Interlocutors/Readers

At this point in our discussion, we believe it is necessary to establish (or at least to begin here) a true and deep cultural contact with this North American scholar, Peter McLaren. As interlocutors, we are familiar with critical pedagogy in its North American incarnations. We are sympathetic to it but are not acritical of it. And we want to engage with it, and its leading proponent, across the Americas.

It is true that McLaren is one of the rare First World scholars who has dared to pursue a very deep, strong and passionate intercultural relationship with Latin American scholars, while at the same time maintaining his own identity. Beginning in the 1990s, he undertook this task courageously, and since that time, many of his books have been translated into Spanish, and his lectures have been heard by Latin American scholars and students throughout the hemisphere. At the same time, Peter has studied and drawn on the work of many Latin Americans—and other internationalists—including Freire, Macedo, Guevara and de Alba.

The number of essays, articles, books and lectures that McLaren has produced is truly amazing. Even websites treating his work and ideas have proliferated. Additionally, he has been consulted and studied by Latin American students and scholars from various disciplines, and his ideas have been incorporated by these scholars into their own essays, articles, books and lectures.

As McLaren (2000) has noted, a strong academic, intellectual and political intercultural relationship has been created. There has been, he says, an "approximation of inter-culturality." However, this relationship positions McLaren in the margins of cultural contact in the same way that his Latin American interlocutors and readers remain similarly positioned: cultural contact between his work and ours has not occurred.

As de Alba et al. (2000) claim:

> Cultural contact has appeared at various times in human history and it is possible to know its characteristics from its historicity. The present historic moment, widely understood as a postmodern condition of existence, is an important context for analysis of cultural contact, especially from a standpoint that considers postmodern existentiality.... Cultural contact refers to the exchange of cultural goods and the interrelationship between groups, sectors and individuals of different cultures. Consequently, cultural contact uses different semiotic codes that produce changes in the different subjects that participate in it as well as changes in its contexts. These are produced in social spaces with multiple trajectories in which power relationships are exercised. (p. 172)

From this perspective, cultural contact is relational, unequal, conflictive and productive. It is relational because it is generated, produced and defined in the open, and precarious relationships exist among its different elements, as they are constituted and produced among several articulated meaning systems. Its relational character can be understood if we consider that:

> [F]rom an historical point of view it...involves different semiotic codes or language games of those who participate in a process of cultural contact, and the language games of some participants are more powerful than others.... Inequality acts as both an obstacle to establishing communication and as an external dislocating element of language games themselves. (de Alba et al., 2000, p. 172)

Cultural contact is conflictive since it is produced when different language games come into conflict:

> The subjects involved in it have structural difficulties in establishing communication.... [T]hey must construct elements of meaning that work as bridges among the semiotic codes of their respective cultures, yet at the same time attempt to keep the constitutive irruptive traits of their identity. (de Alba et al., 2000, p. 172)

Finally, cultural contact is productive because

> The relationality, the conflictive and the unequal character, allows and accelerates the dislocation of subjects' identities that takes place during cultural contact. Multiple interpellations are produced among the subjects. Floating signifiers proliferate, and through mechanisms of identification, new elements, new condensations and meanings are generated. New semiotic and semantic elements permit not only communication among cultures and their subjects but also permit the transformation of subjects and cultures. In the case of long and intense periods of cultural contact, this becomes the space where it is possible to generate new meaning configurations (with nodal points), which permits the emergence of new cultures. (de Alba, 2000, p. 90)

Three of the four features mentioned above as characteristics of true "cultural contact" have occurred, we believe, in the intercultural relationship produced between Peter McLaren and his Latin American interlocutors. Interculturality has undoubtedly been relational and unequal, and at times (as we have seen from Orozco's [1998] work) it was conflictive, but this relation has not been "productive." Why might this be? One answer could be that although both McLaren and his Latin American interlocutors take what is useful from one another for their purposes, it is only with difficulty that they resignify what they are receiving.

There has not yet been, we believe, a real discussion that enables Mexican and Latin American scholars to produce new symbolic and cultural elements, as well as new ontological, epistemological and political perspectives and points of view. As McLaren has pointed out, in speaking of identities, it is possible to promote the academic linkage of intercultural scholars, provided we are able to cross the cultural boundaries and negotiate and create new and hybrid identities. In other words, this project of Latin and North American productive interculturality and co-learning—specifically around the work of McLaren—will be possible only if we assume intercultural and multicultural perspectives and take the risk of entering into new cultural contacts.

There exists an important agenda that we must undertake, that is, the construction of new multicultural or cultural contacts. Perhaps we will reach this goal in the future, working on common projects and within common and shared struggles, and opening our minds in order to listen to the other. In these ways we can construct new meanings that might produce new, emancipatory possibilities, and allow us to hold on to the possibility and promise of utopias in this globalized world.

References

Althusser, L. (1967). *La revolución teórica de Marx* [The Marx's theoretical revolution]. Mexico City, Mexico: Siglo XXI Editores.

Buenfil, R.N. (Ed.). (2000). *En los márgenes de la educación: México a finales del milenio* [At the margins of education: Mexico at the end of the millennium]. Mexico City, Mexico: Plaza y Valdés Editores.

de Alba, A. (2000). Educación: Contacto cultural, cambio tecnológico y perspectivas postmodernas [Education: Cultural contact, technological change and postmodern perspectives]. In R.N. Buenfil (Ed.), *En los márgenes de la educación: México a finales del milenio* (pp. 87-112). Mexico City, Mexico: Plaza y Valdés Editores.

de Alba, A., González-Gaudiano, E., Lankshear, C., & Peters, M. (2000). *Curriculum in the postmodern condition.* New York: Peter Lang.

Gómez-Sollano, M. (2000). Problemática de la formación en la postcrisis: Una lectura epistémico-pedagógica [Professional formation's problems within the postcrisis: An epistemic-pedagogical reading]. In R.N. Buenfil (Ed.), *En los márgenes de la educación: México a finales del milenio* (pp. 165-186). Mexico City, Mexico: Plaza y Valdés Editores.

Laclau, E. & Mouffe, C. (1985). *Hegemony and socialist strategy: Towards a radical democratic politics.* London: Verso.

McLaren, P. (1994). Critical pedagogy, political agency and the pragmatics of justice: The case of Lyotard. Available on-line at http://www.ed.uiuc.edu/EPS/Educational-Theory/Contents/44_3_McLaren.asp.

———. (2000). *Ché Guevara, Paulo Freire, and the politics of hope: Reclaiming critical pedagogy.* On-line at http://www.che-lives.com/home/modules.php?name=Content&pa=showpage&pid =14.

Orozco, F. (1998). La crítica en el discurso de los docentes mexicanos: Hallazgos y Desafíos. In H. Zemelman et al. (Eds.), *Investigación institucional desde el enfoque crítico social.* México: Colegio de México.

Zemelman, H. et al. (1987). *Investigación institucional desde el enfoque crítico social.* México: Colegio de México.

Chapter 5

Revolutionary Possibilities: Multicultural Professional Development in Public Schools

Pepi Leistyna

Educators and cultural workers need to have access to important and influential work in critical social theory and cultural studies in order to help them better understand, critique and transform the myriad social injustices and undemocratic practices that continue to fester in schools. In the early 1990s, back when I first began graduate school, I had the good fortune of meeting Peter McLaren. It was the strategic mentoring of Donaldo Macedo that began to put me in contact (theoretically, intellectually and personally) with important educators such as Peter, as well as Paulo Freire, Henry Giroux, bell hooks, Stanley Aronowitz, Antonia Darder, Robert Bahruth and Noam Chomsky, among others. Without the outside influence of these progressive and criticalist educators, I would probably never have made it through the mundane mud of Harvard.

I was caught within the depoliticized zone of the Harvard Graduate School of Education, where making claims to scientific objectivity was a means to discourage substantive debates over such pressing issues as white supremacy, economic exploitation, patriarchy and heterosexism. As a private corporation and educational institution, with a multi-billion dollar endowment, Harvard (which I refer to as "the pillars of the republic") represents a very selective form of truth, and those who have maintained the institution have managed to obfuscate its exclusionary practices by promoting and defending a belief in "objectivity," "certainty" and a "scientific" basis for the study of social reality. From this perspective, knowledge and reason are interpreted as neutral and universal, rather than the products of particular ideologies and interests. Within these modernist clutches, multiple voices cannot be heard because the notion of "objective truth" implies that only one voice and one view of social reality exists and thus merits legitimacy.

Inside this factory of cultural reproduction, where conformity and malaise abounded, I found McLaren's alternative work, such as *Cries from the Corridor* (1980), *Schooling as a Ritual Performance* (1986), *Life in Schools* (1989) and *Critical Pedagogy and Predatory Culture* (1995) enormously refreshing and invaluable. Given that the logic of transnational capitalism has been driving educational policy and practice, there was (and continues to be in books such as *Revolutionary Multiculturalism* [1997] and *Ché Guevara, Paulo Freire, and the Pedagogy of Revolution* [2000]) a rare sincerity and courage in McLaren's work, where terms like oppression, capitalist exploitation and liberation are not wrapped up in some domesticated language that bleeds into silence the pains that these very words are intended to name.

Examining schooling not as a neutral process, but rather as a form of cultural politics, critical multiculturalists like McLaren were effectively arguing that, as microcosms of the larger society, educational institutions reflect and produce social turmoil by maintaining dominant beliefs, values and interests—cultural identities—through particular teaching practices and bodies of knowledge that are legitimized in the classroom. Guided by centuries of work in critical social theory (e.g., Marx, the Frankfurt School, poststructuralism, Feminism, etc.), critical pedagogues were working to reveal that educational practices and knowledge are always produced within particular social and historical conditions, and therefore any understanding of their production and dissemination must be accompanied by an investigation of their relation to ideology and power.

As I was experientially, empirically and theoretically convinced of the reproductive role of traditional institutional, pedagogical and curricular practices in education, my doctoral research turned to what were considered more progressive approaches to democratizing schools. Caught in the middle of the culture wars of the 1990s, *Multicultural Education* was the buzzword of the day.

Setting my sights on researching an actual implementation of multicultural alternatives to traditional schooling, I designed a descriptive ethnographic dissertation around a system-wide infusion of multicultural education in an inner-city public school district. I immediately realized that over the years, multicultural education had come to mean many different and even contradictory things. I thus went in search of a typology of multicultural camps that would ideologically situate the parameters of each so that I could use such a lens to read the work being accomplished within the school system. Having already categorized the various multicultural approaches as *Conservative, Liberal, Left-Liberal* and *Critical & Resistance Multiculturalism,* McLaren offered just the heuristic that I needed (1997).

I came to understand how the first three of these models in McLaren's typology are caught up in maintaining the status quo: the first, through a deficit-model orientation to cultural differences in the classroom (with a religious fervor for the "gifts" of "common culture," "standard language" and standardized testing); the second, taking the stance that all humans are equal and should be able to compete on a level playing field within a capitalist society (the main reformist goal being to promote positive relations among groups in schools by encouraging tolerance and unity); and the third, emphasizing cultural differences and authenticity in a culturally relativististic and essentializing manner.

It was McLaren's fourth approach—*Critical & Resistance Multiculturalism* (which he also refers to as *Revolutionary Multiculturalism*) that would set the stage for the analysis of my research.[1] In this radical model, *culture* was not being reduced to a list of books, materials, artifacts and social practices produced outside of history, economics and intergroup relations. Instead, culture was understood as embodying the lived experiences and behaviors that are the result of the unequal distribution of power along such lines as race, class, gender, sexuality and ability. That is, culture is shaped by the lived experiences and institutional forms organized around diverse elements of struggle and domination. As people interact with existing institutions and social practices in which the values, beliefs, bodies of knowledge, styles of communication and biases of the dominant culture are imposed, they are often stripped of their power to articulate and realize, or are forced to rearticulate their own goals.

When it comes to multicultural professional development, a major problem with *Liberal* approaches to the classroom is that the attitudes and beliefs of educators are often taken for granted. In fact, many well-intentioned educators, working from such conceptual frameworks, naively believe that they can be more welcoming just by miraculously leaving their own cultural baggage and biases at the schoolhouse door. Rather than confronting any potentially negative, inhibiting and exclusionary ideologies that inevitably enter the classroom, they are, in many cases, rendered invisible. The idea that personal politics can be left at the door gives the erroneous impression that teachers can in fact be neutral distributors of information, and that objective truth is attainable.

Even in *Left Liberal* models, the need to question the affective domain of teachers is often translated into an innocuous call for individuals to be more sensitive to differences and more inclusive.

From a critical multicultural perspective, teachers are viewed as working and speaking from within historically and socially determined relations of power and privilege that are based on such markers as their race, class, ability, sexuality and gender. Diametrically opposed to ignoring educators' attitudes and beliefs, critical multiculturalists call for the ongoing process of self-reflection and self-actualization. This evolving awareness, which I now refer to as *presence of mind,* is intended to help us not only to understand the social nature of our own cultural assumptions, and how they may affect the educational process, our students and the school's overall social relations, but also the asymmetries of power that exist within the institutions where we work and live.

In the spirit of *Critical Multiculturalism,* professional development needs to create a space that allows for a more critical and democratic exchange of ideas in which everyone's location, experiences and perceptions in their private and public lives become the point of departure for dialogue and a text for debate. In examining the social construction of knowledge, values and interaction across difference, the idea is not for the process to be abusive by silencing participants or placing their identities on trial. Rather, the process is to be unsettling only to the degree that it forces all of those involved to recognize and challenge their role in accepting and perpetuating oppression of any kind. It was with this analytic lens that I approached the three years (eventually eight years) of data involving professional development in "Changeton."[2]

Forging Change

Hoping to accommodate the demographic shifts and mitigate the antagonistic social relations in their school community and to help ensure cross-cultural understanding (among students, faculty and staff), academic success, and overall school/community harmony, an effort was being made by the Changeton school district to create a system-wide multicultural education program to combat the racism, cultural strife and exclusionary practices that were plaguing their schools and city. A volunteer group, referring to itself as the Multicultural Central Steering Committee (the "CSC"), had been established in order to shape and direct what the seventeen members hoped would provide a foundation for working toward what they described as "the affirmation of diversity through educational equity and social justice."

At the time this research was initiated, the city of Changeton's estimated population was 74,449 whites, 12,028 African Americans, 1,589 Asian Americans, 5,860 Latino/as, 269 Native Americans and 4,453 designated "Others." In addition, there were more women than men, over 13,000 people living in poverty, and the annual crimes committed in the city totaled 6,895, with 1,156 violent acts.

The educational system in the city was comprised of fifteen elementary schools, four middle schools, and one high school. Of a total school enrollment of 14,015, students were 13.6% Latino/a, 29.7% African American, 3.0% Asian American, and 53.2% white. One in every fourteen students in Changeton was limited-English proficient.

Adding to the system's status of probation with the state because of its inability to effectively desegregate the schools, Changeton had high annual dropout rates, especially among racially subordinated and low-income youth(s)—9.9% (or 296 students). The high school lost nearly a tenth of its population the year that the research began (and the dropout rate for ninth graders was estimated at 12-14%). The retention rate (those held back) in high school was 11.5%.[3]

The development of the Multicultural Central Steering Committee was a direct response to such statistics. It was also a critical reaction to public attitudes of the likes expressed by a union representative who proclaimed that "The local gene pool in Changeton should be condemned...."

The CSC, whose members reflect a diversity of racial, ethnic, religious and professional backgrounds, and includes teachers, guidance counselors, administrators and specialists in Adult, Bilingual and Special Education, has been officially sanctioned by the Superintendent of Schools to direct this system-wide effort. The committee members have been given the responsibility of extracting from their own individual experiences, as well as from the bounty of research and literature on cultural diversity, ideas that they think will help their city's schools.

As professional development should be a major component in any model of multicultural education, it is admirable that the CSC was willing to go through so much trouble, with no pay and an almost-nonexistent budget, to attempt to educate their school system's faculty and staff in the area of cultural diversity. The CSC understood the negative impact that educators can have on students' self-image and academic achievement, as well as on overall school social relations. As such, the group labored diligently to conceptualize and implement workshops that would raise awareness about multiculturalism.

Throughout their 54 meetings—including 20 subcommittee gatherings and 5 in-services, the CSC's central focus was on changing the negative attitudes and biases of their faculty and staff. As revealed in their written Mission Statement and their individual lists of goals, sensitivity training (which implied sensitizing teachers to other cultures) and the affirmation of diversity were viewed with the utmost importance: "Teaching culturally different groups requires more than sensitivity, it requires placing equal value on all students. The committee should be involved in providing retraining to all staff; i.e., sensitivity workshops." Strategies to ensure that sensitivity and affirmation would come to fruition would preoccupy the committee and consume their energies for the next three years.

Unfortunately, working from a theoretical model limited to issues of sensitivity and affirmation can create three fundamental problems. First of all, such a model can individualize and thus psychologize discrimination and oppressive practices, abstracting one's identity from its ideological, sociohistorical and institutional construction. Second, a sensitivity model often functions through the lens of "cultural relativism"—from which all cultures are valued equally and uncritically. Cultural relativism not only limits the possibilities for critical dialogue, but it also allows discriminatory values, beliefs and actions to go uncontested. Third, an exclusive focus on sensitivity and affirmation has the propensity to restrict awareness of the complexities of cultural politics. These issues will be illustrated through the CSC's work, and recommendations will be provided throughout the discussion as to what could be done additionally to extend the possibilities of multicultural professional development.

It is important to note that while the level of criticism throughout this chapter is extensive, the goal of such research analysis is by no means intended to dismiss the crucial work being done by the CSC, or to ridicule the individual contributions of its members. On the contrary, in deconstructing their work, the task at hand is to approach theoretically the complex social conditions that produce the disheartening statistics that gave rise to the committee in the first place. Such analysis is thus undertaken with the utmost optimism; however, hope for the future requires awareness of the grim realities of so many students in this country and the reconcilable limitations of mainstream efforts to democratize schools in the United States.

Abstracting the Political from the Psychological

Centered on a *Liberal* approach to professional development, which focuses on fostering positive interpersonal and intergroup interactions in schools by encouraging tolerance and unity, the Central Steering Committee concentrated on transforming individual psyches and thus directed its professional development energies toward "changing attitudes," "self-reflection," "asking yourself questions," "self exploration," "addressing personal prejudice" and "self-examination, awareness and sensitivity."

Most multiculturalists would agree that self-actualization and prejudice reduction are essential to social change, and that educators need to reflect critically on the assumptions that they carry about themselves, learning, different cultures, and so forth. However, discrimination was being dealt with by the CSC as if the abusive treatment of students and their poor academic performance were the end result of an educator's ignorance, personal affective character or individual values and beliefs, rather than the product of historically and socially sanctioned practices and conditions that produce such dispositions and subjectivities. Epitomizing the tendency to individualize discrimination and extract the psychological from the social in the CSC's deliberations, an African American, male member stated, "Some don't know, some don't care and some are truly racist."

Comments such as "We need to teach these kids to work and keep the system going…" and, "They [young African American males] are bright and talented, but they turn outside rather than inside the system…" risk communicating that the society is systemically structured to accommodate everyone, if educators could just get individual obstacles and the resulting student resistance out of the way of the existing educational process. In other words, if people were given the opportunity to learn in an environment that is welcoming, then everyone would stay in school and eventually succeed in the larger society. It would be inaccurate to tell students that if they study hard—assimilating mainstream values and beliefs—they will automatically succeed in the larger discriminatory society: many of them already know, intergenerationally, that this simply isn't true.

The central problem/limitation with pathologizing individual behavior is that self-actualization and prejudice reduction in and of themselves do not point out where the *self* or the discriminatory tendencies come from. It also risks implying that people are biologically predisposed to do the things that they do, driven by some innate fear and disdain of the unknown. The committee needs to explore in greater depth how schools, the media and other institutions nationwide function to legitimate particular experiences and world views at the expense and distortion of others. Developing a sense of the social and political realities that shape people's lives shouldn't be limited to "unlearning" what people have come to know, because it is also imperative to identify how such values and beliefs were produced, distributed and consumed. As one white, female member of the CSC suggested in the Multicultural Committee Draft of Goals questionnaire, "We need experiential activities and opportunities to recognize and evaluate the ideological influences that shape our thinking about schooling, society, ourselves and diverse others."

Educators need to understand that peering within oneself, disconnected from the rest of the world, a person is unable to make the links to the larger sociopolitical reality that shapes the psychological. Only in critical dialogue with the world around them can educators begin to understand what is within. A Latina at one of the in-services emphasized the importance of engaging the socially sanctioned industries of values and beliefs: "These are more than individual acts of meanness, it took a long time for it to become systemic....In reverse, it will take a long time to get back to individuals." In addition, near the end of the third year, an African American in-service facilitator informed the CSC that "Educators need to examine the values and the institutions such as slavery that shape our society."

The committee needs to articulate the linkages among macro-level political, economic and social variables, the formation of identities (including their own), and subordinated groups' academic performance at the micro-level classroom. In other words, in order to rupture the fallacy of education as the great equalizer, the group should explore the ways in which schools reflect the larger social order. In this way the CSC can continue its important goal of prejudice reduction and self-actualization while moving beyond its original premise that the institutions that structure society are okay, including their own school system, and it is simply the people who needed changing.

Taking the Reigns of Social Theory

Theory is a way of interpreting, criticizing and unifying established generalizations about the world. The important risk to be aware of with theorizing is that there is a fine line between generalizing and stereotyping, which is precisely why people need to be critical of all of their assumptions, regardless of any empirical justifications. However, deterring people from analyzing and scrutinizing the world around and within them is a major shortcoming in any project of change.

An African American, female, in-service facilitator encouraged the Central Steering Committee and the representatives from the school-based committees to voice their individual opinions: "We need to share and speak with 'I' statements, from our own personal experience—'I believe,' 'I think,' so we can get out of the practice of generalizing." While it is extremely important for individuals to come to voice around their own life histories, and to avoid any perpetuation of stereotypes, people nonetheless need a language with which they can examine and establish social patterns. Educators who embrace what the facilitators were calling for in the individualization of experience and history make it virtually impossible to analyze what it means to be exposed to a particular cultural reality or group history. As such, it is difficult to understand how "I" is more often than not the product rather than the creator of meaning.

Without critical social theory, the group is likely to conclude that the central goal should be to look for mechanical strategies for responding to discriminatory incidents. An example of this occurred when a white, male principal, eager to confront harsh behavior from some members of his staff, stated, "I want to know strategies that teachers can use if they hear a racist remark in the teachers' lounge!" Before searching for an efficient technical response, which needless to say is a vital step toward intervention, educators should first be apprenticed into theorizing oppressive behavior—all human behavior for that matter—and then act upon discriminatory tendencies from a more informed position.

In order to affirm and engage the complexity of diverse human histories and perceptions, a fundamental tenet of critical multicultural education—when it comes to professional development and/or teaching—is the inclusion of facilitators' and in-service participants' voices in the learning process. This type of democratic participation calls into question everyone's identity, experiences and the assumptions that guide one's actions. In listening to and engaging opinions and values that are made public, the idea is not for in-service facilitators or teachers to be disparaging or censorious. Rather, interaction through dialogue is meant to leave people ill at ease to a point where everyone acknowledges and takes responsibility for their complicity in perpetuating forms of discrimination.

The Dangers of Cultural Relativism

It is difficult to address multiculturalism without first establishing a working definition of culture—how it is produced and what in turn it works to create and maintain. Overall, the committee was working toward solutions to enhance educational success by embracing cultural relativism—in which all differences are equally acceptable. The Central Steering Committee Mission Statement is comprised of language that echoes this goal. The committee speaks of "appreciation of all cultures," being "inclusive," having a "common purpose," that "a celebration of diversities promotes unity," placing "equal value on all students," "acceptance," and promoting "staff respect for and sensitivity toward the diverse backgrounds of students and their families." The affirmation of diversity is extremely important if multicultural education of any kind hopes to gain the initial trust and participation of all groups in society. However, the celebration of difference can create an interactive process within which it is virtually impossible to engage all cultures around their strengths and shortcomings.

One young man, from a group of multiracial adults who had either dropped out, been pushed out or kicked out of Changeton schools, described his predicament in an interview: "At one point, I juss started sellin' guns for a livin'. Went to jail a couple times; moved to Providence; had a kid; got tired of sellin' drugs out there; came back over here; went to jail again."

Trapped in a language of affirmation, the liberal multicultural educator would be compelled to romanticize this world view. There is no room for critique, cultural analysis and ethical intervention. In fact, what usually happens in mainstream multicultural classrooms is that students never hear of this harsh reality in the shape of formal learning, because teachers rarely investigate the existential realities of their students and the compressed poverty, disenfranchisement, police brutality and racism that shape these kids' lives and self-concept. As the Social Studies Chair, a white woman, stated, "They [teachers] think that these kids come from Nobel [the capital city of the state]....We go out to the bus stop to show people that these kids live here...." Multicultural education and professional development should be used as a way to prepare teachers and learners with exactly what they will need in order to excavate their history and cultural roots, and consequently the social nature of the self. It is only then that real substantive personal transformation and social agency can occur. In other words, it is only then that a society can begin to work against the culture of violence that it creates.

When professional development is based on in-service games, role plays or ideas such as cultural fairs, all of which are generally sanitized of any engagement with the core of society's intergroup antagonisms, it can never achieve any kind of critical awareness among educators, or students for that matter. The CSC, brainstorming for ideas for a faculty workshop, mentioned developing a convention that would use passports to move from one exhibit to another. The advocates of this creative and potentially informative idea should also propose visiting a ghetto where people actually live. As one Changeton youth interviewed during the research describes, "The ghetto is everywhere, the hood ain't no joke and there's no way out." The facilitators of such a multicultural event should pose the question to educators, in order to encourage them to theorize culture, of what it is like to survive in a dilapidated housing project where drugs, violence and hunger are everyday realities. They need to explore what it means to take care of sick parents, the feeling of having no school books, the inevitable ramifications of not trusting public education, what it's like to have your imprisoned brothers' mug shots posted around town, the experience of seeing battery acid poured all over someone's face because of a gang deal gone bad, finding your mother's boyfriend dead in your house from an overdose of drugs, what it feels like to get stabbed or shot or beaten by the police—all social realities described by the local youths interviewed.

In order to extend the virtues of multicultural professional development, in-service facilitators and workshop participants must also move beyond internationalizing multiculturalism and reducing diversity to issues of immigration (as many of the country's disenfranchised children have been here for generations and/or are on the tail end of U.S. domestic and foreign policy) by limiting the discussion to life back in some other country that many children have never even seen. What would be crucial here is to develop a deeper understanding of what defines culture so as to be able to move beyond an ahistorical sense of values, beliefs, group ethos, language and practices, and to understand how these elements are produced within abuses of power. In this way, educators can move beyond Flag Day, Japanese doll day, food festivals, and so on, that reduce the complexities of culture to aesthetics and fun. Within the clashes of cultural capital—different language, cognitive and learning styles, values and beliefs, literacies, knowledge, and so forth—educators can also begin to address the kinds of academic failure that are endemic to Changeton. Multicultural professional development should thus be working to apprentice teachers into being ethnographers so that they can begin to understand the communities which they are intended to serve and what their students are bringing to the arena of formal learning.

Understanding Difference

Throughout its work, the Central Steering Committee often made reference to difference (e.g., "We are afraid of difference" and "We should see these kids not as culturally disadvantaged, but as different"). However, the committee needs to define what exactly the term implies and to recognize that difference only exists in relationship to a referent. The critical question is: What are the defining parameters of that referent, that is, of the person/group who is speaking?

The concept of *difference* in the United States is generally not examined in ways that name and call into question the dominant referent group—the invisible norm of the white, upper-middle-class, heterosexual, healthy, Christian male by which all others are evaluated and positioned. Educators are not simply individuals making random comparisons in the world. In reality, everyone is marked by group membership, whether or not that connection is understood or perceived as such. Whites, for example, are marked by membership in a category that has historically been used as the referent for negatively evaluating other racial groups. It is precisely these social markings that shape identities and points of reference that are far too often taken for granted, or seen as universal/human.

The first three multicultural in-services that the CSC developed and participated in did not take up the issue of difference, that is, beyond a relativistic approach—which is surprising given that the outside organizations that facilitated the sessions had the word "difference" in their names. At the first workshop, one of the facilitators, after categorically separating the group, asked if the participants felt labeled. One white male claimed, "It made everyone feel like a minority." Others made reference to feeling "manipulated" or "segregated" and that they "didn't like to be white or non-white." Some were uncomfortable with the social-class differentiation. The general consensus among the in-service participants was that "I felt good about some categories, and bad about others."

In order for this exercise to be more productive, there needs to be a profound discussion of how these divisions among groups are legitimated in society, thus moving the experience into something more than just psychologically driven sensations. Otherwise, the end result will be much like that of an African

American, male committee member's relativistic stance inspired by this apolitical and ahistorical separation exercise: "We all mixed in the differences and belonged with each other at one point, we all have differences and commonalities." This *Left Liberal* celebration of otherness unfortunately disregards the difference between experiences as well as the complex relations that exist between them.

There were a number of opportunities during this first workshop to tease out some crucial points about the struggle over identity and difference. For example, when a woman sat down in the middle of the floor, explaining to the larger group: "I was born in the U.S. My family is from Cape Verde. They originated in Europe (Italy). Where am I? When I changed my descriptor, they changed my minority status."

Or, back at the central administration building, the Head of the Bilingual Education Department explained to the CSC: "America wants you to come here and fit into categories that are already established and millions of people are marked other." These types of situations—pedagogical moments—provide ample opportunity to explore the history of socially and institutionally sanctioned racist and segregationist practices in the United States. Taking advantage of such pedagogical moments is crucial if teacher education is to move past the mere acceptance of differences and help educators explore and deconstruct the sociopolitical formations that give rise to those differences.

Remapping the Comfort Zone

In developing in-services for teachers throughout their school system, the Multicultural Central Steering Committee talked about comfort and feeling free to speak and share experiences. At one point in their workshop preparations, a Cape Verdean male informed the facilitator that he wanted to be able to talk about all groups and issues without emphasizing the negative—"nothing negative, no violence, we are working on that." One of his white, Jewish, female colleagues agreed: "We shouldn't deal with all the negatives such as lynchings, rather, we need to accentuate the contributions of different groups." The Social Studies Department Chair, who would soon resign from the Committee, immediately rejected this position: "I'm tired of dancing around with food and simple curriculum changes, and I don't like the idea of a fair, it trivializes multicultural education, as does Black History Month and Martin Luther King Jr. Month!"

One of the in-service facilitators, while trouble-shooting with the committee on what to do in the first workshops, stated, "We can tailor the day to make everyone feel good." She told the CSC, "There are some things that you don't want in the first session; some issues are difficult for the people that are in denial of living in a multicultural world." This assurance of comfort was again reiterated when the same facilitator opened the in-service discussion with some words about "the need for safety and feeling comfortable" when dealing with diversity. This strategy of interaction resulted in a variety of issues and tensions going unaddressed and thus uncontested.

Subsequent to the facilitator's opening statement about safety and comfort, she introduced an article on white privilege. After reading the essay aloud, some whites at the in-service voiced the opinion that they didn't think that their position was necessarily a privilege. There was general agreement among the group that "We don't want to shift the blame to white males in multicultural education." One woman argued: "There is a backlash against the white male... What is the purpose of this in-service and the CSC? I think it's tolerance... Math, science and language have no color....We need concrete strategies to go back with."

If given the opportunity, in-service participants who were challenged and felt under attack tried to move, perhaps unconsciously, away from the point of analysis. This movement was often done in a call for practical solutions and materials. Unwilling to engage the ideological construction of whiteness, this particular individual (from the above quote) not only requests "concrete strategies" but also wants to move out of the political and into what she believes to be neutral and objective ground—"Math, science and language have no color."[4]

Along these same lines, confronted with issues of white supremacy, another white woman expressing frustration with the in-service exclaimed: "I don't feel that I'm getting anything here that I can use! I can't know everything about all groups, religions or cultures. All students need certain things. Let's talk about that and their similarities." A call for harmony and not engagement, this comment risks a translation such as: "I am not comfortable with where this is going. Let's talk about something else—abstract educational needs and materials, for example." If all kids have certain needs, and those needs are empathy, respect, encouragement and to be treated with integrity, then that requires naming and engaging their experiences across racism, sexism, homophobia, classism, linguisism, and so forth. This participant's comment risks implying that students' needs have nothing to do with cultural politics. Perhaps using her position of privilege to avoid an analysis of the harsh realities that many people face, the speaker wanted to turn to a discussion of *similarities*, which risks the translation of: "Let's only talk about what you have in common with me so that I am not uncomfortable."

After the above statement was made, the facilitator took the floor, pointing out how the literature on privilege evoked "feelings of anger, confusion and uncomfortableness." She added that this was "not simply a white/black thing" and that "gender, class and sex were also important issues." What appeared to be a prime opportunity to discuss how the struggles over identity and difference cut across individual categories disappeared after this statement. It was as if the facilitator were using other categories to divert the group away from the tensions that were building around racial issues. Referring to the temporary discomfort, she argued that these feelings need to be dealt with, especially when working with students—"We want students to be comfortable, then they will do better." However, in leaving the in-service participants' comments untouched, she didn't confront the assumptions and potential biases of the people directly in front of her. In this sense, the facilitator seems to be falling prey to a laissez-faire practice. In other words, whatever the group wants, it gets, and in this case, that is to avoid discussion of volatile issues.

If comfort were a strategy for keeping everyone open minded at the in-service, members of the CSC, after years of working together, should have challenged their colleagues' assumptions and statements once they were back at the central office debriefing over the workshops. In support of what they had just experienced with the in-service organization, and avoiding confrontation altogether, an African American committee member exclaimed: "We recognized that we do have a problem and not to simply place blame… There are things that you have to be aware of, that came out in the exercises." Chiming in on the theme of blame, a white principal informed the group that some people were upset because they felt that the Europeans were not mentioned at all. He also brought up the issue of white male-bashing, pointing out that "Many people don't support multiculturalism because they feel that it's against white males and females… Their concern is that we should not shift the blame from one group to another."

The willingness to embrace a culprit-less world invoked a huge contradiction in the committee's logic: up until this point, it seemed as if the social institutions were functional, and once negative teacher attitudes were changed, schools would cater to all students. Suddenly it sounded as if no one was to blame, that people are the products of what they have inherited from history and institutions. As an African American, male, in-service facilitator added, "I'm not blaming anyone for that [discrimination] today," arguing that people in present-day society "have inherited such conditions."

After the professional development in-services, most Committee members felt that the workshops were "non-threatening," "comfortable," "inclusive" and "built on our sensitivity and camaraderie." It is more than likely that the participants were comfortable because of the tendency to avoid the really difficult issues and tensions among the group, as well as those in their schools, city, state, nation and world.

The Committee's future work should explore the ways in which people breathe life into existing institutions and socially sanctioned practices, which in turn breathe life into people. Insisting that there is no one to blame risks shifting the power of human agency to historical determinism. In this uncritical sense, people become objects of history (passive recipients) and not subjects (shapers) capable of engaging and transforming both themselves and the world around them.

Color-Blindness

Whiteness has played a significant role in shaping ethnic patterns, social identities and institutions in the United States. However, whiteness has paradoxically been able to mask itself as a category. The underlying evasive ideology that informs the social construction of whiteness is strategically infused such that those who for whatever reason buy into its logic are unable, or simply unwilling, to see and thus name its oppressive nature.

By not recognizing whiteness as a racial identity, most whites see themselves as race-free and less ethnic than "Others" and consequently take for granted the privileges they secure by such an ideologically charged (yet purposefully invisibled) racial marker.

Limited to a liberal multicultural discourse of sensitivity, affirmation and comfort, and simultaneously an approach to multicultural education that focuses on the universal human experience and not a politics of identity and difference, members of the Central Steering Committee embraced such ideas as "unity and common purpose," "working with teachers to help them view everyone as innately equal," "the concept of oneness," "not pigeonholing them [racially subordinated students] as black or brown," "I value all of my students in the same way, [all groups] go under one umbrella" and "We are the same under the skin." The CSC also celebrated the fact that the high school was selling t-shirts that said "Be Color Blind."

Although such efforts are meant with the best intentions, not naming and working with the ideological markers of difference across race, class, gender, sexuality, and so forth, can have detrimental results. Educators can't value "all" students if they deny any engagement with their diverse life experiences that are the very products of those socially constructed categories. Educators shouldn't rely on what appears to be an objective and just way of dealing with all students—the idea that "I value all people as human beings," if they truly hope to work toward significant social change. Because of the fact that the process of racialization (ascribing behavioral characteristics to racial groupings) begins at an early age, by no means should experiences be denied or artificially homogenized in the name of equal treatment.

What is ironic is that in the very article that the in-service participants were required to read twice, the author Peggy McIntosh (1990) asserts: "I think that whites are carefully taught not to recognize white privilege....My schooling gave me no training in seeing myself as an oppressor, as an unfairly advantaged person, or as a participant in a damaged culture." This social construction of not seeing is embodied in the laughter of the two white women at the first all-faculty in-service, who commented to each other in response to the obvious implications of the video *The Eye of the Storm* (more popularly known as "Brown Eyes Blue Eyes"): "It doesn't carry over, we don't see that....It's not racial, they like you or they don't." The CSC should work to approach how such educators disregard the realities of discrimination as expressed by two Changeton youths interviewed:

> *Olavo:* They treat you different man. I had like three classes where I was the only nigga in the room. The teacher used to teach everybody in the class but me. I used to call her, "Can you explain this to me?" She used to like ignore me.
>
> *Roland:* If you Black, the attitude is, "You dumb."

Any depoliticized ahistorical approach to multicultural education can provide window-dressing-type reforms, but simply acknowledging our differences, or avoiding them altogether in a color-blind approach, will not lead to an eradication of the abusive ideological and structural patterns of schools in the United States.

The long-term goal of any political project should be to achieve a world in which biological features such as color, gender and sexual orientation have no negative social significance or unethical meaning. However, such an immediate transition is impossible in that these categories play a major role in the production of social identities, interactions and experience in the United States.

Encouraging Praxis: Reflection and Action

There appeared to be a de facto acceptance among the Central Steering Committee members that an individual's subject position (the place that a person occupies within a set of social relationships) predisposes him or her to theoretical awareness. However, educators should be encouraged to understand that a person's race, ethnicity, gender, social class, and so on, do not predispose critical consciousness—that is, the ability to read the social and political realities that shape people's lives. McLaren (1995) warns of this very pitfall:

> Either a person's physical proximity to the oppressed or their own location as an oppressed person is supposed to offer a special authority from which to speak.…Here the political is often reduced only to the personal where theory is dismissed in favor of one's own personal and cultural identity—abstracted from the ideological and discursive complexity of their formation. (p. 125)

As has been argued, critical forms of multicultural education should invite everyone to explore further the relationship between their own identities and individual experiences, and society's larger historic, economic and ideological constructs, and their inextricable connection to power. Part of this awareness for the CSC should include an examination of gender, sexuality and social class.

Transforming Gendered Identities

During the Central Steering Committee's work, the issue of gender exposed ideological divisions among the participants—divisions that are representative of the larger society. In fact, any call to name discrimination against women (let alone patriarchal domination) as an essential part of their multicultural efforts was met with resistance by a number of men on the committee. Virtually dismissing the importance of understanding gender politics and the production of gendered identities, a Cape Verdean American guidance counselor insisted that

"The Constitution implicitly includes women, you don't know oppression unless you're black!" Not only did this stance create a decontextualized hierarchy of oppression which prioritized issues of race, but it also neglected to engage the multiple and interconnecting relationships of language, gender, race, class, sexuality and so forth. Pitting different groups against each other, and creating a hierarchy of oppression rather than creative multicultural communities of solidarity, is counter-productive. Instead of reproducing such a hierarchy, the CSC should embrace feminist struggles while at the same time challenging the women, who were predominantly white, to address their own racism. White women often hide behind gender issues so as not to have to deal with their own discriminatory beliefs and actions.

Some women on the committee responded to the comment about not knowing oppression: "You don't know what it's like to be a woman, girls are excluded from the curriculum in math and science!"; "Women are not empowered here at the elementary level!"; "Some people have more gender insensitivity than they may recognize, so this area should be included!" This last statement, given by a white woman, is of special importance in that she had just been denied the position of High School Principal for what many citizens interpreted as sexist reasons. The Mayor, who cast the deciding vote, concluded that she lacked the necessary "presence" and "leadership style" to preside over the high school. Nonetheless, such dissent fell by the wayside. In fact, the issue of gender would rarely, if ever again, surface in the Committee's work. The CSC needs to engage more deeply the complexities of the relationship between gender and culture; in other words, how sex-role socialization and the concomitant discourses that situate how boys/men and girls/women are supposed to speak, act, walk, learn, and so on.

Confronting Heterosexism and Homophobia

Throughout the committee's discussions, it appeared as though many members were trying to minimize the importance of sexual politics so that they could justify not having to deal with it (also perhaps a strategy used to ignore disabilities and gender). Sexual orientation was at one point reduced to a matter of gender—"When you say gender, does that include gays? It does for me." Two other Central Steering Committee members argued that gays in fact have a culture: "Those others, gays for example, belong to a culture." "Stay away from group identification—gays are part of a culture, we are including everyone." However, instead of elaborating on the relationship between sexuality and culture, it appeared as though these two racially subordinated men simply used avoiding "group identification" as justification for not naming sexuality in the committee's written statement. Immediately after that, a Cape Verdean American guidance counselor interjected, "Before you know it, AIDS advocates…." It is important to note how "AIDS advocates" risks reinforcing an ideologically coded phrase to imply gays. This is precisely where a white principal declared that he was reluctant to get involved "with every group that comes along…."

At another juncture in the committee's work, addressing gay, lesbian, bisexual and transgendered concerns was considered a risk for the CSC because "The papers will show how you are talking about homosexuality, which will cover up the issue of race." This statement was perhaps being made so as to use fear of a media backlash to dissuade the multicultural committee members from confronting their own assumptions about sexuality. The media would most certainly make a great deal of disparaging noise if the group chose publicly to confront homophobia. In fact, there were already negative assaults by the Changeton press when other, less contentious, multicultural issues were raised in the community and schools. However, the key for the CSC is to be strategic while at the same time honest about the values and beliefs that inform one's/the group's position on an issue. In other words, the committee should anticipate the response of the press and work it to the group's advantage. But participants shouldn't simply erase the realities of sexual politics because of the fierce debates that may emerge. In fact, instigating such polemics would be extremely helpful in educating and including the public in these "culture wars."

An egregious example of the CSC's indifference to sexual politics was manifested during the registration process for an in-service being provided by the Center for Training & Health Education (not organized or related in any way to the Committee's efforts). Part one of the conference was titled "Working and Living in Culturally Diverse Environments," and part two was called "Making Schools Safe for Gay, Lesbian & Bisexual Youth." Not a single member of the CSC expressed the need to better inform themselves about the politics of sexuality. Instead, the committee strategically eliminated any mention of the gay/lesbian section of the workshop advertisement when they went in search of public funds that would support their attendance in the first part of the conference. In addition, the group never actively, or even rhetorically, sought out the Committee membership of an openly gay or lesbian person (or a disabled person for that matter), as they had done with the various racial and ethnic categories.

Multicultural educators need to attempt to develop an approach for honestly addressing sexuality and should explore the connections between sexual orientation and the cultural realities of everyday life. The real tangible tragedy would be to ignore the reality of people like the young man interviewed, a student who had dropped out of Changeton High School, who had turned to drugs and suicide because of his public mistreatment for being gay.

Facing Social Class

The significance of social class emerged early on in the Multicultural Central Steering Committee's work. The issue arose during the drafting of the Mission Statement: "We treat poor kids poorly, what about them?," and "Sensitivity should not be limited to racial and ethnic differences alone, but should include gender, physical and mental challenges, and socioeconomic differences." It also came up in the preparation for the first in-service: "We had a workshop that really made the participants feel class conscious....The people from Borton, in their Brooks Brothers suits, were embarrassed." When asked to separate themselves by social class at the first small in-service, many agreed that it made them feel uncomfortable. However, the CSC needs to develop a deeper theoretical understanding as to how socioeconomic status (beyond the mere quantity of money a person possesses) in part shapes the values, beliefs, worldviews, discourse styles, social relations and actions of people.

The first in-service facilitator included in his speech the history of exploitation of the poor in Changeton. However, his contributions were considered by the CSC to be "a bomb"—that is, a waste of time. The general sentiment was: "Bur was atrocious—he was only going to speak for ten minutes. He talked more about the blue collar stuff, and not about different populations—total irrelevance!"

Capitalism and socioeconomic status should be considered significant issues when dealing with consciousness-raising about multiculturalism. The committee needs to engage the interpenetrating relationship among power, economic resources and social control, and thus explore how schools function as major socializing influences in preparing students for their place in a hierarchically divided labor force, one that includes a degree of poverty. In order to better understand the social realities of their students and communities, the CSC—all citizens of Changeton, for that matter—needs to explore how the struggles of different classes over material and symbolic wealth have shaped the city's past and historical present, as well as the ways in which class antagonisms have historically been used to incite racism and other forms of oppression.

Throughout the three years, there was no mention of the fact that the affluent, white minority in Changeton ran the schools (as they have historically controlled the city), and that many of the faculty and administrators don't actually live in the predominantly blue-collar community. In addition, a discussion should be encouraged of how the CSC members' own social-class lenses have been shaping the ways in which they see their students (and vice versa), the kinds of expectations that they have for them, and the ways in which they have been approaching the entire debate over multiculturalism.

The Changeton youths interviewed during this research recognized the problem of social class and education:

> *Stevie:* You know what I notice, I noticed when I used to go to school, if the teachers knew you came from a nice like middle-class neighborhood, they'd treat you good. They give you special attention. But if they knew you came from the projects or somethin'....
>
> *Carlos:* If you come from a bad neighborhood they make sure you never make it.
>
> *Stevie:* They think that you are a trouble maker.
>
> *Dion:* Automatically, automatically!

The neglect of issues of class and capitalism (and the interconnecting relationships with race and gender) is especially disconcerting given that—as stated earlier—in the very year that the committee would get its start, there were locally 13,000 people living in poverty, and the annual crimes committed in the city totaled 6,895.

One of the most potentially critical activities listed in the Changeton survey data of multicultural projects that were the outcome of the professional development efforts of the CSC was the "World Food Day Awareness Project." The local paper depicted the interdisciplinary project involving math, food and geography as "Students gathered in the computer lab to learn about the challenges facing citizens of far-flung lands trying to survive drought and poverty so they can put food on their family's table."

As about four hundred transnational corporations control two-thirds of the earth's fixed assets, and 70 percent of the world trade, and organizations such as the World Bank, the International Monetary Fund, GATT, the World Trade Organization, NAFTA and the G-8 are shaping the New World Order and forging what McLaren (2000) refers to as the "globalization of misery," students in a course on world hunger should be encouraged to explore how neo-liberalism (i.e., transnational corporate exploitation) and U.S. foreign policy contribute greatly to the very poverty that countries around the planet experience—that they are not as distant as the newspaper article would like people to believe. Students should also be encouraged to examine related environmental issues such as pollution, biotechnology, genetic engineering, agribusiness and sweat shops. In addition, they should learn about and theorize on the poverty and hunger in the United States, and more specifically in Changeton. As almost a quarter of the population of the United States experiences poverty every day, it is by no means "far-flung." Students could begin to understand the high rate of crime and violence in their city, and not so easily fall victim to the racist ideologies that are readily disseminated to explain the problem of cultural deviance within African American and Latino populations; i.e., young black men are vicious and without morals or provocation. In this way courses, as the CSC wanted, could be truly inter-/trans-disciplinary, combining economics (e.g., the political economy of the burgeoning prison industrial complex), science and technology, political science, history, anthropology and ethics. The CSC needs to call for a rigorous analysis of capitalist social relations as they have historically and currently exist.

A Look into the Future

In their efforts to conceptualize and implement professional development for their colleagues, the Central Steering Committee worked tirelessly and altruistically to build a foundation on which multicultural education could become a fundamental part of the overall process of public schooling. Hopefully, the contentious issues left on the table after three years of development will take center stage in the near future. The CSC should certainly continue with its noble job of introducing multicultural education (avoiding the paralysis of "We can't move until we've solved our ideological differences..."). However, they need to be openly honest, and insistent, about naming to the public (in the hope of a wider debate) the very content and detail of those discrepancies.

From the research observations and pedagogical suggestions presented in this chapter,[5] and from exploring the work of important critical pedagogues like Peter McLaren, perhaps educators can open up new doors of possibility for developing the necessary awareness to extend the virtues for multicultural professional development in public schools, and more effectively work to eradicate cultural tensions, low academic achievement and high dropout rates. As a grander goal, educators and students can begin to influence and democratize the larger social realities that shape the very texture of school life. Otherwise, as McLaren (1995) argues, "Multicultural education without a transformative political agenda can just be another form of accommodation to the larger social order" (p. 126).

On the contrary, Peter McLaren's work has been forged with an unwavering commitment to social justice. And with his renewed Marxist theory and political vision, he makes hope a reality and revolutionary pedagogy a possibility. I am grateful that he has played such an influential role in my life, and I'm glad that he is being honored (and critiqued!) with this book of appreciation.

Notes

[1] In an attempt to categorize the myriad theoretical and practical approaches for addressing diversity within schools, other researchers had developed a number of helpful typologies (Gibson, 1976; Pratte, 1983; Sleeter & Grant, 1988). With this particular research project, I am also deeply indebted to Christine Sleeter and Carl Grant for their painstaking research and insight.

[2] The name *Changeton* is a pseudonym, as are all of the other names of towns, cities and people used throughout.

[3] The academic standings throughout Changeton's school system were also bleak: the percentage of high school seniors performing at grade-level goals in math was 25; and in science, 27. Of the 64% of the students who took the SATs that year, the average score was 801—as compared with the state average of 903. In addition, 13.5% of the students throughout the school system, overwhelmingly poor and racially subordinated boys and linguistic minorities, were in Special Education.

[4] Beyond a call for tolerance, educators need to question the privilege that whites have in being in a position to decide who will and will not be tolerated.

[5] In order to answer the research question "How did the Changeton Multicultural Central Steering Committee get created, how did they come to define multicultural education and go about operationalizing this definition?" (i.e., what were their goals, and what strategies did they use to meet these goals?), I used qualitative methods of participant observation and document collection. I sat in on all of the Changeton Multicultural Central Steering Committee meetings (including subcommittee meetings and in-service workshops) and recorded the sessions. I also collected all documents that were shared among the group. The most important data collected for this study consisted of recorded observations of all the CSC meetings (round table discussions, which took place about once per month)—ideas presented, issues raised, points of debate, decisions made. These data, the result of 54 Multicultural Central Steering Committee meetings—including 20 CSC subcommittee meetings and 5 in-services—was central in describing the developments in the group's work. Secondary sources were collected in order to provide more detail and to corroborate the recorded meetings. This consisted of official CSC minutes taken at each meeting by the Committee's chairperson, CSC official progress reports that were publicly distributed and clarification interviews. When information discussed during the CSC meetings was not clear, I

briefly interviewed the person/s after the meeting. For additional triangulation, I also used "member checks": I recognized that my own subjectivities would inevitably come into play in the collection process, analysis and interpretation of the data. In an attempt to achieve a coherent depiction of the CSC's endeavors, during the descriptive stage of this research (capturing what the group discussed and accomplished), I had the CSC's approval to select members to read over my written descriptions of the committee's efforts to make sure that they were, in some respect, on target. This technique allowed the solicitation of alternative perspectives on what transpired.

References

Gibson, M.A. (1976). Approaches to multicultural education in the United States: Some concepts and assumptions. *Anthropology and Education Quarterly*, 7, 7–18.

McIntosh, P. (1990). White privilege: Unpacking the invisible knapsack. *Independent School*, Winter, 31.

McLaren, P. (1980). *Cries from the corridor: The new suburban ghettos.* Agincourt, Ontario: Methuen.

———. (1986). *Schooling as ritual performance.* London: Routledge & Kegan Paul.

———. (1989). *Life in schools: An introduction to critical pedagogy in the foundations of education.* New York: Longman.

———. (1995). *Critical pedagogy and predatory culture: Oppositional politics in a postmodern era.* New York: Routledge.

———. (1997). *Revolutionary multiculturalism: Pedagogies of dissent for the new millennium.* Boulder, CO: Westview Press.

———. (2000). *Ché Guevara, Paulo Freire, and the pedagogy of revolution.* Boulder, CO: Rowman & Littlefield.

Pratte, R. (1983). Multicultural education: Four normative arguments. *Educational Theory*, 33, 21–32.

Sleeter, C. & Grant, C. (1988). *Making choices for multicultural education: Five approaches to race, class, and gender.* New York: Merrill.

Chapter 6

Peter McLaren: One Intellectual in Two Realities

Marcia Moraes

Nowadays, in Brazil, the work of Peter McLaren is going strong and is influential within numerous fields such as education, sociology, political science and philosophy. This has been the case especially since 1992, when his books began to be translated into Portuguese: *Rituais na Escola* (1992) (*Schooling as a Ritual Performance*); *Vida nas Escolas* (1997) (*Life in Schools*); *Multiculturalismo Revolucionário* (2000a) (*Revolutionary Multiculturalism*); and, *Multiculturalismo Crítico* (2000b) (*Critical Multiculturalism*). It has become hard to find anyone from the aforementioned disciplines who is unfamiliar with Peter and his ideas. The recognition of his work is easily seen in all crowded auditoriums each time he comes to Brazil to speak (and it does not matter if he is going to the South, Southeast or Northeast regions of Brazil).

The focus of this chapter is a brief analysis of the reception of McLaren's work in two different contexts: first, in the rural areas of the state of Rio de Janeiro, where I've been working since 1992 with elementary and secondary school teachers in a program called InterCAP/UERJ; second, in a metropolitan area, the city of Rio de Janeiro, where I teach master's classes.

As a starting point for this analysis, I am reminded of Michel Foucault (1980) when he argues that an author is that individual whose writings allow other people to think differently than him or her. That is, an author's work may make possible the production of thoughts and arguments that bring a different perspective to that author's work. This is what constitutes a discursive and, it seems to me, a dialogical perspective.

Teaching Peter McLaren in Rural Areas

The teachers I work with in the rural areas of the state of Rio de Janeiro are people who teach children and teenagers across different grade levels, at the same time, in the same classroom. Many of these students work on farms before or after school hours and come from a very impoverished socioeconomic background. Many students go to school without shoes, and the marks on their small, rough hands are evidence of the hard work they engage in on area farms. In some schools there is only one teacher who, beyond the role of teacher, is also the principal of the school and prepares meals for the students as well.

Textbooks are sent to these public schools by the government, since public education is a governmental responsibility. However, the number of books is frequently not sufficient, considering the quantity of students. Additionally, the content quality of these books is quite poor: they emphasize repetition and structural exercises in all areas of instruction. Furthermore, many of these books present a variety of sexist and racist perspectives. On the other hand, for most teachers in these rural areas, the textbook is the only available material.

With this in mind, the program I coordinate represents an attempt to bring methodological and pedagogical suggestions to teachers so that they can begin to consider diverse ways of teaching without the exclusive support of textbooks. The difficult part of this program is that a vast majority of these teachers do not believe that other ways of teaching—beyond the all-too-common and popular "banking" approach—are possible. At the same time, the major purpose of the program is to give them ways of seeing and questioning constructions of knowledge as they are enacted in schools, as well as to offer diverse methodological perspectives for their work in classrooms.

In this program, my encounter with teachers is called "Critical Pedagogy in Classrooms." The main objective in this course is to explore and discuss the role of critical theory in relation to schooling and learning processes: in relation to epistemological perspectives within the process of creating knowledge and understanding semiotic values of ideology and in relation to the political and social project of possibility and hope for emancipatory democracy. Within these perspectives, McLaren's work is one of the fundamental resources I regularly use. For these purposes, I have the teachers read McLaren's *Life in Schools* (*Vida nas Escolas*) as a major source for understanding the perspectives of critical pedagogy.

Teaching Peter McLaren: Rural Versus Urban

Another setting in which I use McLaren's work is in a master's course I teach entitled "Epistemological Paradigms of Education." In this class, one of the perspectives offered is an analysis of diverse pedagogical epistemologies, including a comparison of traditional, progressive and critical/radical education. And I use McLaren's work to help delineate and understand the purposes of critical pedagogy. Just as in the rural areas, students read *Life in Schools* (*Vida nas Escolas*) as one of the required texts.

Most of the students in this master's class are teachers, or even professors, at private or public universities, but some of them come from other backgrounds and are in the course—and program—simply because they need an MA certificate in order to teach at the university level. Among these students are lawyers, nurses, engineers and so forth. These are people who come from diverse areas, and it is my hope that through this course and their reading of McLaren, they may have a positive first encounter with educational and critical theory.

One of the differences between the rural and the metropolitan groups is that rural-area teachers are prepared at the high school level, while the metropolitan group is composed completely of people who hold undergraduate certificates.

The comparison I would like to highlight here is based on a simple question I asked of both groups as a starting point of our study: "How would you describe briefly the kind of impression or impact McLaren's work gives you?" For this analysis, I recorded and later transcribed the answers. What follows are examples of people's reactions during our first discussion after the readings.

From the Rural Group

> I like the idea of a diary [as used by McLaren in *Cries from the Corridor/Life in Schools* as a reflection and research tool], because it may help me to better understand what I have done with my students.

> I don't think the diary is the point. The point is that I could never imagine someone would write about difficulties in the classroom. Usually people write about good things and not the bad ones. They try to teach us how to be good teachers but they don't say we must change things. Peter talks about the walls and not just the sky.

Well, I think Peter says: Look, we can criticize and make changes.

I thought I was giving chances to my students, but now I know I was repressing their expressions, but I know I must let them criticize the world around them. I did not know how weak and how strong I could be as a teacher. But I have to criticize the world, too. I don't like the way things happen, but now I understand what this whole system is.

I think Peter was very poor when he was young. If he were rich he could never write things we understand and relate to. He demonstrated that I can question things and I cannot be afraid of what I am thinking as a teacher or as a woman.

That's why I think this resistance stuff is something that really happens. I did not know those things in the classroom were resistance. Parents resist, too. They are illiterate but they want homework for their kids. If you say there is no homework they can kill you. I am against homework for many reasons. I can see I resist, too. Some days I just don't wanna teach. Some days I feel weak; I feel I hate my work, but that's the first time I feel I can say this. It is weird, because we teachers are supposed to do good things to our children, but I can see we can do bad things; we can be evil; we can touch their minds in a bad way. I think Peter writes that we can change things if we want to and that we are not perfect models.

You know that part when Peter writes about women? Well, I could not believe it. I was so repressed as a woman, but because I did not know anything about social reproduction; resistance; street-corner culture; and all the stuff Peter wrote about. Well, I said, "I did not know" not because I did not know, but "I did not know" in the sense that I did not have the expressions to say so. Peter gives us that sense. I can say that now "I know" and I feel sad in certain ways. But Peter was sad, too. Maybe critical pedagogy means you must feel sad to change. I don't know. Why don't they teach us everything about critical pedagogy when we are still students?

From the Metropolitan Group

He wrote everything I wish I had written. The educational system must change and educators must change as well. I agree with all he said. I wish he could write more specifically about how to survive in the middle of our principal's demands.

I am just afraid of this empowerment perspective, since many students at the university where I've been working are already rich. I am not sure McLaren addressed what to do with these students within critical pedagogy epistemology.

I can understand his point that teachers and professors are all extremely blind in terms

> of their responsibilities as social agents. His idea of dialectical pedagogy is powerful, but I mean, how does this happen in the classroom? I understand the concepts, but I don't know exactly the ways in which this happens in classrooms at the university level.
>
> What I most like is his perspectives in terms of culture and the aspects that comprise culture. A single reference for culture or difference is a big mistake.
>
> I would like to know how we can work with these new forms of power, as McLaren said, because we are living under a form of liberal power which is more perverse and, at the same time, more efficient. Of course, this is dangerous. For instance, I understand what critical pedagogy is, but I would like to know what I should do in class; I mean, if I want to apply critical pedagogy.

Discussion

From these brief comments we can see that the rural-area group locates itself as part of McLaren's analysis, while people of the master's group speak as if they were not part of the process. That is to say that people of the rural-area group locate their life within the epistemological dimensions of critical pedagogy while people of the master's group speak about social constraints as if they were out there, apart from them.

The fact that people of the master's group seek an application of "recipes" is evident; it is a group that is more concerned with how "to do" critical pedagogy or how to *survive* if they "do" critical pedagogy. In a different vein, the rural-area group is the group that discusses McLaren's perspectives and seeks ways of changing, especially because it is a group that locates and includes itself within McLaren's arguments.

Throughout both courses, McLaren's work is not only extremely helpful, but crucial to the development of important perspectives such as resistance, critical multicultural education and the analysis of economic issues related to society in general, and to education in particular. Furthermore, his work is fundamental within an analysis of the nature of struggles for knowledge, power, culture and resistance, since it offers significant insight into the production and transformation of meaning and histories in schools and society.

Students in the master's class and teachers in rural areas come to understand that the power of truth is ultimately legitimizing, since power cannot be exercised without a discourse of truth. Conversely, there cannot be a discourse of truth that does not have power. The relevance of critical pedagogy in a country like Brazil begs some crucial questions: What is the meaning of truth? What kind of truth do we live in? What methods of subjugation are present that the students must work against in order to legitimize *their* truth and gain power? How has the truth of the powerful become the universalized truth of all people in our society? To examine and attempt to answer these questions is fundamental if we are to overcome the neo-liberal educational agenda. As McLaren (1989) argues:

> Teaching always takes place in relation to a particular regime of truth or dominating logic. Teaching itself functions to produce students and teachers as social and culture subjects.…While it may be true that we can never scope ideology, the teacher must both reveal how subjectivity gets constructed and legitimated through dominant pedagogical discourses and eventually challenge the imaginary relations that students live relative to the symbolic and material conditions of their existence. (p. 240)

From the first moment, the master's group seeks recipes to "do" critical pedagogy. However, it is through a deeper analysis of McLaren's work that allows them to see, for instance, that classroom desks can be placed in circles, but the instructor can still conduct a lecture in which students are passive listeners. In other words, what is relevant is not the way in which classroom desks are placed, but how we can work toward a liberatory pedagogy.

Furthermore, as the first impressions of both groups demonstrate, we can perceive that the master's class is more concerned with methods, while the rural-area group is more connected to the methodology of critical pedagogy. The apparent controversial issue is that when compared to the metropolitan group, teachers in rural areas experienced fewer years in schools. It seems that this perspective destroys two widespread beliefs held especially by some U.S. professors, who have condemned McLaren's language: first, the idea that elementary and secondary school teachers cannot understand McLaren's views because he uses such a sophisticated language and vocabulary; and second, the more years we spend in schools, the more we are able to direct our attention to theoretical supports that inform methodologies.

First Encounters

I first met Peter McLaren in Chicago at the 1991 annual meeting of AERA, in a special homage to Paulo Freire. During this homage to Freire, I could not believe I was in front of two of the most brilliant intellectuals of critical pedagogy: first, Paulo Freire, whose books I had to read by candlelight in the basement of my undergraduate university because of the (U.S.-supported) military repression of the 1970s; and second, Peter McLaren, with whose perspectives I had been familiar since 1990 when I read *Life in Schools,* which a friend had brought me from the United States. Since that time, I have been continuously learning from McLaren's acute intellectuality, from the wisdom of a man who, I truly believe, is one of the major intellectuals of our day.

Some Final Thoughts

In a recent study of data collected from 22 Brazilian states, it was shown that only 0.4% of racist crimes are denounced, and none of the accused was charged or punished at all, even after a variety of criminal evidence was produced. Furthermore, according to official data, the *registered* number of women raped in the state of Rio de Janeiro alone has grown from 17,596 to 34,831 in the last year alone (Moraes, in press). The actual number is, of course, much higher than official statistics indicate.

Such examples are simply basic facts that justify the urgency of McLaren's work. I believe that his arguments and perspectives are crucial for socio-political-educational changes in a country like Brazil. McLaren offers a possible perspective for overcoming social inequalities when he advocates a form of multiculturalism that moves beyond conservative, meta-centric identities. And McLaren's revolutionary multiculturalism moves beyond the liberal monoculturalist "multiculturalism" that fails to address identity formation in a global context. Within this perspective, McLaren argues that instead of asking: Who can speak? We should ask: How can we speak together? And, even more importantly: How can we move the dialogue forward? How can we intertwine our voices? And, what are the modes of collective speech? The revolutionary multiculturalism he advocates is a socialist, feminist multiculturalism that challenges the historically sedimented process through which race, gender, class and sexual identities are produced within this capitalist society. Therefore, as Peter argues, a revolutionary multiculturalism is not an issue of political correctness, but of reconstituting the deep structures of political economy, culture and power in contemporary social arrangements.

McLaren has clearly and rightly argued that critical pedagogy should not be understood as a "boutique" of superficial forms of democratic classroom arrangements, such as discussion circles, teachers serving as facilitators, and so on. These perspectives, according to McLaren, deny the view that in critical pedagogy teachers and students are engaged in an historical discussion of social struggles. Critical pedagogy, as perceived by McLaren, constitutes a dialectical and dialogical process that engages teachers and students in re-framing, re-functioning and re-posing the question of understanding itself. For McLaren, a revolutionary pedagogy is a process in which a subject of history recognizes that she or he exists in a world and is subjected to it. In this way, hidden social meanings can be questioned and reviewed.

For all these reasons, Peter McLaren's work is crucial not only to me and my pedagogical work as a professor in Brazil, but to all individuals located in a politically constructed hell known as the Third World.

References

Foucault, M. (1980). *Power/knowledge: Selected interviews and other writings.* New York: Pantheon.

Freire, P. (1970). *Pedagogy of the oppressed.* New York: Continuum.

———. (2000). *Pedagogia da autonomia.* Rio de Janeiro: Paz e Terra.

Giroux, H. (1988). *Teachers as intellectuals: Toward a critical pedagogy of learning.* New York: Bergin & Garvey.

McLaren, P. (1989). *Life in schools: An introduction to critical pedagogy in the foundations of education.* New York: Longman.

———. (1992). *Rituais na escola: Em direção a uma economia política de símbolos e gestos na educação* [J. Marques & A. Biaggio, Trans.]. Petrópolis: Vozes.

———. (1997). *A Vida nas escolas: Uma introdução à pedagogia crítica nos fundamentos da educação* [L. Zimmer, F. Nonnenmacher, F. Carvalho & J. Bertoletti, Trans.]. Porto Alegre: Artes Médicas.

———. (2000a). *Multiculturalismo revolucionário: Pedagogia do dissenso para o novo milênio* [M. Moraes & R. Costa, Trans.]. Porto Alegre: Artes Médicas.

———. (2000b). *Multiculturalismo crítico* [B.O. Schaefer, Trans.]. São Paulo: Cortez.

McLaren, P., Leonard, P. & Gadotti, M. (Eds.). (1998). *Paulo Freire: Poder, desejo e memórias da libertação* [M. Moraes, Trans.]. Porto Alegre: Artes Médicas.

Moraes, M. (in press). *Ser humana: A mulher em questão.* Rio de Janeiro: DP&A.

———. (in press). *Ser humana: Quando a mulher está em discussão.* Rio de Janeiro: DP&A.

PART FOUR

McLAREN THE MARXIST

Chapter 7

The "Inevitability of Globalized Capital" Versus the "Ordeal of the Undecidable": A Marxist Critique

Mike Cole

I begin this chapter by discussing the way in which globalization and capitalism are presented as natural, inevitable and permanent features of life in the twenty-first century. I then go on to examine postmodernism and Marxism with a view to establishing their respective analyses of the present and their "visions" of the future.

While for capitalists and their political and academic supporters, globalized capital is incontrovertible, for postmodernists, nothing is certain, or indeed even decidable. Hence, no programs for action, or even suggestions about a future world in opposition to capitalism, are possible. It is in this sense that postmodernism is, albeit often unintentionally, conducive to the needs of capital. Marxism, on the other hand, provides both an analysis and a critique of capitalism *and* a vision of a possible new world order, namely, socialism.

The chapter concludes with an evaluation of the contribution of the work of Peter McLaren to these debates. Despite his brief (and in my view regrettable) love affair with postmodernism, it is argued that McLaren, one of the world's leading Marxist academics within the field of educational theory, has played, and continues to play, a central role in the struggle for a just and equitable world.

The Inevitability of Globalized Capital?

"Globalization" became one of the orthodoxies of the 1990s and continues to hold sway into the twenty-first century.[1] It is proclaimed in the speeches of virtually all mainstream politicians, in the financial pages of newspapers and in company reports, and it is common currency in corporation newsletters and shop stewards' meetings (Harman, 1996, p. 3). Its premises are that in the face of global competition, capitalists are increasingly constrained to compete on the world market. Its argument is that, in this new epoch, these capitalists can only do this insofar as they become multinational corporations and operate on a world scale, outside the confines of nation-states. This, its protagonists claim, diminishes the role of the nation-state, the implication being that there is little, if anything, that can be done about it.

While the extent to which globalization is a new epoch is open to question (viz. Cole 1998a, 2005), and the degree to which it has transcended the nation-state is debatable (viz. Harman, 1996; Ascherson, 1997; Meiksins Wood, 1997; Cole, 1998a), Marxists are particularly interested in the way it is used ideologically to further the interests of capitalists and their political supporters (for an analysis, see Cole, 1998a) and of the way in which it is used to mystify the populace as a whole and to stifle action by the left in particular (viz. Murphy, 1995; Gibson-Graham, 1996; Harman, 1996; Meiksins Wood, 1997). Capitalists, and their allies, argue that since globalization is a fact of life, it is incumbent upon workers, given the globalized world market, to be flexible in their approach to what they do and for how long they do it, to accept lower wages and to concur with the restructuring and diminution of welfare states.[2] The adoption of neo-liberalism has given a major boost to globalization, both de facto and ideologically.

Since the globalization of capital is promoted as "inevitable," then—by necessity—capitalism itself must be inevitable. In fact, capitalism is also hailed as natural and indeed coterminous with democracy and freedom. Capitalism presents itself as "determining the future as surely as the laws of nature make tides rise to lift boats" (McMurtry, 2001, p. 2). The fetishism of life, whereby the relationships between things or commodities assume a mystical quality, hiding the real (exploitative) relationships between human beings, makes capitalism seem natural and therefore unalterable. The market mechanism is thus transformed into a natural force unresponsive to human wishes (Callinicos, 2000, p. 125). Capitalism is praised:

> ...as if it has now replaced the natural environment. It announces itself through its business leaders and politicians as coterminous with freedom, and indispensable to democracy such that any attack on capitalism as exploitative or hypocritical becomes an attack on world freedom and democracy itself. (McLaren, 2000, p. 32)

Globalization, heralded as a new phenomenon, attempts to nail the lid on the coffin of a possible different world order. It acts ideologically in that it mystifies what is really going on. The most important task it achieves, in presenting capitalist development as natural, is the reinforcement of the falsehood that nothing can be done. The message of globalization is that the world is now like this, and certain measures have to be taken as a result. In essence, states need to acquiesce in the requirements of the global market.[3]

Any notion of workers' struggle, let alone socialist revolution is, at the very least, "old-fashioned" and inappropriate. Those who continue to talk about the overthrow of capitalism are seen as dinosaurs.[4] At the same time, the creative energy of the majority of the working class is being channeled away from confrontation with the global trajectories of capitalism and into safer cultural pursuits. Marxists refer to this phenomenon as the creation and nurturing of false consciousness.[5]

Thatcherism and Reaganomics were crucial not only in laying the foundations for the neo-liberal revolution, but also, in Thatcher's case in particular, in discrediting socialism. The collapse of the Soviet Union is used to back up the claim that socialism is no longer viable.[6]

So where might we look for alternative interpretations of our world in the twenty-first century? In the rest of this chapter, I will analyze the contributions of postmodernists, on the one hand, and of Marxists on the other.

Postmodernism and the Ordeal of the Undecidable

Postmodernism certainly provides an antidote to "naturalness," "inevitability" and "permanence." Leading British postmodernist Elizabeth Atkinson defines postmodernism as:

- Resistance toward certainty and resolution;
- Rejection of fixed notions of reality, knowledge or method;
- Acceptance of complexity, of lack of clarity, and of multiplicity;
- Acknowledgement of subjectivity, contradiction and irony;
- Irreverence for traditions of philosophy or morality;

- Deliberate intent to unsettle assumptions and presuppositions;
- Refusal to accept boundaries or hierarchies in ways of thinking; and,
- Disruption of binaries, which define things either/or. (2002, p. 74)

In a critique of what she refers to as "economistic Marxism" (Lather, 2001, p. 187), postmodern feminist Patti Lather's stated intention is to challenge "the masculinist voice of abstraction, universalization, and the rhetorical position of 'the one who knows,' what Ellsworth calls 'The One with the *right* Story'" (p. 184). To counter what Lather refers to as Marxists' "insistence on the 'right story'" (p. 184), she proposes "a thinking within Jacques Derrida's 'ordeal of the undecidable,'" with "its obligations to openness, passage and non-mastery" where "questions are constantly moving and one cannot define, finish, close" (p. 184). Derrida's (1992) position is that "a decision that didn't go through the ordeal of the undecidable would not be a free decision" (cited in Parrish, 2002, p. 1). Richard Parrish explains:

> Any claim—discursive position—is a universal claim that in order to be universal must continually re-found itself. Any position, even the position that universal positions are impossible, is a universal claim and is therefore considered iterable universally. This universal iterability denies in its structure the legitimacy of counter-claims made by others, thus denying others as independent sources of meaning. (Parrish, 2002, p. 1)

Lather attempts to link Derrida with Marx by bringing to our attention that in her book *Getting Smart* she ended the section on "post-Marxism" with Foucault's prophecy that "it is clear, even if one admits that Marx will disappear for now, that he will reappear one day" (Foucault; cited in Lather, 1991, p. 45). However, she rejects what she sees as Marxists' "discourse of mastery/transparency/rationalism and repositioning of economistic Marxism as the 'master discourse of the left'" (Lather, 2001, p. 187). Rather than return to historical materialism (the belief that the development of material goods necessary to human existence is the primary force which determines social life),[7] Lather's interest is in "a praxis of not being so sure" (p. 184), "a praxis in excess of binary or dialectical logic" (p. 189). This "post-dialectical praxis" is about "ontological stammering, concepts with a lower ontological weight, a praxis without guaranteed subjects or objects, oriented toward the as yet incompletely thinkable conditions and potentials of given arrangements" (p. 189).

In fact, Lather's adoption of such a "praxis" does not reposition Marxism; it leaves its domain entirely. (See below for a discussion of dialectical praxis in the context of the Labour Theory of Value.) For Lather, nothing is certain or decided. Citing Derrida, Lather asserts that undecidability is "a constant ethical-political reminder…that moral and political responsibility can only occur in the not knowing, the not being sure" (Lather, 2001, p. 187). Lather's academic efforts are informed by Alison Jones (1999), who concludes "with a call for a 'politics of disappointment,' a practice of 'failure, loss, confusion, unease, limitation for dominant ethnic groups'" (Lather, 2001, p. 191). Lather and Jones are claiming to be anti-colonialist in supporting Maori students in their wish to break up into "discussion groups based on ethnic sameness" (p. 190).

While it is always vital to challenge the colonialism and racism of dominant groups (viz. Cole, 2003), it is not clear how Jones's list of negative politics and practices (disappointment, failure, loss, confusion, limitation) is helpful in such a quest. In addition, since Lather believes that "all oppositional knowledge is drawn into the order against which it intends to rebel" (Lather, 1998, p. 493), it is difficult to see what possible progressive potential is entailed in her and Jones's anti-colonialism or indeed in Lather's overall project. Are these Maori students destined to be drawn into the dominant order (colonialism)? In the meantime, is "undecidability" all postmodern teachers have to offer them? In fact, all that Lather provides, by way of conclusion, is an assertion that there are "forces already active in the present" and that we will "move toward and experience the promise that is unforeseeable from the perspective of our present conceptual frameworks" in the pursuit of "a future that must remain to come" (Lather, 2001, p. 192)

Any defender of social injustice would surely be delighted to hear that Patti Lather, who like so many of her postmodern contemporaries was arguing in the early 1980s that "feminism and Marxism need each other" (Lather, 1984, p. 49) and that "the revolution is within each and every one of us and it will come about" (1984, p. 58), now posits the contradictory position that the future is an open book, with some progressive potential, and in which all opposition is drawn into the dominant order. This is neither conducive to progressive social change nor to social justice, and it is indicative of the way in which postmodernism acts as an ideological support for national and global capital (Cole & Hill, 1995, 2002; Cole, 2003, 2004a).

An Alternative Vision: The Case for Socialism

In stark contrast to the defenders and promoters of globalized capitalism, and providing a positive acclamation for the future denied by the postmodernists,

Meiksins Wood has argued that: "the lesson that we may be obliged to draw from our current economic and political condition is that a humane, 'social,' truly democratic and equitable capitalism is more unrealistically utopian than socialism" (Meiksins Wood, 1995, p. 293).

Increased awareness of the plight of the majority of humanity in the aftermath of the events of September 11, 2001, provides some degree of space to argue for the alternative vision of socialism. In contradistinction to the arguments of Thatcher and Straw, for example, for the Left, it is not socialism itself that has been discredited, but rather the dictatorships of Eastern Europe (and elsewhere) that claimed to be socialist. As Callinicos (2000) has argued, Marxists must break through the bizarre ideological mechanism in which every conceivable alternative to the market is seen as not viable because of the collapse of Stalinism (p. 122) or anti-democratic dictatorial "state socialism."

As Birchall (2000) points out, there have actually been only a few major revolutions in modern history, far too few from which to deduce any absolute principles. "No self respecting scientist would base a scientific law on so few experiments" (p. 22). As he puts it, "I can spin a coin and get 'tails' five times in a row—but that scarcely proves all coins will come down tails" (p. 22).

Analyzing the French and Russian revolutions and the Spanish Civil War, Birchall concludes that if any general lesson can be drawn, it is not that revolution leads to tyranny, as claimed by capitalists and their supporters, but rather that failure to complete a revolution opens the way to tyranny (2000, p. 22). So what are the chances of a truly democratic socialist world order, as envisaged by Marx? Have developments within advanced global capitalism ruled this out? Has capitalism finally triumphed?

Capitalism is, in reality, a messy business. Things rarely run smoothly. Indeed, the trajectory of capital's social universe forces it to crash continually against the limits of its own constitution and existence. However, this destructive movement rests entirely on workers' capacity to labor, their labor power; hence, wherever capital is, so is labor, "aiding, abetting and nurturing its development…holding its hand as it bites us" (Rikowski, 2001b, p. 11). Capital cannot become "not-capital." "However, labour can become labour…unlocked from its value-form" (p. 11). The only viable future for the working class is a socialist one. "This is a future *with* a future, a future that is possible for us on the basis of the implosion of capital's social universe" (p. 11).

Marx's Labour Theory of Value (LTV), for example, explains most concisely why capitalism is objectively a system of exploitation, whether the exploited realize it or not, or indeed, whether they believe it to be an issue of importance for them or not. The LTV also provides a solution to this exploitation. It thus provides dialectical praxis—the authentic union of theory and practice.

According to the LTV, the interests of capitalists and workers are diametrically opposed, since a benefit to the former (profits) is a cost to the latter (Hickey, 2002, p. 168). Marx argued that workers' labor is embodied in goods that they produce. The finished products are appropriated (taken away) by the capitalists and eventually sold at a profit. However, the worker is paid only a fraction of the value she or he creates in productive labor; the wage does not represent the total value she or he creates. We appear to be paid for every single second we work. However, underneath this appearance, this fetishism, the working day (as under serfdom) is split in two, into socially necessary labor (and the wage represents this) and surplus labor, labor that is not reflected in the wage. This is the basis of surplus value, out of which comes the capitalist's profit. While the value of the raw materials and of the depreciating machinery is simply passed on to the commodity in production, labor power is a peculiar, indeed unique commodity, in that it creates new value. "The magical quality of labour-power's…value for…capital is therefore critical" (Rikowski, 2001c, p. 11). "[L]abour-power creates more value (profit) in its consumption than it possesses itself, and than it costs" (Marx, 1966, p. 351). Unlike, for example, the value of a given commodity, which can only be realized in the market as itself, labor creates a new value, a value greater than itself, a value that previously did not exist. It is for this reason that labor power is so important for the capitalist, in the quest for capital accumulation. It is in the interest of the capitalist or capitalists (nowadays capitalists may, of course, consist of a number of shareholders, for example, rather than outright owners of businesses) to maximize profits, and this entails (in order to create the greatest amount of new value) keeping workers' wages as low as is "acceptable" in any given country or historical period, without provoking effective strikes or other forms of resistance. Therefore, the capitalist mode of production is, in essence, a system of exploitation of one class (the working class) by another (the capitalist class).

Whereas class conflict is endemic to—and ineradicable and perpetual within—the capitalist system, it does not always or even typically take the form of open conflict or expressed hostility (Hickey, 2002, p. 168). Fortunately for the working class, however, capitalism is prone to cyclical instability and subject to periodic political and economic crises. At these moments, the possibility exists for socialist revolution. Revolution can only come about when the working class, in addition to being a "class-in-itself" (an objective fact because of the shared exploitation inherent as a result of the LTV) becomes a "class-for-itself" (Marx, 1976). By this, Marx meant a class with a subjective awareness of its social class position, that is to say, a class with "class consciousness"—including its awareness of its exploitation and its transcendence of "false consciousness."

Marx argued that if and when the working class has become a "class-for-itself," it has the potential to seize control of the means of production, the economy, and take political power. Seizure of the economy would constitute such a socialist revolution (Hill & Cole, 2001, p. 147). This, of course, is not an easy option, but it is the working class that is most likely to be at the forefront of such a revolution.

As Michael Slott (2002) has put it with great clarity:

> Marxists have understood perfectly well that there are many obstacles to the working class becoming a universal agent for socialism. At the same time, Marxists have argued that, because of the particular interests, collective power, and creative capacities that are generated by workers' structural position in society, the working class is more likely to be at the core of any movement of social transformation. (p. 419)

For Marx, socialism (a stage before communism—that state of existence when the state would wither away and we would live communally) was a world system in which "we shall have an association, in which the free development of each is the condition for the free development of all" (Marx & Engels, 1977, p. 53). Such a society would be democratic (as such, socialism as envisaged by Marx should be distanced from the undemocratic regimes of the former Soviet Bloc) and classless, and the means of production would be in the hands of the many, not the few. Goods and services would be produced for need and not for profit.[8]

The Work of Peter McLaren

So what has Peter McLaren got to do with the above analyses? In an article I wrote with Dave Hill, we took Peter McLaren to task for his defense of postmodernism as a progressive force; in particular, his claim that "critical resistance" postmodernism is an effective appropriation by the Left of "Ludic postmodernism" (McLaren, 1994, p. 199).[9] The article (Cole & Hill, 1995) was published in June, and three months later, Peter (a long-standing and close friend and comrade of mine) and I met up and spent an evening together in

Halle, Eastern Germany, where unemployment was at a record high since they closed down the chemical plant and where, incidentally, nearly everybody we spoke too wanted the old GDR back.[10] Peter tried to convince me that all he was doing was incorporating certain ideas from poststructuralism into his Marxist beliefs. I argued, on the contrary, that in embracing postmodernism, Peter, like Lather (above), was leaving the terrain of Marxism altogether. Soon after our meeting, an account of which he subsequently published (McLaren, 1997, pp. 100–101), Peter ended his love affair with postmodernism and reverted to a full-blown re-engagement with Marxist theory and practice (though with some residual respect for certain aspects of postmodernism).

The extent to which this decision was influenced by our night in Halle is less important than the major contribution Peter (e.g., McLaren, 2000) and his co-writers (most notably Ramin Farahmandpur—cf. McLaren & Farahmandpur, 2002a, 2002b) are making to the revival of Marxism.[11]

In *Ché Guevara, Paulo Freire, and the Pedagogy of Revolution* (2000), McLaren returned decisively to the camp of historical materialism and democratic (as opposed to Stalinist) socialism. In this book, there are trenchant critiques of global capitalism (in which, to be fair, he also engaged in his postmodern phase) combined with a commitment to a socialist future and incisive critiques of postmodernism. Thus, following Ché, McLaren talks about his "outrage at the casualness and detachment with which capitalism destroys human lives—disproportionately the toilers of the world and the dark-skinned populations—and insulates the rich against compassion and accountability" (2000, p. 42) and about the need for capitalism to be overthrown, since only socialism can transform the human heart (p. 204).

McLaren states that he does not reject "all postmodern theory" (2000, p. xxiv), which "in some instances…may be more productive for understanding aspects of social life than current Marxist theories admit" (p. xxv). Nevertheless, he castigates "those voguish hellions of the seminar room, [for whom] postmodernism is the toxic intensity of bohemian nights…[and] the proscribed, the immiserated, and the wretched of the earth simply get in the way of their fun" (pp. xxiv–xxv). His revulsion of postmodernism's contempt for socialism is scathing: "an unwanted interloper from the past…a dusty, washed-up, homeless intruder who approaches you on your way to your cappuccino stand, demanding that you pay attention to his unshaven face and running eyes" (p. 191).

However, Peter is quietly optimistic about the future. He perceives a new fomenting social consciousness, signaled most dramatically by the recent protests against the World Trade Organization in Seattle, Quebec City and Genoa. As he puts it:

> I'm not suggesting that young people today can't be found palavering happily with their friends in front of mind-numbing television game shows, but I am more convinced than ever that the dialectical contradictions and internal relations of capitalism are becoming more glaring and less accepted by young people as an historical inevitability. They know that capitalism brooks no opposition to its imperialist demands. (McLaren, 2003, p. 14)

Peter's recent re-engagement with Marxism and his almost total abandonment of postmodernism have gone far from unnoticed by leading postmodernists. Indeed, Patti Lather's attack on (conventional) Marxism (Lather, 2001) critiqued above is directed at Peter McLaren (specifically, at a paper by him published in *Educational Theory* [McLaren, 1998]). His is the "the masculinist voice of abstraction, universalization, and the rhetorical position of 'the one who knows,' what Ellsworth calls 'The One with the right Story'" (2001, p. 184). His is the "discourse of mastery/transparency/rationalism and repositioning of economistic Marxism as the 'master discourse of the left'" (p. 187).

For Lather, McLaren's call for revolutionary pedagogy amounts to "a boy thing" (2001, p. 184), altogether "too strong, too erect, too stiff" (1998, p. 490) as opposed to a "girl thing" favored by Lather (2001, p. 184). This "girl thing" is about deconstruction.

To facilitate thinking within "the ordeal of the undecidable," postmodernists engage in an endless and relatively ahistorical process of deconstruction, in order to challenge

> the educator, the researcher, the social activist or the politician not only to deconstruct the certainties around which they might see as standing in need of change, but also to deconstruct their own certainties as to why they hold this view. (Atkinson, 2002, p. 75)

This sounds fine, but what do these constituencies actually do to effect meaningful societal change once their views have been challenged? What is constructed after the deconstruction process? Unlike McLaren, who is most clear that what needs constructing is democratic socialism, postmodernists provide no answer. This is because postmodernism is not capable of providing an answer (Hill, 2001a; Rikowski, 2002, pp. 20–25). Deconstruction "seeks to do justice to all positions…by giving them the chance to be justified, to speak originarily for themselves and be chosen rather that enforced" (Zavarzadeh, 2002, p.

8). Indeed, for Derrida (1990, p. 945), "deconstruction *is* justice" (italics added). Thus, once the deconstruction process has started, justice is already apparent, and there is no discernible direction in which to head. Lather, in declaring on the first page of the Preface to her book *Getting Smart: Feminist Research & Pedagogy With/In the Postmodern* her "longtime interest in how to turn critical thought into emancipatory action" (1991, p. xv), is in fact wasting her time. After over two hundred pages of text, in which indications are made of the need for emancipatory research praxis, in which proclamations are made of how the goals of research should be to understand the maldistribution of power and resources in society, with a view to societal change, we are left wondering how all this is to come about.

Deconstruction without reconstruction typifies the divorce of the academy from the reality of struggle on the ground. Postmodernism cannot provide strategies to achieve a different social order, and hence, in buttressing capitalist exploitation, it is essentially reactionary. This is precisely what Marxists (and others) mean by their assertion that postmodernism serves to disempower the oppressed and uphold global capitalism.[12]

In her attempt to present the case that "[p]ostmodern deconstruction…is not the same as destruction" (2001, p. 77), Atkinson cites Judith Butler who argues that "to deconstruct is not to negate or to dismiss, but to call into question and, perhaps most importantly, to open up a term…to a reusage or redeployment that previously has not been authorized" (1992, p. 15; cited in Atkinson, 2002, p. 77).

This is precisely what Marxism does. The difference is that Marxist concepts—for example, the fetishism inherent in capitalist societies, whereby the relationships between things or commodities assume a mystical quality hiding the real (exploitative) relationships between human beings—provide a means of both analyzing that society, understanding its exploitative nature and pointing in the direction of a non-exploitative society. The LTV is a good example of such a concept.

Postmodernists are clearly capable of asking questions, but, by their own acknowledgment, they have no answers. As Glenn Rikowski has put it, this leads one to ask: Just what is the postmodernist attitude toward explanation?

> Truly political strategies require explanation (of what went wrong, why the analysis and/or tactics failed, etc.) so that improvements can be made. Do postmodernists have a notion of improvement (of society, of political strategies)? If they do, then they need explanation. I

> don't think they are interested in either and hence can't have a political strategy for human betterment (cited in Cole, 2003, p. 495).

To this I would reiterate that postmodernism could be liberating to individuals and to local groups. But to be politically valid, an analysis must link "the small picture" to "the big picture." As McLaren argues, "all oppressed groups should come together in an effort to struggle against inequality in all its odious manifestations" (2000, p. 202). However, this is not enough. A socialist vision is required. He cites Raya Dunayevskaya, who argues that "without a philosophy of revolution, activism spends itself in mere anti-imperialism and anti-capitalism, without ever revealing what it is *for*" (p. 202). Postmodernism, again by its own admission, can neither bring people together nor provide a solution to their oppressions and to their struggles. It is thus antithetical to social justice and social change (Cole, 2003, 2004a).

The work of McLaren as a whole has, perhaps, been most influential in North America in the realm of critical pedagogy (and multicultural education).[13] However, in *Ché Guevara, Paulo Freire, and the Pedagogy of Revolution* (2000), McLaren seems to break from this tradition. Indeed, the pedagogical implications of McLaren's return to a Marxist paradigm are expressed in a key question: "How do educators assume a model of leadership that can resist global capitalist exploitation and create a new social order?" (p. 91). For McLaren, this is formable neither in terms of the critique that postmodernism provides, nor with critical pedagogy, which, with its political ally, multicultural education, is no longer an adequate social or pedagogical platform. Only revolutionary pedagogy puts power and knowledge on a collision course with their own internal contradictions and gives a provisional glimpse of a new society freed from the bondage of the past, and this, McLaren argues, can only be grasped in the dialectical thinking of revolutionary thinkers such as Ché and Freire. For them, capitalism is neither natural nor inevitable and is, in fact, the antithesis of freedom and democracy. Ché and Freire, as McLaren argues, have never been needed more than at this moment in history.

The whole issue of the role of education in social transformation is extremely problematic. Indeed, Lather notes that while McLaren:

> Acknowledges the failures of the educational Left in the United States to effect change not only in global capitalist relations but also in its more specific target of schooling, [he]...then goes on to call for more of the same in terms of "dare the schools build a new social order?" (Lather, 2001, p. 186)

On the one hand, massive ideological apparatuses mask the tyranny of capitalism. Louis Althusser argued that in the present era, the Educational Ideological State Apparatus (Educational ISA) is the most important apparatus of the state for transmitting capitalist ideology (Althusser, 1971). As is argued above, in order for it to function effectively and to protect its interests, capitalism needs to prevent the working class from becoming a "class-for-itself." This is a twofold process. First, a concept of the world is fostered in which capitalism is seen as natural and inevitable; second, "false consciousness" is nurtured, whereby consciousness is channeled into non-threatening avenues (e.g., commercial ones) (Cole, 2004b). It is important for capitalism that the education system does not hinder this process. Indeed, the current ideological requirements of capitalism are that the education system play an active role both in facilitating the growth of consumerism (a material as well as an ideological benefit for capitalists) and in naturalizing capitalism itself. This takes the form of both bringing business into schools and of using schools to promote business values. This process has accelerated greatly in Britain under New Labour (Allen et al., 1999; Cole et al., 2001; Hill 2001a, 2001b; 2005a, b) Rikowski, 2001d). In schools and colleges throughout the world, people are being miseducated (Cole, 2004c; Hill, 2003, 2004a, b, c).

However, on the other hand, the Educational ISA is neither total nor all-encompassing. While recognizing the limitations of the power of schools and teachers, I do consider that teachers have a valid role to play in challenging dominant inequalities and in raising consciousness in the quest for a more egalitarian economic, social and educational system. Socialist teachers in Britain have consistently challenged and continue to challenge the "businessification" of education and education for compliance. This takes the form of organized resistance from activists within the teacher unions, campaigning groups such as the Socialist Teachers Alliance (www.socialist-teacher.freeserve.co.uk), the Hillcole Group (www.ieps.org.uk.cwc.net/hillcole.html) and the Promoting Comprehensive Education Network. In addition, teachers, both individually and in groups, are creating and opening up space within the National Curriculum and the Hidden Curriculum[14] to challenge education for compliance (Cole et al., 1997; Hill & Cole, 1999; Hill & Cole, 2001; Hill, 2001a, 2004d; Cole, 2004c; Cole, [ed.] 2004). However, these remain marginal and relatively isolated pockets of resistance. One must presume that this is also the case in the United States and that McLaren's clarion call is aimed at a small group of left-wing activists, who, nevertheless, will be eager to increase their influence in any way possible. Socialist teachers will continue to challenge false consciousness in whatever way seems appropriate in any given situation. Here is not the place to discuss various strategies to achieve this, but for an analysis, see Hill, in this volume; see also Cole et al. (2001).[15]

Conclusion

I would like to conclude with a few recent and current facts about the state of globalized capitalism in the United States, the United Kingdom and the “developing world.” As far as the United States is concerned, during the 1980s the top 10% of families increased their average family income by 16%, the top 5% by 23% and the top 1% by 50%. At the same time, the bottom 80% all lost something, with the bottom 10% losing 15% of their incomes (George, 2000; cited in McLaren & Pinkney-Pastrana, 2001, p. 208). The poverty rate rose from 11.7% in 2001 to 12.1% in 2002, while the number of poor increased also by 1.7 million to 34.6 million (U.S. Bureau of the Census, 2003).

In Britain, the latest figures show that the wealthiest 1% own 22% of wealth, while the wealthiest 50% own 94% (*Social Trends*, 2003). This means that the poorest half of the population own only 6% of all wealth (Hill & Cole, 2001, p. 139). With respect to income in Britain, the bottom fifth of people earn less than 10% of disposable income, and the top fifth over 40% (*Social Trends*, 2002, p. 97). Over one in five children in Britain does not have a holiday away from home once a year because their parents cannot afford it (p. 87).

As far as the “developing world” is concerned, for two decades poverty in Africa and Latin America has increased, both in absolute and relative terms. Nearly half the world’s population is living on less than $2 a day, and one fifth live on just $1 a day (World Development Movement, 2001). The turning over of vast tracts of land to grow one crop for multinationals often results in ecological degradation, with those having to migrate to the towns living in slum conditions and working excessive hours in unstable jobs (Harman, 2000). There are about 100 million abused and hungry “street kids” in the world’s major cities; slavery is re-emerging, and some 2 million girls from the age of five to fifteen are drawn into the global prostitution market (Mojab, 2001, p. 118). It was estimated that over 12 million children under five would die from poverty-related illness in 2001 (World Development Movement, 2001). Approximately 100 million human beings do not have adequate shelter, and 830 million people are not “food secure,” i.e., are hungry (Mojab, 2001, p. 118). It has been estimated that, if current trends persist, in the whole of Latin America, apart from Chile and Colombia, poverty will continue to grow in the next ten years at the rate of two more poor people per minute (Heredia; cited in McLaren, 2000, p. 39).

In fact, the world is becoming polarized into central and peripheral economies, with the gap between rich and poor, between the powerful and the powerless, growing so large that the 300 largest corporations in the world account for 70% of foreign direct investment and 25% of world capital assets (Bagdikan, 1998; cited in McLaren, 2000, p. xxiv) and the combined assets of the three richest people in the world exceeds the combined GDP of the 48 poorest countries combined. At the same time, the combined assets of the 225 richest people is roughly equal to the annual incomes of the poorest 47% of the world's population (Heintz & Folbre, 2000; cited in McLaren & Farahmandpur, 2001, p. 345) and eight companies earn more than half the world's population (World Development Movement, 2001). As if to underline these massive global injustices, and as an indication of the amount of disposable capital available for states in the capitalist west, the United States and Britain have spent hundreds of billions of dollars on the invasion and occupation of Iraq.

Despite the assertions of the advocates of and apologists for global capital, this obscene state of affairs is neither inevitable nor irreversible. And all the postmodernists have to offer are strictly local remedies and uncertainty, lack of clarity and unsettled assumptions, neatly encapsulated by "the ordeal of the undecidable." While the subjectivities they are so keen to bring to center stage are important, only Marxism has an alternative vision of the future. This vision can and has been extended beyond the "brotherhood of man" concept of early socialists, to include the complex subjectivities of everyone. Socialism can and should be conceived of as a project where subjective identities, such as gender, "race," ability, non-exploitative sexual preference and age all have high importance in the struggle for genuine equality (Cole & Hill, 1999a, p. 42).[16]

Given the huge benefits that accrue to capitalists in the process of global capital accumulation, any movements which are seen as challenging or even resistant to capitalism are met with intense state brutality, as witnessed by the reactions to the recent and ongoing anti-capitalist protests (viz. Rikowski, 2001d). It is therefore necessary, whether the postmodernists like it or not, for women and men to be "strong, erect and stiff" (Lather, 1998, p. 490; Lather, 2001, p. 187) rather than "not being sure" (Lather, 2001, p. 187) in their resistance to global capitalism. Inability to rise to the occasion, however, is not the reason mass movements for social change cannot be successful. As Callinicos puts it, despite the inevitable intense resistance from capital, the "greatest obstacle to change is not...the revolt it would evoke from the privileged, but the belief that it is impossible" (2000, p. 128).

Challenging this climate requires courage, imagination and will power inspired by the injustice that surrounds us. Beneath the surface of our supposedly contented societies, these qualities are present in abundance. Once mobilized, they can turn the world upside down (Callinicos, 2000, p. 129).

Echoing the assertion of Meiksins Wood (cited above) that a humane, "social," truly democratic and equitable capitalism is more unrealistically utopian than socialism (1995, p. 293), I would argue that it is socialism alone that can provide a just and equitable future.[17] While postmodernism can subvert established beliefs by its very essence, it is not able to offer an alternative to the barbarities of capitalism. It is for this reason that Peter McLaren's re-adoption of Marxist theory and practice is most welcome.

Notes

1. The analysis that follows draws on Cole (1998a) and (2005).
2. As Rikowski (2001a) explains, since other areas of profit-making look increasingly risky (e.g., the "dot-com" businesses) and profit rates are declining in traditional areas, corporate capital looks to the public sector for expansion. In addition, the nations who are signatories to the World Trade Organization's (WTO) General Agreement in Trade in Services (GATS) are committed to opening up public services to corporate capital (p. 1). This comprises an interrelated two-pronged attack on and threat to the concept of "the welfare state."
3. Ironically, the capitalist class and their representatives who used to deride what they saw as the metaphysic of "Marxist economic determinism" (economic processes determine all else, including the future direction of society) are the ones who now champion the "world-wide market revolution" and the accompanying *inevitability* of "economic restructuring" (McMurtry, 2000). It needs to be pointed out that there are those who argue that, although inevitable, globalization can be tamed. British Prime Minister Tony Blair, for example, advocates global capital as "a force for good." For a critique of this position, see Cole (2005).
4. If socialism is not perceived as a threat, this is not, of course, the case with Islamic fundamentalism, which is currently perceived as a real threat, at least to Western capitalism.
5. Current manifestations of false consciousness are signified by the diversion of the creative energy of the working class into alcohol and drugs, pubs, clubs, pop music, chat shows, football, soaps, play stations, videos and DVDs. Significantly, concerned about the general decline in news audiences, ITV, the commercial terrestrial channel aimed specifically at Britain's working class, wants the news to concentrate more on "leisure, consumer and show business news" (Wells, 2001, p. 1). At the same time, that technological supremo of our age, the Internet, which has enormous potential of playing a role in working-class liberation and can be used, and in many cases is being used, in progressive ways, has enabled a further detour. Rather than being used as a source of liberatory knowledge, however, it is often being used in a further quest for trivia. On a much more sinister note, the Internet is being increasingly used as a site of oppression as well. Examples of this latter role are the numerous "race hate" websites and, in the case primarily of men, increasingly violent pornography (Amis, 2001).
6. This was starkly reiterated by British foreign secretary Jack Straw in an article entitled "Globalization Is Good for Us": "[S]ince the collapse of the Soviet Bloc, there is no longer a coherent ideology on offer" (*The Guardian,* September 10, 2001). It is worth recalling that we were told by the spokespersons for capitalism (Margaret Thatcher and Ronald Reagan among them) that this collapse would bring freedom and democracy. If it has, it has also brought homelessness, unemployment, gangsterism, drugs and child pornography.
7. As historical materialists, Marxists analyze the progression of society from primitive communism, through slavery and then through feudalism to capitalism. It is only under capitalism, they argue, that the productive forces of society are such that socialism becomes a vi-

able option. It is only then that "to each according to her or his needs" is technically possible.

8 It is ironic that the countries of the former Soviet Bloc were falsely designated "communist" by the West. In reality (despite the fact that many had a number of positive features—full employment, housing for all, free public and social services, and so on) they were undemocratic dictatorships with special privileges for an elite and drudgery for the many. If anything, these Eastern European societies were deformed socialist states, far removed from Marx's vision of "the higher phase of communist society" (that would come after the temporary phase of socialism). In communist society "labour is no longer merely a means of life but has become life's principal need." "All the springs of co-operative wealth flow more abundantly…[and the guiding principle is] from each according to his ability, to each according to his needs" (Marx, *Critique of the Gotha Programme*, 1875; cited in Bottomore & Rubel, 1978, p. 263). In a communist world, the "original goodness" of humanity is realized, and "the private interest of each" coincides "with the general interest of humanity" (Marx, *The Holy Family*, 1845; cited in Bottomore & Rubel, 1978, p. 249). Of the ten countries I have visited that claimed or claim to be socialist, for me, Cuba is closest to what I perceive to be the spirit of socialism. I believe socialists can learn a lot from the experiences of that society.

9 Peter's argument is not a new one, either within educational theory or outside it. "Ludic postmodernism" is based, for example, on the writings of Baudrillard (1984), where in "total hopelessness" (cited in Gane [Ed.], 1993, p. 95) we playfully survive among the remnants of life (p. 95). "Resistance postmodernism," on the other hand, is claimed to be fundamentally theoretically different from Ludic postmodernism and to be a challenge to the status quo; in Atkinson's (2002) words, to be "something of a shock" (p. 78) to the establishment, in that it reveals the sub-texts and textual silences (p. 80). (Surrealism and other art forms performed and continue to perform similar functions, as do, for example, certain alternative comedians.) However, as subversive as these art forms may be, they do not provide directions for change. Hill's position and mine was (and is) that the "two postmodernisms," despite some progressive and radical potential for "resistance postmodernism," are in fact one and that postmodernism is, in essence, reactionary. We argue that postmodernism's essential reactionary nature relates to its denial of the possibility of the meta-narrative, in its having no agenda for social change (Cole & Hill, 1995; see also Cole & Hill, 1999a, 1999b, 2002; and Cole, 2003, 2004a). Atkinson (2003) has recently attempted to link "Ludic" to "resistance postmodernism." As she puts it, postmodernism can act as a form of resistance by pitting its "Ludic…playful…ironic…restless, shape-shifting dance…against the ludicrous" (p. 5). She concludes by stating that she wants fun and resistance combined: "I want more than Carnival…once a year. I want to hear the voices from the margins; to ask the questions which arise from uncertainty, hybridity and multiplicity. I want to speak the unspeakable and have awful thoughts. I want to ask the questions that open up the trouble" (2003, p. 12). (For a critique, see Cole, 2004a.)

10 As stated above, I would on the whole dissociate myself from anti-democratic dictatorial "state socialism" or Stalinism in its various guises as practiced there. The conception of Marxism advanced in this chapter is distant from many practices which have been enacted in Marx's name. My belief is in democratic socialism (where modernity fulfils its promise of equality and liberty, or égaliberté, as Balibar describes it; cited in Callinicos, 2000, p. 22).

11 Peter has written of our time in Halle:

> My time spent with you was a profound step in getting my work back on track to Marx. No question about that...listening to your talk in Halle, spending time with you, experiencing East Germany with you, that really shook me...it was a major moment, perhaps the key single moment; then, of course, the next step was reading over the criticisms of my work by you, Dave [Hill] and Glenn [Rikowski]...and then the correspondence among us by e-mail...and I began to reeducate myself with the help of comrades such as yourself, reading *Capital*, and a half dozen other books of Marx, Marx and Engels, and also Hegel (via the Marxist humanist tradition of *News and Letters*/Dunayevskaya) putting myself on a program of study and dialogue with other Marxists, working with Ramin [Farahmandpur] and other Marxist students...and I began reading the Open Marxist folks via Glenn, getting into Glenn's work on the labor theory of value...and reading major Marxist journals like *Science and Society*, and then finally meeting Peter Hudis of *News and Letters* and hanging out with him in LA and learning a lot. (personal correspondence, 2002)

McLaren's love affair with postmodernism still reverberates. Thus in a recent edition of the very influential *British Journal of Sociology of Education*, Michael Slott mounts a critique of critical postmodernism, citing the work of Peter, along with Henry Giroux and Stanley Aronowitz, as exemplars of that genre. To be fair to Slott, he does provide an endnote citing McLaren (1998 and 2000) as signifying "a return to Marx" (Slott, 2002, p. 424, endnote 2). Yet this endnote in no way attests to the impact of McLaren's work over the last decade in making Marxism visible in educational debates throughout the United States. McLaren is one of the most visible Marxists writing in the United States at the present time.

12 On a trip to South Africa in 1995, I was asked to present a Marxist critique of postmodernism at a seminar attended by some leading South African postmodernists. Having spent considerable time in the townships and squatter camps, I asked what postmodernists could do for their inhabitants and was met with stony silence.

13 Peter's considerable influence in the Americas in the ongoing development of critical multiculturalism has never had much purchase in the UK, where the debates have centered more on multicultural education versus antiracist education (e.g., Cole 1998b; Short & Carrington, 1998; Cole, 1998c; Waller et al., 2001, pp. 165–166).

14 Since 1988, England and Wales have had a prescribed core National Curriculum from ages 5 to 16. (This has been modified by successive New Labour legislation.) The Hidden Curriculum refers to everything that goes on in educational institutions outside of this formal curriculum.

15 On a note of more general resistance to capitalism, McLaren has recently written on his experiences of resisting the current (April 2003) invasion of Iraq:

> Strolling through Hollywood
>
> I make it no secret that I am fighting the urgings to go back to Canada, urgings which I have daily, though I took out US citizenship several years ago. I will make every effort to remain in the belly of the beast and do my anti-war, anti-capitalist globalization work here, despite how nauseating it is to live here at this time. My efforts, I trust, will bear more fruit here, than if I were to leave. The confrontations at anti-war marches and rallies are one thing—there are the cops, plus counter-demonstrators, and most of us are prepared. Quite another experience is just walking the streets on your way to the bookstore, or on your way to meet friends in the local coffee shop. Or trying to work away frustration on the tread mills in the local gym. Being confronted by (usually) young people for just walking

> the streets of Hollywood and West Hollywood with a medium-sized STOP BUSH pin in the lapel of my jean jacket, certainly tests the nerves, but it also tests the limits of my ability to restrain my own anger and outrage. In three weeks, I have come close to blows five times. Fortunately for this 55 year-old body, it did not come to that...if it did, these hands might not be in any position to punch out this message on the keyboard. A few weeks ago I was loudly berated for wearing my Ché shirt in a West Hollywood gym, when I was approached by a fist-shaking, jaw-jutting, vein-popping, lung-clearing Hulk (who I admit surprised me by knowing who Ché was, and recognizing that Ché was not "pro-USA"). That ended in the Hulk storming off, and me giving an impromptu anti-war teach-in in the sauna, which went surprisingly well. In the last two weeks, at the local coffee shop (only seconds from my home on foot) I have been the object of screaming assaults by different parties whom I did not know, and twice I have been singled-out for loudly expressed derision (the last time was 20 minutes ago) simply for walking past some local pubs around noon with the medium size STOP BUSH pin in the lapel of my otherwise unremarkable jean jacket. Yesterday my wife was asked to leave the gym equipment she was occupying and go to another area of the gym by a group of muscled men, because they overheard her talking to a friend and criticizing the war (in relatively muted tones I might add). The belligerence is staggering. And this in a city (West Hollywood) whose city council took a public position against the invasion of Iraq. I can imagine what comrades across the country are facing.

Peter McLaren (personal email correspondence, April 14, 2003).

16 Class, however, remains central. This is demonstrated clearly by the ongoing occupation of Iraq. While the conflict may be gendered and racialized in various ways, and while this occupation is a part of the project of American Imperial hegemony (Cole, 2004c), it is ultimately about class and capitalism: about the privatization of basic services in Iraq; about the ownership and control of oil—in short, about increasing the global profits of capital at the expense of the working class, about squeezing out more and more surplus value from the labor of workers. (See the discussion on the LTV above.)

17 Alex Callinicos has written of the requirement to revive "utopian imagination—that is...our capacity to anticipate, at least in outline, an efficient and democratic non-market form of economic co-ordination" (2000, p. 133)—"to give serious attention to models of democratic socialist planning...[to] a much more decentralized system of planning in which information and decisions flow horizontally among different groups of producers and consumers rather than vertically between centre and productive units" (p. 123). Callinicos' "utopian imagination" echoes Paulo Freire's discussion of the "revolutionary imagination":

> This is the possibility to go beyond tomorrow without being naively idealistic. This is Utopianism as a dialectical relationship between denouncing the present and announcing the future. To anticipate tomorrow by dreaming today. The question is...Is the dream a possible one or not? If it is less possible, the question for us is how to make it more possible. (Freire & Shor, 1987, p. 187)

By contrast, the notion that liberal democracy can continue to buffer us from the worst excesses of capitalism and enable us to exist as civilized beings regardless of capitalism's deepening and expanding contradictions remains "an utterly ridiculous utopia" (Allman, 2001, p. 13)

References

Allen, M., Benn, C., Chitty, C., Cole, M., Hatcher, R., Hirtt, N. & Rikowski, G. (1999). *Business, business, business: New Labour's education policy*. London: The Tufnell Press.

Allman, P. (2001). Education on Fire. In M. Cole, D. Hill, & P. McLaren, *Red chalk: On schooling, capitalism and politics*. Brighton: Institute for Education Policy Studies.

Althusser, L. (1971). *Lenin and philosophy and other essays*. London: New Left Books.

Ascherson, N. (1997). Don't be fooled: Multinationals do not rule the world. *Independent on Sunday*, 12 January.

Amis, M. (2001). A rough trade, *The Guardian Weekend*, 17 March.

Atkinson, E. (2002). The responsible anarchist: Postmodernism and social change. *British Journal of Sociology of Education*, 23, (1), 73-87.

Bagdikan, B.H. (1998). Capitalism and the information age. *Monthly Review*, 50, (7), 55-58.

Birchall, I. (2000). "Revolution? You must be crazy!" *Socialist Review*, no. 247, December, 20-22.

Bottomore, T. & Rubel, M. (1978). *Karl Marx: Selected writings in sociology and social philosophy*. Harmondsworth: Pelican Books.

Callinicos, A. (2000). *Equality*. Oxford: Polity.

Cole, M. (1998a). Globalization, modernisation and competitiveness: A critique of the New Labour project in education. *International Studies in Sociology of Education*, 8, (3), 315-332.

——— . (1998b). Racism, reconstructed multiculturalism and antiracist education. *Cambridge Journal of Education*, 28, (2) 37-48.

——— . (1998c). Re-establishing antiracist education: A response to Short and Carrington. *Cambridge Journal of Education*, 28 (2), 235-238.

——— . (2003). Might it be in the practice that it fails to succeed?: A Marxist critique of claims for postmodernism as a force for social change and social justice. *British Journal of Sociology of Education*, 24 (4), 487-500.

——— . (2004a). Fun, amusing, full of insights, but ultimately a reflection of anxious times: A critique of postmodernism as a force for resistance, social change and social justice. In J. Satterthwaite, E. Atkinson & W. Martin (Eds.), *Educational counter-cultures: Confrontations, images, vision* (pp. 19-34). Stoke on Trent, UK & Sterling, USA: Trentham Books.

———. (2004b). Rethinking the future: The commodification of knowledge and the grammar of resistance. In M. Benn & C. Chitty (Eds.) *For Caroline Benn: Essays in education and democracy.* London: Continuum.

———. (2004c). "Rule Britannia" and the new American Empire: A Marxist analysis of the teaching of imperialism, actual and potential, in the English school curriculum. *Policy Futures in Education,* 2 (3).

———. (2005). New Labour, globalization and social justice: The role of education. In G. Fischman, P. McLaren, H. Sunker & C. Lankshear (Eds.), *Critical theories, radical pedagogies and global conflicts.* Lanham, Maryland: Rowman and Littlefield.

Cole, M. & Hill, D. (1995). Games of despair and rhetorics of resistance: Postmodernism, education and reaction. *British Journal of Sociology of Education*, 16, (2), 165-182.

Cole, M. (Ed.). (2004). *Education, equality and human rights: Issues of gender, 'race', sexuality, special needs and social class,* 2nd Edition. London: Routledge/Falmer.

———. (1999a). Into the hands of capital: The deluge of postmoderism and delusions of resistance postmoderism. In D. Hill, P. McLaren, M. Cole & G. Rikowski (Eds.), *Postmodernism in educational theory: Education and the politics of human resistance* (pp. 31-49). London: The Turnfell Press.

———. (1999b). Ex-left academics and the curse of the postmodern. *Education and Social Justice*, 3 (1), 28-30.

———. (2002). 'Resistance postmodernism'-progressive politics or rhetorical left posturing?. In D. Hill, P. McLaren, M. Cole & G. Rikowski (Eds.), *Marxism against postmodernism in educational theory.* Lanham, Maryland: Lexington Books.

Cole, M., Hill, D. & Shan, S. (1997). *Promoting equality in primary schools.* London: Cassell.

Cole, M., Hill, D., Rikowski, G. & McLaren, P. (2001). *Red chalk: On schooling, capitalism and politics: Mike Cole, Dave Hill and Glenn Rikowski in discussion with Peter McLaren.* Brighton: Institute for Education Policy Studies.

Derrida, J. (1990). The force of law: The mystical foundation of authority. *Cordozo Law Review,* November.

Freire, P. & Shor, I. (1987). *A pedagogy for liberation: Dialogues on transforming education.* Basingstoke: Macmillan Education.

Gane, M. (Ed.). (1993). *Baudrillard live: Selected interviews.* London: Routledge.

Gibson-Graham, J.K. (1996). Querying globalization. *Rethinking Marxism*, 9, Spring, 1-27.

The Guardian, September 10, 2001.

Harman, C. (1996). Globalization: A critique of a new orthodoxy. *International Socialism*, 73, 3-33.

———. (2000). Anti-capitalism: Theory and practice. *International Socialism*, 88, 3-59.

Hickey, T. (2002). Class and class analysis for the twenty-first century. In M. Cole (Ed.) *Education, equality and human rights* (pp. 162-181). London: Routledge/Falmer.

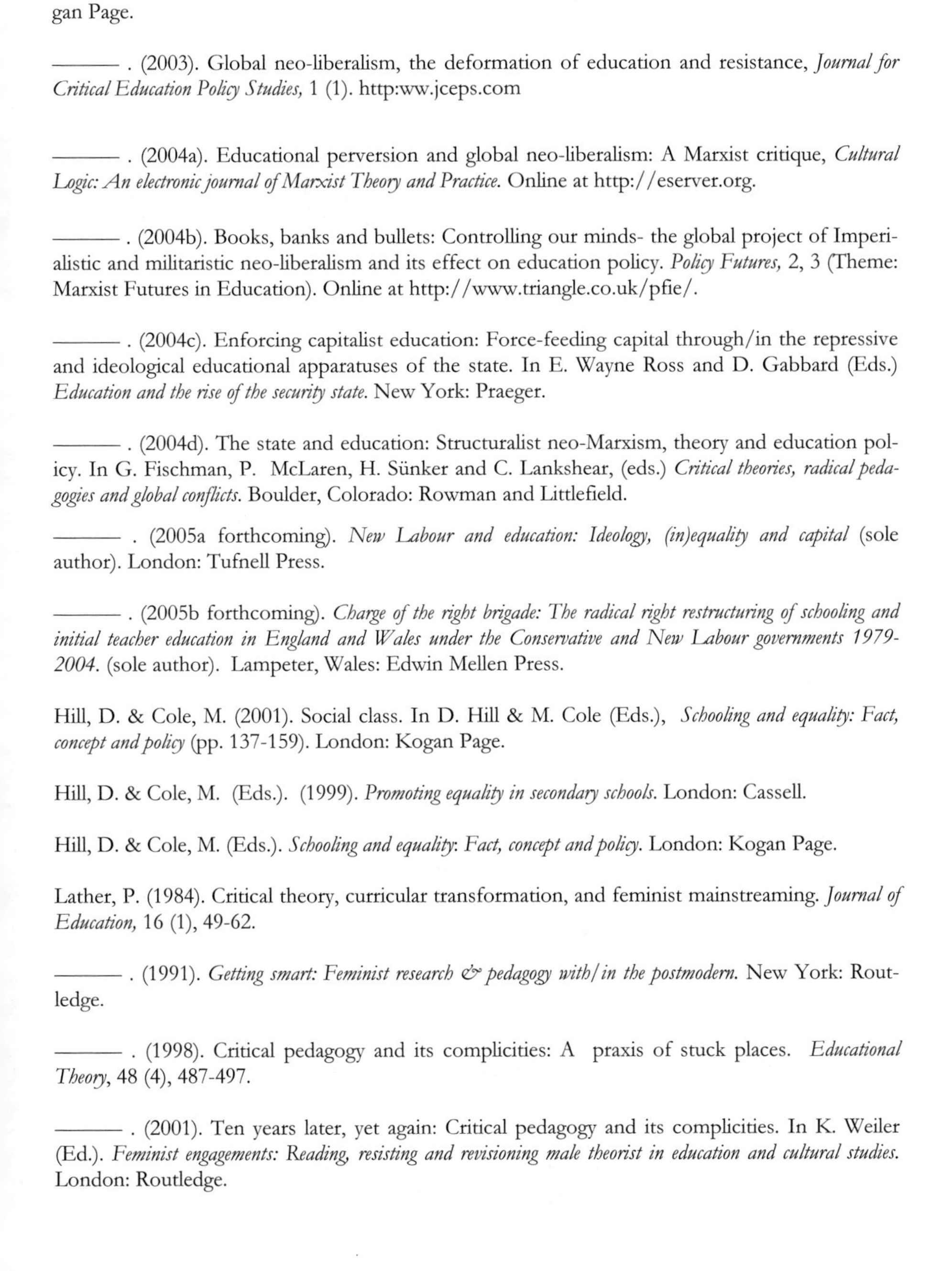

Hill, D. (2001a). State theory and the neo-liberal reconstruction of schooling and teacher education: A structuralist neo-Marxist critique of postmodernist, quasi-postmodernist, and culturalist neo-Marxist theory, *British Journal of Sociology of Education,* 22 (1), 135-155.

———. (2001b). Global capital, neo-liberalism, and privatization: The growth of educational inequality. In D. Hill and M. Cole (Eds.). *Schooling and equality: Fact, concept and policy.* London: Kogan Page.

———. (2003). Global neo-liberalism, the deformation of education and resistance, *Journal for Critical Education Policy Studies,* 1 (1). http:ww.jceps.com

———. (2004a). Educational perversion and global neo-liberalism: A Marxist critique, *Cultural Logic: An electronic journal of Marxist Theory and Practice.* Online at http://eserver.org.

———. (2004b). Books, banks and bullets: Controlling our minds- the global project of Imperialistic and militaristic neo-liberalism and its effect on education policy. *Policy Futures,* 2, 3 (Theme: Marxist Futures in Education). Online at http://www.triangle.co.uk/pfie/.

———. (2004c). Enforcing capitalist education: Force-feeding capital through/in the repressive and ideological educational apparatuses of the state. In E. Wayne Ross and D. Gabbard (Eds.) *Education and the rise of the security state.* New York: Praeger.

———. (2004d). The state and education: Structuralist neo-Marxism, theory and education policy. In G. Fischman, P. McLaren, H. Sünker and C. Lankshear, (eds.) *Critical theories, radical pedagogies and global conflicts.* Boulder, Colorado: Rowman and Littlefield.

———. (2005a forthcoming). *New Labour and education: Ideology, (in)equality and capital* (sole author). London: Tufnell Press.

———. (2005b forthcoming). *Charge of the right brigade: The radical right restructuring of schooling and initial teacher education in England and Wales under the Conservative and New Labour governments 1979-2004.* (sole author). Lampeter, Wales: Edwin Mellen Press.

Hill, D. & Cole, M. (2001). Social class. In D. Hill & M. Cole (Eds.), *Schooling and equality: Fact, concept and policy* (pp. 137-159). London: Kogan Page.

Hill, D. & Cole, M. (Eds.). (1999). *Promoting equality in secondary schools.* London: Cassell.

Hill, D. & Cole, M. (Eds.). *Schooling and equality: Fact, concept and policy.* London: Kogan Page.

Lather, P. (1984). Critical theory, curricular transformation, and feminist mainstreaming. *Journal of Education,* 16 (1), 49-62.

———. (1991). *Getting smart: Feminist research & pedagogy with/in the postmodern.* New York: Routledge.

———. (1998). Critical pedagogy and its complicities: A praxis of stuck places. *Educational Theory,* 48 (4), 487-497.

———. (2001). Ten years later, yet again: Critical pedagogy and its complicities. In K. Weiler (Ed.). *Feminist engagements: Reading, resisting and revisioning male theorist in education and cultural studies.* London: Routledge.

Marx, K. (1976) [1847]. The poverty of philosophy. In K. Marx and F. Engels, *Collected works, Vol. 6*. London: Lawrence and Wishart.

Marx, K. (1966) [1894]. *Capital, vol. 3*. Moscow: Progress Publishers.

Marx, K. & Engels, F. (1977) [1847]. *Preface to the German edition of the Manifesto of the Communist Party*. In Karl Marx and Frederick Engels: Selected works in one volume, London: Lawrence and Wishart.

McLaren, P. (1994). Multiculturalism and the postmodern critique: Towards a pedagogy of resistance and transformation. In H. Giroux and P. McLaren (Eds.), *Between borders: Pedagogy and the politics of cultural studies*. London: Routledge.

———. (1997). The ethnographer as postmodern flaneur: Critical reflexivity and posthybridity as narrative engagement. In P. McLaren (Ed.). *Revolutionary multiculturalism: Pedagogies of dissent for the new millennium*. Boulder, Colorado: Westview Press,.

———. (1998). Revolutionary pedagogy in post-revolutionary times: Rethinking the political economy of critical education. *Educational Theory*, 48 (4), 431-462.

———. (2000). *Che Guevara, Paulo Freire and the pedagogy of revolution*. Oxford: Rowman and Littlefield.

———. (2003). *Life in schools: An introduction to critical pedagogy in the foundations of education*, 4th Edition. Boston, MA: Allyn & Bacon.

McLaren, P. & Farahmandpur, R. (2001). Educational policy and the socialist imagination: Revolutionary citizenship as a pedagogy of resistance. *Education Policy: An Interdisciplinary Journal of Policy and Practice*, 15 (3), 343-378.

———. (2002a). Breaking signifying chains: A Marxist position on postmodernism. In Hill, D., McLaren, P., Cole, M. & Rikowski, G. (Eds.). *Marxism against postmodernism in educational theory*. Lanham, MD: Lexington Books.

———. (2002b). Recentering class: Wither postmoderism?: Towards a contraband pedagogy. In D. Hill, P. McLaren, M. Cole & G. Rikowski (Eds.), *Marxism against postmodernism in educational theory*. Lanham, Maryland: Lexington Books.

McLaren, P. & Pinkney-Pastrana, J. (2001). Cuba, yanquizacion, and the cult of Elian Gonzalez: A view from the "enlighttened States." *Qualitative Studies in Education,* 14 (2), 201-219.

McMurtry, J. (2000). Dumbing sown with globalization: The ideology of inevitable revolution. *Economic Reform,* August, 8-9.

———. (2001). Education, struggle and the left today. *International Journal of Educational Reform,* 10 (2), 145-162.

Mojab, S. (2001). New resources for revolutionary critical education. *Convergence*, 34 (1), 118-125.

Murphy, P. (1995). A mad, mad, mad world economy. *Living Marxism*, 80 (June), 17-19.

Parrish, R. (2002). Some thoughts on Derrida and Nietzsche, Department of Political Science, University of Wisconsin-Madison. On-line at http://polisci.wisc.edu.

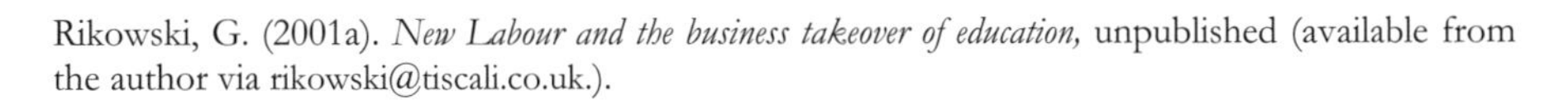

Rikowski, G. (2001a). *New Labour and the business takeover of education,* unpublished (available from the author via rikowski@tiscali.co.uk.).

———. (2001b). *After the manuscript broke off: Thoughts on Marx, social class and education.* Paper delivered to the British Sociological Association Education Study Group Meeting, 23 June (available from the author via rikowski@tiscali.co.uk.).

———. (2001c). The importance of being a radical educator in capitalism today. Guest lecture in Sociology of Education, The Gilian Rose Room, Department of Sociology, University of Warwick, Coventry, 24 May (available from the author via rikowski@tiscali.co.uk.).

———. (2001d). *The battle in Seattle: Its significance for education.* London: The Turnfell Press.

———. (2002). Prelude: Marxist educational theory after postmodernism. In D. Hill, P. McLaren, M. Cole & G. Rikowski (Eds.), *Marxism against postmodernism in educational theory* (pp. 15-32). Lanham, MD: Lexington Books.

Short, G. & Carrington, B. (1998). Reconstructing multicultural education: A response to Mike Cole. *Cambridge Journal of Education*, 28, (2), 231-234.

Slott, M. (2002). Does critical postmodernism help us "name the system"? *British Journal of Sociology of Education,* 23 (3), 414–425.

Social Trends. (2002). No. 32. London: The Stationery Office.

Social Trends. (2003). No. 33. London: The Stationery Office.

U.S. Census Bureau (2003). On-line at http://www.census.gov/.

Wells, M. (2001). ITN cuts jobs and shifts towards lifestyle news, *The Guardian*, 22 November.

Wood, E.M. (1995). *Democracy against capitalism.* Cambridge: Cambridge University Press.

———. (1997). Capitalism, globalization and epochal shifts: An exchange (reply to A. Sivanandan). *Monthly Review*, 48, 21-32.

Waller, T., Cole, M. & Hill, D. (2001). Race. In D. Hill & M. Cole (Eds.), *Schooling and equality: Fact, concept and policy* (pp. 161-185). London: Kogan Page.

World Development Movement. (2001). *Isn't it time we tackled the causes of poverty?* London: World Development Movement.

Zavarzadeh, M. (2002). On "class" and related concepts in classical Marxism, and why is the post-al Left saying such terrible things about them? Article available on-line at http://www.etext.org/Politics/AlternativeOrange.

Chapter 8

The Revolutionary Critical Pedagogy of Peter McLaren

Ramin Farahmandpur

The world runs amok as global carpetbaggers looking to become the world's latest centillionaires take advantage of the results of enhanced rights for corporations worldwide. These results include privatization, budget cuts, outsourcing and labor "flexibility," which have come about because of the engineered absence of government regulation on the production, distribution and consumption of goods and services. This, in turn, is largely brought about by global neoliberal economic policies. Stacking the shelves of Planet Mall with goods shaped for designer lifestyles becomes the operative strategy. Following in the wake of push-cart, no-frills, bootstrap capitalism is the cultural flotsam and jetsam produced by the Starbucking and Wal-Marting of the global landscape, as the tyranny of the market ruthlessly subjects labor to its regulatory forces of social and cultural reproduction in the unsustainable precincts of the capitalist market.

Under the tutelage of neo-liberialism's economic engineers, Milton Friedman and Friedrich Von Hayek, the 1980s and 1990s became a showcase for an orchestrated conservative and right-wing backlash against the civil rights of working-class minority groups, immigrants, women and children. This has spilled over into the new millennium with a series of scandals that has involved, among others, the Enron and WorldCom corporations. Recently in the United States we have witnessed a series of democratic "victories" for proponents of Propositions 21, 209, and 227 in California, propositions aimed at welfare "reform" and "managed care" as well as increasing the executions of criminals and massively expanding the prison industry.

It is not surprising that the privatization of health care, reduction in social services for the poor and the "Martha Stewartization" of Wall Street's school of ethics coincide with the stagnation of wage growth and declining economic prosperity for most working-class men, women and children. These recent trends are also associated with the vanishing middle class in the United States. Given such a scenario, democracy seems perilously out of reach. Indeed, the frontiers of human freedom are being pushed back as "free" market forces—under the leadership of Dick Cheney and his understudy, George Bush, Jr.—are being pushed forward.

The Decline of Marxist Scholarship and the Rise of the New Right

In the late 1970s and early 1980s, radical scholars working in the field of sociology of education stood at a peculiar historical crossroads. For one, they were forced to withstand the New Right's onslaught—its single-minded, ruthless attacks on the welfare state—orchestrated by the aerosol figure of Ronald Reagan and his army of renegade storm troopers composed of Christian fundamentalists, corporate raiders and Wall Street moguls. At the same time, the United States, Japan and Germany vigorously enforced neo-liberal social and economic reforms on Third World and developing countries as a short-term remedy to the deepening structural crisis of global capitalism (Brenner, 1998).

Faced with the cynical intellectual mood of the late 1970s and the early 1980s, scores of radical scholars joined the rank and file of the new wave of post-Marxists, neo-Marxists and cultural Marxists. A large number of radical scholars roundly dismissed Marxism as an "outmoded" and unfashionable nineteenth-century meta-narrative that had failed to accommodate the postindustrial consumer society. Instead, these scholars embraced what they claimed to be far more "open-ended" and far less "deterministic" radical sociological frameworks, which included, for instance, neo-Gramscianism, postmodern theory, poststructuralism and postcolonial theory. By the end of the 1980s, with the "cultural turn" in full swing, radical scholars allied themselves with the followers of such celebrated academic brigands as Jean Baudrillard, Jacques Derrida, Jean-François Lyotard, Ernesto Laclau and Chantal Mouffe, who ebulliently announced the death of Marxism.

In the course of my own research studies in classical Marxist social theory, I decided to engage in a rigorous re-examination of the most recent developments and trends in Marxist scholarship in the field of sociology of education. Although I agreed with most of the theoretical perspectives proffered by the leading radical scholars, I became increasingly alarmed by and suspicious of the emerging radical approaches to educational reform. I am referring particularly to a number of scholars who signaled the declining significance of class politics after the publication of *Schooling in Capitalist America* (1976). My suspicion, with respect to this shift, was further confirmed when I examined the main body of literature in the field of sociology of education of the 1980s and 1990s.

To my surprise, I discovered that feminist and critical-race theorists alike had become generally disillusioned with class politics. Having criticized Marxism's "class essentialism," these scholars explored new theoretical vistas, such as the social construction of race and patriarchy, in order to examine the underlying causes of social oppression. Many scholars extensively incorporated postmodern and poststructural theories in order to examine how race, class and gender oppressions are maintained and reproduced in society. Disenchanted by class politics, radical scholars further concentrated on the prospects of the new social movements. Peter McLaren's (1986) cautionary synthesis of critical pedagogy and postmodern theory, and his attempt to warn the Left of the possible entrapments of postmodern and poststructural theory, remained largely unheeded by a large number of scholars on the Left. It seemed that only a few scholars, such as Brosio (1990, 2000) and Berlowitz and Chapman (1978), continued to work within a Marxist framework. McLaren (1998) later joined the ranks of Marxist scholars (e.g., Rikowski, 1997; Hill & Cole, 1995), only to be attacked for his emphasis on class struggle (see Lather, 1998; Gur-Ze'ev, 1998; Biesta, 1998).

Currently, a significant amount of scholarship coming out of graduate schools of education across the United States continues to operate from within the parameters drawn by capitalist social relations of production. Today's much-celebrated radical scholarship in the field of sociology of education has largely failed to challenge and offer a vigorous critique of capitalist social relations of production (e.g., Apple, 1993, 1996, 2001). After identifying the shift from class politics to identity politics, I became drawn into developing a sustained critique of that segment of the Leftist scholars who had largely abandoned class politics.

The Rise of the Revisionist Movement

Regrettably, most (if not all) radical scholars have downplayed the significance of class politics by severing its ties from the ideological, political and cultural foundations of capitalism (McLaren & Farahmandpur, 2000, 2001a, 2001b, 2001c). Seduced by the avant-garde overtures of postmodern, poststructural and cultural theories, scholars have truncated the political economy of schooling with their terse dismissal of class struggle as a central element of the project associated with social transformation (McLaren & Farahmandpur, 2000, 2001a, 2001b, 2001c). In addition to postmodernists and poststructuralists, other scholars working in the precincts of cultural politics have summarily dismissed the working class as the appointed agents of social change. Most of the recent scholarly material produced by radical scholars in the field of political economy has been tainted by the work of post-Marxists Laclau and Mouffe (1985), the exponents of "radical democracy" as well as the leading champions of the new social movements: the appointed agents of anti-capitalist struggles (Boggs, 1995; Croteau, 1995).

A case in point is the much-celebrated work of Michael Apple. Arguably the leading "mainstream" Marxist scholar in North America, Apple has straddled these "paradigm shifts" (Kuhn, 1962) by positioning himself within the neo-Marxist and post-Marxist frameworks. Along with other theorists, Apple (1993, 1996, 1999, 2001) has dismissed the centrality of class struggle in efforts at educational reform. Although he acknowledges the significance of class as a key variable in the perpetuation of inequality in education and schooling of children, Apple has nevertheless remained a trenchant critic of "traditional" and classical Marxists for their overtly "economistic" and "deterministic" analyses of schooling.

Despite the best efforts of Marxist and neo-Marxist education theorists to provide an analysis of capitalist schooling (Anyon, 1980; Gonzales, 1982; Harris, 1982; Price, 1986; M. Sarup, 1978; R. Sarup, 1983; Sharp, 1980, 1988; Strike, 1989; Willis, 1977; Youngman, 1986), by the early 1980s it had become abundantly clear that a Marxist approach to schooling had lost much of its appeal among progressive scholars on the Left. In the United States, only Michael Apple (1993, 1996, 1999) and Jean Anyon (1980, 1994)—along with less visible scholars like Richard Brosio (1990, 2000)—remained among a handful of Marxist scholars who continued to stress the significance of social class.

In the late 1970s, as the New Left gained momentum inside the corridors of graduate schools of education, a number of Marxist-Leninist theorists anticipated the shift from class politics toward postmodernism and cultural politics. Berlowitz and Chapman (1978) identified a "new historical revisionist" trajectory within the scholarship of Samuel Bowles, Herbert Gintis, Michael Katz, Joel Spring and David Tyack (Cole, 1988; Karabel & Halsey, 1977; McDonald,

1988). To this list we might add Michael Apple (1985, 1986) and Henry Giroux (1981, 1983, 1991, 1992) and the early work of Peter McLaren (1986, 1989, 1995, 1997).

Although by the 1990s class analysis became peripheral in the body of work produced by most scholars, Michael Apple remained one of a handful of scholars who consistently worked within a neo-Marxian framework of class analysis. Yet despite his criticisms of postmodernism and poststructuralism, Apple's (1993, 1996, 1999) recent work on class has been compromised by neo-Marxist and post-Marxist assumptions.

According to Berlowitz and Chapman (1978), the main objective of the new historical revisionists has been to dismiss the central role of the working class in the struggle against capitalism. The new historical revisionists relied on a combination of radical functionalist and neo-Marxist theories to explain how schools are implicated in reproducing capitalist social relations of production (Berlowitz, 1977; Liston, 1988). This explanation is evident in the work of Bowles and Gintis (1976), who assigned the working class a marginal role as agents of social change (Berlowitz, 1977; Föner, 1978).

To their credit, historical revisionists working within the precincts of post-Marxism in the past two decades have enriched the field of sociology of education with their scholarly contributions. Most scholars working within fields as diverse as reproduction theory, resistance theory, postmodern theory, feminist theory and cultural politics have shown how schools "function" to reproduce existing social relations through cultural domination. Yet by failing to underscore the centrality of class politics, historical revisionists have not been able to overcome the confinements of radical functionalism (Berlowitz, 1977). In fact, a number of scholars, including Michael Apple (1993, 1996, 1999), have openly dismissed class politics and the vanguard role of the working class in the arena of social change.

Trapped within the radical functionalist model of social reproduction that frequently characterizes the working class as passive social agents, the new historical revisionists have overlooked the successful battles that the working class has waged in the name of democratic schooling (Liston, 1988; Berlowitz & Chapman, 1978; Sharp, 1988). Instead, these post-Marxist scholars have upheld a political ideal that is frequently associated with new social movements and "democratic pluralism."

The Rebirth of Marxist Scholarship in Education

In the 1980s and 1990s, working-class men and women experienced a massive assault by neo-liberal social and economic policies, which were accompanied by deregulation, unrestricted access to consumer markets, downsizing, outsourcing, flexible arrangements with respect to labor practices, intensification of competition among transnational corporations, an increasing centralization of economic and political power and, finally, an accelerating class polarization. In the United States and abroad, the emergence of neo-liberal social and economic policies has led to the centralization and concentration of capital in the hands of multinational corporations. The means to this end have been achieved through corporate mergers, the increased exploitation of labor, anti-union activities and the reduction of corporate taxes in an effort to prevent the falling rate of profit caused, in part, by competition between Japanese and German manufacturing industries (Britain, 1998).

In the 1990s, it became strikingly clear that neo-liberal economic policies (those that favor an unfettered access to markets, a cut in social services and the dismantling of the welfare state) had failed to fulfill the promise of economic growth and stability, not only in developing countries, but in Western industrialized nations as well. Beyond that, these policies have also contributed to the environment of intensified class polarization and the globalization of poverty. The Asian financial crisis in 1997 is a case in point, demonstrating that the transition toward economic globalization followed by deregulation and privatization of state- and public-owned industries has not been as successful as the champions of the market economy had initially envisioned.

Recent efforts to dismantle the welfare state in order to reduce federal and state spending on social services has been met with some success for multinational corporations that are seeking cheaper labor markets and raw materials in the competitive global market economy. Furthermore, the problem of high unemployment has temporarily been resolved with the expansion of the service-sector economy in the United States and the exportation of manufacturing jobs to Third World countries. The result of these practices has been declining wages, lower standards of living and increasing social and economic polarization in the United States.

In responding to the social and political shifts to the right, a small yet increasingly visible group of scholars, who identify their work within the Marxist tradition, have moved to renew and revamp class politics in the field of sociology of education (Allman, 2001; Cole & Hill, 1995, 1996; Cole, Hill & Rikowski,

1997; McLaren, 2000; McLaren & Farahmandpur, 1999, 2000, 2001a, 2001b, 2001c; Raduntz, 1999; Rikowski, 1996, 1997, 2001; Sharp, 1988). These Marxist scholars have found the political implications of post-Marxism (i.e., postmodernism, poststructuralism, cultural politics) woefully problematic. They maintain that the politics associated with radical democracy are, at best, a form of liberal pluralism in disguise and, at worst, a reactionary form of politics afflicted with an extreme form of skepticism (Sokal & Brichmont, 1998). Finally, Marxist scholars have forewarned that in the absence of a well-developed Marxist theory of class exploitation, it would be difficult—if not impossible—to uncover the underlying causes of inequalities in education and the schooling of children that are associated with the structural contradictions of the class system under capitalism.

Situating the Work of Peter McLaren

The Early Work

McLaren's earliest work, *Cries from the Corridor* (1980), remains one of the most influential ethnographic studies to have emerged from the early 1980s literature on schooling. Along with Paul Willis' groundbreaking ethnographic study of working-class culture of high school students in England, *Learning to Labor* (1977), Paul Corrigan's *Schooling the Smash Street Kids* (1979), and Robert Everhart's *Reading, Writing, and Resistance: Adolescence and Labor in a Junior High School* (1983), McLaren's *Cries from the Corridor* is an original contribution to the field of critical ethnography that documents the everyday life experiences of inner-city school children in Toronto, Canada. It was a precursor to McLaren's highly acclaimed, full-length ethnographic study, *Schooling as a Ritual Performance* (1986). Teaching in the 1970s, at the height of the post–World War II economic boom, McLaren offered through his diaries a rare glimpse into the little-known world of teaching and learning experiences of working-class immigrant students. When McLaren's unorthodox teaching style and leftist politics provoked his university to cancel his teaching contract in 1985, he took up a professorship in the United States at the invitation of Henry Giroux. One of McLaren's first projects upon his arrival in the United States was to integrate the diaries of *Cries from the Corridor* (1980) into a longer foundational education textbook, which he titled *Life in Schools* (1989). By drawing upon the life experiences of his Canadian students, McLaren masterfully brought into the foreground the fundamental contradictions of capitalist schooling in the larger North American context (see Bowles & Gintis, 1976). In essence, *Life in Schools* captured the darker side of capitalism by showing how democracy fails to live up to its promise.

To McLaren's surprise, *Cries from the Corridor* (1980) had become a best-selling book in Canada. The book's success generated an unparalleled measure of public controversy and debate among educators, scholars and policymakers both in North America and abroad. It is also to McLaren's credit that he listened to the critics of his book, not only Marxists but also the very community members about whom he wrote. He incorporated what he learned into the pages of *Life in Schools* (1989). McLaren's key insight was that he had not provided a sociopolitical context for readers so that they could make critical sense of what he was writing about. Without such a context, readers could easily "blame the victims" of McLaren's story. That McLaren had the foresight and courage to address the limitations of his first book is a testament to his commitment as a critical scholar.

Finally, McLaren's ethnographic study of one Catholic school was among the early studies that introduced poststructuralism and postmodernism to the field of education. In *Schooling as a Ritual Performance* (1986), McLaren studied working-class students at a Catholic school in Toronto, Canada. In examining the day-to-day classroom practices and interactions among students and teachers of a Catholic school, McLaren incorporated Victor Turner's study of ritual practices. In addition, McLaren utilized Foucault's study on the birth of new social institutions under capitalism by examining the relationship between schooling and the body, as a site of discipline and control. McLaren identified "Catholicism" and the "good worker" as two root paradigms emphasized in Catholic schools in an effort to socialize students and enable them to become "good citizens."

The Seduction of Postmodernism and Poststructuralism

McLaren's journey toward Marxism began by traversing the rough and uncharted vast terrain of postmodern and poststructural theories. In both *Critical Pedagogy and Predatory Culture* (1995) and *Revolutionary Multiculturalism* (1997), McLaren experimented, and even at times flirted, with postmodern and poststructural approaches to educational theory and practice. He brazenly explored and examined the longstanding tensions and debates that exist between the culturalist and materialist approaches to schooling, in addition to the pressing philosophical debates over structure and agency.

One of McLaren's major undertakings in *Critical Pedagogy and Predatory Culture* (1995) was to liberate the progressive, or critical, variants of postmodernism from its more conservative strands. In so doing, McLaren engaged in a sustained critique of conservative forms of postmodernism that included, among others, ludic postmodernism (the works of Derrida, Lyotard, Baudrillard are representative of this trend that reduces politics to textual practices); spectral postmodernism (or "superstructuralism," which privileges culture over social relations of production); and skeptical postmodernism (which endorses "epistemological relativism" and "ontological agnosticism"). McLaren (1995) combined progressive elements of postmodern theory with Marxism under the banner of oppositional or critical postmodern theory. He asserted that signs were not merely free-floating entities existing in ethereal spaces, de-linked from social practices. Rather, McLaren (1995) saw signs as an arena of social, political and material contestation. In other words, "difference" is not merely a logic of language, discourse or textual practices, but the effect of social conflicts among dominant and subordinate groups. Along with oppositional and "critical postmodernism," McLaren (1995) endorsed "resistance postmodernism," which placed identity, power and language in a social, historical and materialist framework. Finally, it should be mentioned that in fusing modernist and postmodernist theories, McLaren's objective was to arm teachers with a language of critique so that they could link issues of power, language and identity to their everyday teaching practices in the classroom.

In a concerted effort to develop a theoretical framework that would include both cultural and materialist approaches to schooling, in *Revolutionary Multiculturalism* (1997) McLaren articulated a postmodern Marxist approach to educational theory and practice. In his view, postmodern Marxism transcended the inflexibility of Marxism that was enshrouded in discourses of modernity. Further, McLaren became concerned with some of the critiques of post-Marxists, who argue that Marxism is inflicted with discourses that are associated with reductionism, determinism and economism. As such, he made a concerted effort to dissociate his work from orthodox and vulgar variants of Marxism that had been influential in Bowles and Gintis' *Schooling in Capitalism America* (1976). Thus, McLaren (1997) believed that a postmodern Marxist approach would be flexible enough to accommodate both political economy and cultural politics.

Finally, while most radical and progressive-minded scholars remained seduced by postmodern and poststructural theories that had besieged much of academia in the 1980s and 1990s, McLaren (1995, 1997) was quick to recognize the entrapments of such "post-al" theories. He recognized that capital works as a "structuring force," which penetrates all aspects of social life. Later, McLaren expressed an urgency for recentering political economy by critiquing capitalist social relations of production. Of course, there is no question that McLaren acknowledged that Marxist pedagogy had to be a pedagogy that was anti-racist, anti-sexist and anti-homophobic.

McLaren's Marxist Reorientation

McLaren's (2000) most recent work is a much-needed analysis that calls for the creation of new revolutionary collective struggles by embattling the destructiveness of neo-liberal globalization. In contrast to postmodern and post-Marxist scholars, who have hastily written off Marxism as a failed totalitarian ideology of the twentieth century and have relegated it to the dustbin of historical relics, McLaren has rediscovered his revolutionary roots by re-engaging Marxist social theory. McLaren's criticism of global capitalism, privatization and the neo-liberalization of life centers on the current social, economic and political turmoil that has engulfed the world. To initiate the struggle against capitalism, McLaren offers an approach that he refers to as "revolutionary critical pedagogy." Outfitted with the fundamental principles of Marxism, class struggle and historical materialism, the objective of McLaren's revolutionary critical pedagogy is to prepare the critical educator as the revolutionary agent of class struggle in the battle against capital.

To its credit, McLaren's *Ché Guevara, Paulo Freire and the Pedagogy of Revolution* (2000) offers educators a much-anticipated Marxian analysis of schooling in an era in which most scholars have abandoned Marxian class analysis altogether. Yet it would be undercutting McLaren's own critical advice if we overlooked the limitations of his work. For example, teachers and teacher educators will be disappointed to discover that while McLaren's book is rich in Marxian analysis of capitalist schooling, it fails to offer concrete examples which made his now-famous ethnographic scholarship in *Life in Schools* (1989) the cutting-edge educational analysis of capitalist schooling in the 1980s and 1990s (including *Cries from the Corridor*, 1980).

Of course, this is not an argument against theoretical work. Teachers have often complained that critical pedagogy is too theoretical or too abstract to have any concrete application inside their classrooms. In most cases, teachers have used their personal experiences (as well their students' experiences) to guide their pedagogical practices in the classroom. However, as critical theorists have frequently stressed, experience alone fails to offer an accurate account of how teachers are positioned in relation to one another, and how they are situated within the social relations of production. This is because experience is mediated through commodity production. Thus, it is important for teachers to incorporate theory to inform their pedagogical practices. As Cyril Smith (1996) notes:

> Theory is a form of thinking which reflects that inhuman shell in which our lives are covered, taking it for granted that humanity can never escape. Marx's struggle for communist revolution is centered on revealing this imprisonment, allowing us to regard it from a human standpoint and to find a way out. Instead of "seeking science in his mind" and presenting a theory, Marx wanted to free our consciousness from these shackles. It is that insight which must be recaptured if communism is to be regenerated. (p. 136)

In short, many critical pedagogists would argue that logical and rational thinking is central in grasping and penetrating what Marx has referred to as the "thing in itself."

Second, it is unclear to what extent teachers in the United States are willing to embrace a Guevarean politics, not to mention the continuing nagging debate between the Marxist-Leninist and Trotskyite camps over the most effective political strategies and tactics the working class should employ to challenge capitalist social relations of production. In addition, Guevarean revolutionary politics raises other important questions, including:

- What were the main political and ideological differences between Fidel and Ché?
- Was Ché correct in pursuing a militant internationalist strategy?
- Did Ché miscalculate in his attempt to organize the Bolivian peasants?
- Should he have placed his efforts in mobilizing more politically organized sectors of the Bolivian working class (i.e., industrial workers)?

Finally, many Marxist scholars, including McLaren (1995, 1997, 2000), have rightly criticized the dogmatism that has haunted orthodox Marxism for the last several decades. However, there is a tendency among a number of critical theorists to straddle the "voluntarist idealism" of Maoism and Guevareanism. To cite one example, Mao was optimistic that social conditions could be transformed by willpower alone. That optimism was also reflected in the revolutionary struggles of Ché Guevara, who believed that guerrilla warfare in the countryside, alongside the Peruvian peasants, could ignite a social revolution in that region of the world. However, as John Molyneux (1995) maintains, both ideologies ignore the social conditions that determine the nature of class struggle and social revolution. Unlike Marxist humanists, historical materialists believe that capitalism cannot be overthrown by voluntaristic struggles and actions alone. Instead, revolutions are only possible under certain social and historical conditions, and even then they require an organized, working-class movement armed with a revolutionary consciousness. Despite these criticisms, my intention in highlighting these shortcomings of McLaren's recent work is to strengthen its Marxian roots and to align it more closely to its avowedly historical materialist direction.

Recentering Marx; Reinventing Critical Pedagogy

Why should teachers and teacher educators at colleges and universities trouble themselves with reading *Capital*? What does *Capital*, Marx's Magnus Opus—which took him nearly 40 years of his life to complete and covers more than 1,000 pages—reveal to us? More important, why has Marx become so unfashionable among scholars and professors in academic circles across the United States? Why is it that universities are all too eager to offer courses on postcolonialism, postmodernism, poststructuralism and cultural studies, but they are far less willing to provide any serious forums or seminars in which Marx's *Capital* can be critically discussed, debated and studied? What does Marx, who stood as one of the leading "declassed intellectuals" of the nineteenth century, reveal that has made him a pariah in the eyes of the academic establishment?

Aside from his theory of historical materialism, Marx's other great scientific discovery was the theory of surplus value. Marx's (1969) social and economic theories of class and his analysis of capitalist exploitation pivot around his labor theory of value. Marx argued that the value of any commodity is determined by the socially necessary labor time that is used in its production. He used the term "socially necessary labor time" because the labor time required to create a commodity depends in part on society's level of technological progress and the development of its forces of production. In Marx's labor theory of value, commodities are exchanged in the market for prices that correspond to the necessary labor time embodied in them. Surplus value is realized when a commodity is exchanged or sold for more than its labor value. The labor theory of value provides the basis for Marx's argument that workers are exploited under capitalism. Through the power of capital ownership, the capitalist is able to pay the worker less than the market value of the commodities produced, with the surplus value captured by capital and re-invested to increase the means of production.

Furthermore, Marx's (1969) labor theory of value illuminates the existing tensions and contradictions between labor and capital. Marx offered a glimpse into the cryptic world of capital. Here we can see how class relations and class exploitation are rendered invisible and hidden from our senses. Trafficking Marx's labor theory of value back into the radical educational theory provides us with a penetrating insight into the workings of capital as a social relation, and into how teachers, as productive laborers, are implicated in reproducing social relations of production. It also provides us with a vantage point from which to observe capital as a social relation between the two main classes in bourgeois society—the capitalist class and the working class.

Marx, Commodity Production and Its Implications for Educators

In the first chapter of *Capital*, Marx digs beneath its ideological camouflage to demystify capitalism. Marx's *Capital* can be described as a guiding torch that illuminated the riddles and mysteries of capitalism, which had thus far eluded our senses. Marx explains that the commodity is an "external object" that exists exterior to our physical bodies. He further extends his analysis by proffering that the commodity not only exists apart from "us," but it also confronts us as an alien object, standing in opposition to "us," or "against us" (Holloway, 2001). As such, the commodity "negates" and "denies" our very own humanity. In fact, the commodity can be described as a dehumanizing and alienating force that derives much of its existence from our laboring bodies and from our capacity to labor in the production of surplus value. The commodity, we should stress, is the product of human labor. Not surprisingly, the commodity, which is equal to the work that is expended on its production, is of our own "doing" (Holloway, 2001)

Moreover, Marx explicitly stated that the commodity exists apart from us (Holloway, 2001). A careful reading of the first lines of *Capital*, in which Marx writes: "The commodity is, *first of all*, an external object, a thing which through its qualities satisfies human needs of whatever kind" (p. 125), raises the question of why Marx inserts the words "first of all" in the sentence. As we shall see, there is an implicit meaning to Marx's intention (Holloway, 2001).

Furthermore, Marx writes that the commodity exists exterior to our physical bodies, and we are "negated subjects" (Holloway, 2001). Yet the commodity originates and arises from our laboring bodies, which is the source of value. This is because workers are also the producers of commodities. Thus it is undeniable that there is an ever-present conflict between the commodity as an object standing apart from us and the commodity as an object that arises from within us, and, hence, is a product of our labor (Holloway, 2001).

In the first instance, because the commodity exists exterior to us, we stand as negated and passive subjects (Holloway, 2001). In the second instance, however, because we are producers of these commodities, we also assert ourselves as active subjects (Holloway, 2001). Social change can thus be described as the outcome of the conflict between the dual nature of our passive and active subjectivities. In other words, we are the embodiment of the contradictions between labor and capital as well as being positioned between use-value and exchange-value. In the first instance, we are "denied" and violated by the very product of our labor: namely, the commodity. In the second instance, our labor can strike back by negating the negation of our labor, which exists in the form of the commodity. Thus, not only do our laboring bodies produce their own negation in the form of the commodity, but they also create the conditions by which it is possible to negate their own negation through the act of "doing." In expressing the two contradictory movements in commodity production, Holloway (2001) writes:

> In the first place is domination, the denial of our subjectivity, of our humanity. In the second place is the possibility of liberation, of self-emancipation. The possibility of changing the world lies in the tension between the first and the second place, between form and content, between denial and that which is denied. Both despair and hope are there in the opening words of *Capital*, as they must be in any honest reflection on capitalism....In this movement of despair and hope, despair is in the first place, in the superficial understanding of things as they are. Hope lies in the piercing of the first place, the recuperation of that which is invisible in the first place, that which exists in the mode of being denied. In the first place, our doing is denied, replaced by being. The movement of hope is the recovery of doing, of the doing that is denied by the first place. This movement is the movement of criticism, understood as genetic criticism, as the attempt to trace the origin of phenomena in social doing. Marx presents us with the horror of a commodity that negates doing, that presents itself as being, and then immediately takes us beyond that horror to show us its origin in doing, to show us the real

> presence of that which is denied in the first place, and not only its presence but the absolute dependence of that which denies on that which is denied. (p. 67)

This raises a number of important pedagogical questions regarding the role of teachers and teacher educators in the struggle for building a democratic society. For example, how can teachers participate in the class struggle? How can critical pedagogy be transformed into a vehicle for social change? How do we, as teachers in public schools and teacher educators in graduate schools of education, move beyond the pedagogical spaces of despair and fear, which embrace an uncritical and blind view of the social world, and refuse to engage, critique and question how we live our lives? How can we develop the courage to create and develop pedagogical spaces of hope that can penetrate everyday social practices, and that have the potential to unmask the workings of capitalist social relations of production through the practice of ideology-critique? For teachers and teacher educators, these are among the many questions that McLaren's revolutionary critical pedagogy raises. What is certain is that McLaren's re-alignment with Marxist social theory has inspired and has made it possible for a new generation of critical educators to re-engage with Marxism.

References

Allman, P. (2001). *Critical education against global capitalism: Karl Marx and revolutionary critical education.* Westport, CT, & London: Bergin & Garvey.

Anyon, J. (1980). Social class and the hidden curriculum of work. *Journal of Education*, 26, 67–92.

———. (1994). The retreat of Marxism and socialist feminism: Postmodern and poststructural theories in education. *Curriculum Theory*, 24(2), 115–133.

Apple, M.W. (1985). *Education and power.* Boston: Ark Paperbacks.

———. (1986). *Teachers and texts: A political economy of class & gender relation in education.* New York & London: Routledge.

———. (1993). *Official knowledge: Democratic education in a conservative age.* New York: Routledge & Kegan Paul.

———. (1996). *Education and cultural politics.* New York: Teachers College Press.

———. (1999). *Power, meaning, and identity: Essays in critical educational studies.* New York: Peter Lang.

———. (2001). *Educating the "right" way: Markets, standards, God, and inequality.* New York & London: Routledge/Falmer.

Berlowitz, M. (1977). [Review of the book *Schooling in capitalist America: Educational reform and the contradictions of everyday life.*] *Urban Education*, 12(1), 103–108.

Berlowitz, M.J. & Chapman, F.E. (1978). Introduction: Fourth Midwest Marxist Scholars Conference. In M.J. Berlowitz & F.E. Chapman (Eds.), *The United States educational system: Marxist approaches* (pp. ix–xvi). Minneapolis: Marxist Educational Press.

Biesta, B.J.J. (1998). Say you want a revolution....Suggestions for the impossible future of critical pedagogy. *Educational Theory*, 48(4), 499–510.

Boggs, C. (1995). *The socialist tradition: From crises to decline.* New York & London: Routledge.

Bowles, S. & Gintis, H. (1976). *Schooling in capitalist America: Educational reform and the contradictions of economic life.* New York: Basic Books.

Brenner, R. (1998). The economics of global turbulence. *New Left Review*, 227, 1–264.

Britain, C.P. (1998). Capitalist crises & global slump. *Political Affairs*, 77(11), 16–25.

Brosio, R.A. (1990). Teaching and learning for democratic empowerment: A critical evaluation. *Educational Theory*, 40(1), 69–81.

———. (2000). *Philosophical scaffolding for the construction of critical democratic education.* New York: Peter Lang.

Cole, M. (Ed.). (1988). *Bowles and Gintis revisited: Correspondence and contradiction in educational theory.* London: The Falmer Press.

Cole, M. & Hill, D. (1995). Games of despair and rhetorics of resistance: Postmodernism, education and reaction. *British Journal of Sociology of Education*, 16(2), 165–182.

———. (1996). Postmodernism, education and contemporary capitalism: A materialist critique. In M.O. Valente, A. Barrios, A. Gaspar & V.D. Theodoro (Eds.), *Teacher training and values education* (pp. 27–68). Lisbon: Departmento de Educacao da Faculdade de Ciencias da Universidade de Lisboa.

Cole, M., Hill, D. & Rikowski, G. (1997). Between postmodernism and nowhere: The predicament of the postmodernist. *British Journal of Educational Studies*, 45(2), 187–200.

Corrigan, P. (1979). *Schooling the smash street kids.* London: Macmillan.

Croteau, D. (1995). *Politics and the class divide: Working people and the middle-class Left.* Philadelphia: Temple University Press.

Everhart, R. (1983). *Reading, writing, and resistance: Adolescence and labor in a junior high school.* Boston: Routledge & Kegan Paul.

Föner, S.P. (1978). The role of labor in the struggle for free compulsory education. In M.J. Berlowitz & F.E. Chapman (Eds.), *The United States educational system: Marxist approaches* (pp. 93–104). Minneapolis: Marxist Educational Press.

Giroux, H.A. (1981). *Ideology, culture, and the process of schooling.* Philadelphia: Temple University Press.

———. (1983). *Theory and resistance in education: A pedagogy for the opposition.* South Hadley, MA: Bergin & Garvey.

——— . (1991). Modernism, postmodernism, and feminism: Rethinking the boundaries of educational discourse. In H.A. Giroux (Ed.), *Postmodernism, feminism, and cultural politics* (pp. 1–59). Albany: State University of New York Press.

——— . (1992). *Border crossings: Cultural workers and the politics of education.* New York & London: Routledge.

Gonzalez, G.G. (1982). *Progressive education: A Marxist interpretation.* Minneapolis: Marxist Educational Press.

Gur-Ze'ev, I. (1998). Toward a nonrepressive critical pedagogy. *Educational Theory*, 48(4), 463–486.

Harris, K. (1982). *Teachers and classes: A Marxist analysis.* London: Routledge & Kegan Paul.

Hill, D. & Cole, M. (1995). Marxist state theory and state autonomy theory: The case of "race" education in initial teacher education. *Journal of Education Policy*, 10(2), 221–232.

Holloway, J. (2001). Why read Capital? *Capital & Class*, 75, 65–69.

Karabel, J. & Halsey, A.H. (Eds). (1977). *Power and ideology in education.* New York: Oxford University Press.

Kuhn, T. (1962). *The structure of scientific revolutions.* Chicago: University of Chicago Press.

Laclau, E. & Mouffe, C. (1985). *Hegemony and socialist strategy: Toward a radical democratic politics.* London & New York: Verso.

Lather, P. (1998). Critical pedagogy and its complicities: A praxis of stuck places. *Educational Theory*, 48(4), 487–498.

Liston, K.P. (1988). *Capitalist schools. Explanation and ethics in radical studies of schooling.* New York: Routledge & Kegan Paul.

Marx, K. & Engels, F. (1969). *Selected works*, Vol. 1. Moscow: Progress.

McDonald, P. (1988). Historical school reform and the correspondence principle. In M. Cole (Ed.), *Bowles and Gintis revisited: Correspondence and contradiction in educational theory* (pp. 86–111). London: The Falmer Press.

McLaren, P. (1980). *Cries from the corridor: The new suburban ghettos.* Toronto: Methuen Publications.

——— . (1986). *Schooling as a ritual performance. Toward a political economy of educational symbols and gestures.* London & New York: Routledge.

——— . (1989). *Life in schools: An introduction to critical pedagogy in the foundations of education.* New York: Longman.

———. (1995). *Critical pedagogy and predatory culture: Oppositional politics in a postmodern era.* London and New York: Routledge.

———. (1997). *Revolutionary multiculturalism: Pedagogies of dissent for the new millennium.* Boulder, CO: Westview Press.

———. (1998). Revolutionary pedagogy in post-revolutionary times: Rethinking the political economy of critical education. *Educational Theory*, 48(4), 431–462.

———. (2000). *Ché Guevara, Paulo Freire, and the pedagogy of revolution.* Lanham, MD: Rowman & Littlefield.

McLaren, P. & Farahmandpur, R. (1999). Critical pedagogy, postmodernism, and the retreat from class: Toward a contraband pedagogy. *Theoria*, 93, 83–115.

———. (2000). Reconsidering Marx in post-Marxist times: A requiem for postmodernism? *Educational Researcher*, 29(3), 25–33.

———. (2001a). Class, cultism, and multiculturalism: A notebook on forging a revolutionary multiculturalism. *Multicultural Education*, 8(3), 2–14.

———. (2001b). Teaching against globalization and the new imperialism: Toward a revolutionary pedagogy. *Journal of Teacher Education*, 52(2), 136–150.

———. (2001c). Educational policy and the socialist imagination: Revolutionary citizenship as a pedagogy of resistance. *Educational Policy*, 15(3), 343–378.

Molyneux, J. (1995). Is Marxism deterministic? *International Socialism*, 68, 36–73.

Price. B.F. (1986). *Marxism and education in late capitalism.* London & Sydney: Croom Helm.

Raduntz, H. (1999). A Marxian critique of teachers' work in an era of capitalist globalization. A paper presented at the AARE-NZARE Conference. Melbourne, Victoria, November–December, 1999.

Rikowski, G. (1996). Left alone: End time for Marxist educational theory? *British Journal of Sociology of Education*, 17(4), 415–451.

———. (1997). Scorched earth: Prelude to rebuilding Marxist educational theory. *British Journal of Sociology of Education*, 18(4), 551–574.

———. (2001). *The battle in Seattle.* London: Tuffnell Press.

Sarup, M. (1978). *Marxism and education.* London: Routledge & Kegan Paul.

Sarup, R. (1983). *Marxism/structuralism/education: Theoretical developments in the sociology of education.* London & New York: The Falmer Press.

Sharp, R. (1980). *Knowledge, ideology and the politics of schooling.* London: Routledge & Kegan Paul.

———. (1988). Old and new orthodoxies: The seductions of liberalism. In M. Cole (Ed.), *Bowles and Gintis revisited: Correspondence and contradiction in educational theory* (pp. 189–208). London: The Falmer Press.

Smith, C. (1996). *Marx at the millennium.* London & Chicago: Pluto Press.

Sokal, A. & Brichmont, J. (1998). *Fashionable nonsense: Postmodern intellectuals' abuse of science.* New York: Picador.

Strike, K. (1989). *Liberal justice and the Marxist critique of education.* New York: Routledge & Kegan Paul.

Willis, P. (1977). *Learning to labor.* Farnborough, England: Saxon House.

Youngman, F. (1986). *Adult education and socialist pedagogy.* London: Croom Helm.

Chapter 9

Critical Education for Economic and Social Justice: A Marxist Analysis and Manifesto

Dave Hill

In this chapter I set out a series of progressive egalitarian policy principles and proposals that constitute a democratic Marxist manifesto for schooling and teacher education for economic and social justice. This is based on a democratic Marxist theoretical framework[1] and on a structuralist neo-Marxist analysis.[2]

I recognize the structural limitations on progressive and socialist action through the ideological and repressive apparatuses of the state acting on behalf of capital. However, this chapter calls for transformative change throughout teacher education, throughout schooling and education, by other cultural workers within the ideological state apparatuses of education and the media and throughout the wider social context. In this chapter, I suggest a series of specified principles and a program for critical and socialist educators through which to engage the Radical Right. In the chapter, I examine the Radical Right in both its Conservative and in its revised social democratic ("Third Way"; in the UK, "New Labour," in the USA, "Clintonite") manifestations.

Prologue: Peter McLaren's Influence on My Thought

In my writing I have been influenced by the developing Marxist critique of Peter McLaren. This has taken place in four phases. The first phase, 1989 to 1991, was after I ceased to be an elected Labour Party representative and regional labor union official. (This was because of a deterioration in my hearing; I am now partially hearing disabled.) I was coming out of a twenty-five-year period as a local labor union leader and local leader of the Labour Party.[3] I spent much of the late 1960s/1970s/1980s as a street/strike activist within teacher and other trade unions. I had been, for a time, a construction worker, like the rest of the men in my family. In fact, I worked part-time with my brothers and my dad on various building/construction sites till I was in my thirties (very different social relationships, work regimes, and cultural capitals compared to my teaching and lecturing jobs!). I was also active in the local Labour Party in Brighton. In the 1980s in the UK, the Labour Party still had a very strong socialist current.[4] The late 1970s and the 1980s had also been, for me, a period of organizational and street activism, within the anti-racist Anti-Nazi League and on the picket lines of various labour unions on strike. But I lost too much of my hearing to be able to continue in the Council chambers.

So I decided to pursue socialist/Radical Left ideals and activism through my teaching and writing. This included not only writing but co-writing, collaborative writing, setting up (with Mike Cole) the Hillcole Group of Radical Left Educators in the UK[5] and founding the independent Institute for Education Policy Studies.[6] I also decided to do a PhD, a Marxist analysis of the restructuring of teacher education and schooling in England and Wales.

In 1989, looking for stimulus, I did a tour of Radical Leftist educators in the United States and Britain: Mike Apple, Henry Giroux, Peter McLaren, Christine Sleeter and Susan Melnick. All of them very kindly hosted me, partly, I guess, because I was, as a Radical Left activist, relatively untutored in terms of academic writing. Until then, my reading, from my first days as a teacher activist in inner-city London, had consisted mainly of daily, weekly and monthly left-socialist, Marxist, Trotskyite publications, as well as policy publications from the Labour Party through the 1970s and 1980s. I had only just started reading Mike Apple, Geoff Whitty, Peter McLaren, Henry Giroux and Madan Sarup.

By 1989 I was just starting to publish. My first academic piece of polemicized Marxist analysis was *Charge of the Right Brigade: The Radical Right's Assault on Teacher Education & Training* (1989). Prior to that my writing had been short pieces in Left political magazines and newspapers in Britain such as *Labour Weekly, New Socialist, Tribune* and local publications such as *Brighton Labour Briefing*, and in writing pamphlets/booklets against the Conservative cuts, for example, for the Socialist Educational Association.

The U.S. academics hosted me during my search for a PhD supervisor who would be simpatico to my beliefs and analysis. (In the end, I chose a UK-based supervisor, Geoff Whitty, now Director of the London University Institute of

Education, and incidentally a Director with the courage to openly contribute to socialist debate.)

On my tour, I stayed with Peter and Jenny McLaren for around a week, sleeping in their study in Oxford, Ohio, while Peter was working at the University of Miami. (Fifteen years later, in 2004, I was to reprise this, sleeping in his study in his Hollywood home for a few days.) I had contacted him on the basis of reading his *Life in Schools* (1989) and on the basis of his work on critical pedagogy and teachers as critical transformative intellectuals with Henry Giroux (Giroux & McLaren, 1986, 1989). Their writing, individual and joint, blew my mind with its power, vibrancy and hope. As a street and union activist during the mid- and late 1980s, I was then becoming dispirited by the then-current pessimism and determinism of Marxist reproduction theorists within lecture halls and within the Academy. So the utopianism and hope and vigor excited and emboldened my own theoretical and political-educational struggles, especially since the passion and vision were grounded, as in Peter's *Cries from the Corridor* (1980) and then, in the theorized version published as *Life in Schools* (1989), in the sort of teaching and learning I recognized from my own family upbringing and from my own schoolteaching in Brixton, London. That's why I got in touch with him. (Now, though, I express the need for caution about the facility of socialist transformation through education. I adopt a more materialist perspective than that deriving from a neo-Gramscian dominant ideology perspective (see note 2, while still seeing the need for dreams and utopias, and the need to analyze and organize to work towards and achieve those utopias).

The second phase of our relationship was during the mid-1990s. This was when Mike Cole, Glenn Rikowski and I criticized Peter's (and Henry Giroux's) "resistance postmodernism" as non-Marxist. Our critique was, and remains, that ultimately—even if "resistance postmodernism" had progressive moments and intentions—in effect it plays into the hands of reactionary neo-liberalism.[7] Occasionally, Peter and I and Mike Cole met up at various international conferences. These meetings were fruitful, fun and stimulating exchanges, giving us, on all sides, lots to consider.

The third phase was in the late 1990s. Peter, Glenn Rikowski, Mike Cole and I corresponded, co-wrote and co-edited, commenting on each other's work. In particular, Glenn and Peter had been having a number of e-interchanges, for example in the web pages of *The Commoner* and *Hobgoblin*, the journal of Marxist-Humanists. Some of these e-interchanges are reproduced on the website of the Institute of Education Policy Studies: www.ieps.org.uk.

Together, the four of us wrote *Red Chalk: On Schooling, Capitalism and Politics* (Cole et al., 2001). This developed out of an interview Peter did with the three of us British Marxists (McLaren, Cole, Hill & Rikowski, 2001) in his regular interview column in the *International Journal of Education Reform.* We also co-wrote and co-edited *Postmodernism in Educational Theory: Education and the Politics of Human Resistance* (Hill et al., 1999), a Marxist critique of postmodernism and neo-liberalism published in the UK, and the heavily revised version, *Marxism Against Postmodernism in Educational Theory* (Hill et al., 2002), published in the United States.

The current, fourth phase of the relationship between us and Peter is his work, sometimes in collaboration with Ramin Farahmandpur and Glenn Rikowski (and with many others more recently such as Gregory Martin, Nathalia Jaramillo, Noah de Lissavoy, Valerie Scatamburlo d'Anibale and Jill Pinkney-Pastrana) on the centrality of social class analysis and on revolutionary pedagogy, "a rematerialized critical pedagogy" (McLaren, 2001, p. 27). This places his work even more within the Marxist-humanist theoretical tradition. This moves his theoretical understanding from critical pedagogy to what he terms "revolutionary pedagogy" and is part of his developing a Marxist analysis and program of resistance to and replacement of neo-liberal globalizing capital. This is exciting stuff—developmental and powerful.[8]

Throughout these four phases, Peter has consistently shown kindness, humor, erudition, anger and commitment to economic and social justice and equality. Sometimes, "things ain't easy" for socialist and Marxist educators and activists. Peter has made it easier, and more comradely. And for a political and theoretical minority, sometimes subject to political discrimination, opprobrium and dismissals, that community of theoretical and emotional support and stimulus has been welcome and necessary.[9] Being a Radical Left/Marxist educator who speaks out can be lonely, if exhilarating. Within the UK the Hillcole Group of Radical Left Educators—comprising twenty or so socialist/Marxist writers from different universities, colleges and schools, co-writing booklets and books[10]—has performed that supportive, nurturing, critical environment. The Hillcole Group was particularly active in the first ten years after Mike Cole and I set it up in 1989. Glenn and Peter in particular in the 1990s have involved international progressive/Marxist/socialist co-thinkers and activists in our thinking such as Helen Raduntz, Shahrzad Mojab, Ramin Farahmandpur, Brian Donovan, Grant Banfield, Helen Colley and Kevin Harris.

In more recent years, working with Peter and his compañeras/compañeros, with the independent Radical Left policy unit of the Institute for Education

Policy Studies,www.ieps.org.uk, and, in particular since it was set up in 2003, with the Journal for Critical Education Studies www.jceps.com, this international co-operation/learning/stimulus/solidarity/corresponding/commenting have extended that supportive critical community. The JCEPS (co-edited by me, Peter and by Pablo Gentili of the Universidade do Estado de Rio de Janeiro), in particular allows us to share experiences, analyses, perspectives and programs with Latin American and North American cameradas/camerados and more widely. The Editorial Advisory Board is incredible! Great comradeship there.

And for my part, I am now involved with both the MarxSIG of AERA, and with the USA based Rouge Forum group, involving E Wayne Ross, Rich Gibson, Sandra Mathison, Richard Brosio among many others. Most recently, the meeting up of just about all of the contributors to this book at AERA 2004, and with Pauline Lipman, and with those involved in the journal Curriculo sem Fronteiras, such as Luis Armando Gandin, has added a much needed global/comparative sharing/informing/critiquing/developing dimension to the necessary tasks of analyzing and critiquing capital and neoliberalism, neo-conservatism, and the necessary development of a true democratic Radical Left/socialist/Marxist organization, programmes and activism. And it's added comradeship. We need that!

Part One: The Restructuring of Teacher Education

Critical Teacher Education

On the relation between radical egalitarian teacher education and securing economic and social justice in society, Allman (2000) suggests that:

> Education has the potential to fuel the flames of resistance to global capitalism as well as the passion for socialist transformation—indeed, the potential to provide a spark that can ignite the desire for revolutionary democratic social transformation throughout the world. To carry the metaphor even further, it does so at a time when critical/radical education, almost everywhere, is in danger of terminal "burn-out." (p. 10)

How far can this transformative potential be realized? The autonomy and agency available to individual teachers, teacher educators, schools and departments of education is particularly challenged when faced with the structures of capital and its current neo-liberal project for education (Cole, 2004b, 2004c,

2005; Hill, 2001a, 2003, 2004b,c,d,e,f). Caution is necessary when considering the degree of autonomy of educators (and, indeed, other cultural workers such as journalists and filmmakers) who fuel the flames of resistance.

But identifying particular characteristics of these structures is to identify a starting point for transformative action. As noted elsewhere,[11] the neo-liberal project for education is part of the bigger picture of the neo-liberal project for global capitalism.[12] Markets in education worldwide, and so-called "parental choice" of a diverse range of schools, are only one small part of the education strategy of the capitalist class, with its business plan *for* education (what it requires education to do) and its business plan *in* education (how it plans to make money from education).[13]

The bigger picture, globally and nationally, enables an overall understanding of how the move toward markets in education relates to the overall intentions and project of transnational multinational capital, and to the policies that governments try to put into practice on their behalf. It shows schools continuing their role, inter alia, as a disciplinary force of the capitalist class. For McLaren (2000), "the major purpose of education is to make the world safe for global capitalism" (p. 196), and:

> What teachers are witnessing at the end of the century is the consolidation of control over the process of schooling and particularly over the certification of teachers in order to realign education to the need of the globalized economy. (McLaren & Baltodano, 2000, p. 35)

This has rendered the social democratic (and the sometimes contradictory liberal-progressive) content and objectives of schooling and initial teacher education in England and Wales, for example, almost unrecognizable, compared with the 1960s and 1970s. Then there was, in many institutions, a real commitment, examining issues of equality and the social and political (if not economic) contexts of education policy.

Detheorized Teacher Education in the UK under the Conservatives and New Labour

One key characteristic of this restructuring is the detheorization of initial teacher education (ITE). Under Conservative and New Labour governments, issues of equity and social justice, let alone economic justice, have been virtually extinguished from the ITE curriculum. Study of the social, political and economic contexts of schooling and education has been similarly hidden and expunged. In England and Wales, and elsewhere, ITE is now rigorously examined and policed. Since the Conservative government introduced new regulations for teacher training and education in 1992/1993 (DFE, 1992, 1993), "how to" has replaced "why to" in a technicist curriculum based on "delivery" of a quietist and overwhelmingly conservative set of "standards" for student teachers.[14] This has impacted on the teaching force, and hence on schooling. Teachers are now by and large trained in skills rather than educated to examine the "whys" and the "why nots" and the contexts of curriculum, pedagogy, educational purposes and structures and the effects these have on reproducing capitalist economy, society and politics.

New Labour has, for example, through its regulations of 1998 (DfEE, 1998), accepted to an overwhelming extent the Radical Right revolution in ITE, as it has in schooling. The Conservative legacy has scarcely been amended in terms of routes into teaching, the changing nature of teachers' work and curriculum and assessment (Hill, 1999a, 2000, 2001c, 2005a, b). Indeed, the National Literacy Strategy for schools, which dominates student teacher preparation for teaching English, has further decontextualized and straitjacketed the teaching of reading (Robertson, 2000; Robertson & Hill, 2001). For millions of working-class children in particular, education has become uncritical, basic-skills training.

When placed in the context of what could have been done to promote critical reflection and a more egalitarian curriculum for ITE, New Labour changes since 1997 are very modest. Conservative government policy on ITE has been sustained almost in toto, based as they are on a neo-conservative cultural nationalism and authoritarianism and a neo-liberal competitive, individualist antiegalitarianism.

Education policy effecting this detheorization of teacher education is an aspect symptom of the project of capital, which requires the suppression of oppositional, critical and autonomous thought. As McMurtry (1991) has noted, this requirement is particularly inappropriate for education, leading to "opposite standards of freedom," since:

> Freedom in the market is the enjoyment of whatever one is able to buy from others with no questions asked, and profit from whatever one is able to sell to others with no requirement to answer to anyone else. Freedom in the place of education, on the other

hand, is precisely the freedom to question, and to seek answers, whether it offends people's self-gratification or not. (p. 213)[15]

This occurs with the "systematic reduction of the historically hard won social institution of education to a commodity for private purchase and sale" (1991, p. 216), where the "commodification of education rules out the very critical freedom and academic rigor which education requires to be more than indoctrination" (1991, p. 215). Rikowski makes the significant link from the large-scale movement to local self-awareness:

> Capitalist social relations, and capital, as a social force, have *deepened* since Marx's time. Today: *the class struggle is everywhere*...capital is everywhere—including within "the human" itself. Scary stuff! Education is implicated in the capitalization of humanity—and we have to face up to this. (Cole, Hill, McLaren & Rikowski, 2001, p. 20; see also Rikowski, 2001c, 2001d)

Part Two: Radical Left Principles for Education and for ITE

The Radical Left and Education

In the face of this Conservative and New Labour restructuring of ITE in England and Wales, Marxist, socialist and Radical Left teacher educators share principles and policies for counter-hegemonic theory and practice in teacher education. I now proceed to define a set of Radical Left principles for re-theorized egalitarian education as a whole in Table 1, then in Table 2, 4 and 5 a set of principles and proposals for the ITE curriculum.

There is some debate within the Radical Left over the specific policies suggested, notably over questions of the degree of student-based pedagogy and course development. The following four principles for education as a whole are, however, widely accepted by the Radical Left.

Table 1: List of Four Overarching Radical Left Principles for Education

---

- Vastly increased equality (of outcome).
- Comprehensive provision (i.e., no private or selective provision of schooling).
- Democratic community control over education.

- Use of the local and national state to achieve a socially just (defined as egalitarian), anti-discriminatory society, rather than simply an inegalitarian meritocratic focus on equal opportunities to get to very unequal outcomes.

These four overarching Radical Left principles for education as a whole are expressed through the following fourteen principles:[16]

Table 2: Radical Left Principles for Education

---

1. More resources and funding for education (e.g., through higher rate of tax on profits and on the rich, and by spending less on defense) resulting, for example, in smaller class sizes.
2. An end to selection in schooling and the development of fully comprehensive schooling and further and higher education system, i.e., a change in the structures of schooling and education.
3. An end to the competitive market in schooling.
4. Commitment to egalitarian policies aimed at achieving vastly more equal outcomes regardless of factors such as social class, gender, "race," sexuality or disability and the egalitarian redistribution of resources within and between schools, by way of positive discrimination for under-achieving individuals and groups.
5. A curriculum that seeks to transform present capitalist society into a democratic socialist one.
6. Opposition to some key aspects of liberal-progressive education, such as non-structured learning and minimal assessment of pupils/school students and reliance on the Piagetian concept of "readiness."
7. An egalitarian and anti-elitist common curriculum.
8. An egalitarian and anti-elitist informal (hidden) curriculum.
9. The teacher as authoritative, democratic and anti-authoritarian, engaging in critical pedagogy, with a commitment to developing critically reflective political activists committed to struggling for economic and social justice and equality inside and outside the classroom.
10. Increasing local community democratic accountability in schooling and further and higher education (e.g., local education authority/school district powers) and decreasing those of "business," capital and private enterprise.
11. Local community involvement in the schools and colleges.
12. Increasing the powers of democratically elected and accountable Local Government (Local Education Authorities/school districts) with powers to redistribute resources, control quality, and to engage, *inter alia*, in the development and dissemination of policies for equality (e.g., anti-racist, anti-sexist, anti-homophobic

policies and policies seeking to promote more equal outcomes for the working class and the disabled).

13. A schooling system, the aim of which is the flourishing of the collective society, the community, as well as the flourishing of the individual.
14. Fostering cultures within the classroom and within school and further education/higher education workplaces that are democratic, egalitarian, collaborative and collegiate (i.e., replacing what is sometimes a brutalist, managerialist culture with a more open and democratic one).

Probably the most complete expression of radical Left education policy-principles and detailed legislative proposals for education as a whole—its organization, principles, content—are the two Hillcole Group books: *Changing the Future: Redprint for Education* (1991) and *Rethinking Education and Democracy: A Socialist Alternative for the Twenty-first Century* (1997).

Below, I set out two more recent and brief examples of Radical Left education programs deriving from socialist and Marxist principles, and in opposition to Conservative and New Labour policy and principles in education. The first is the Socialist Party's (formerly "Militant") statement and manifesto for the local elections in England and Wales of June 2004. It is as follows:

> No Privatisation! No Cuts! Vote for A Socialist Alternative! Privatisation is becoming the norm in Britain's schools. New Labour's latest "new" idea is for City Academies. These schools are private companies, which only have to raise £2 million sponsorship, and then receive 100% state funding! At the same time we are witnessing the abolition of comprehensive education and the wholesale reintroduction of selective schools. Comprehensive education, based on the development of all-round skills, was an attempt to partially overcome the greed and anarchy of the market which, of course, favours the children of the rich. Despite the limitations of the comprehensive system, its abolition will be a severe step backwards.
>
> The Socialist Party stands for: (1) free, high quality education for all, from nursery to university; (2) a massive increase in public spending to provide the increased staffing, smaller class sizes, good quality resources needed to ensure the best education and individual support for every child; (3) all schools being brought under local democratic control; and, (4) a democratically planned equitable admissions policy based on genuinely comprehensive, coeducational, neighbourhood schools. (The Socialist, 2004)

As a second example, the (Marxist) Socialist Alliance education policy, contained in its manifesto for the 2001 British general election was presented as follows.

Table 3: Socialist Alliance Education Manifesto, 2001 (UK General Election)

- Improve pay and conditions for teachers and other education workers;
- Stop and reverse Private Finance Initiative and Public-Private Partnership schemes in education;
- Abolish Education Action Zones;
- There should be a comprehensive review of the national curriculum, to involve (among others) teaching unions and experts chosen by them;
- Abolish league tables and the current testing system;
- End charitable status and tax privileges for Eton, Harrow and other private schools;
- Abolish private education;
- Since the Tories destroyed the school meals service, a million children living in poverty do not have access to a free school meal—for many the main meal of the day. We say all children should have free nutritional breakfast and lunch at school;
- For free after-school clubs and play centers for all that need them;
- Ensure provision of a full range of arts, sports and sex education in all schools;
- Of course, education is not just about children. Young people and adults at colleges and universities—and the staff who work in them—have also suffered under both the Tories and Labour, which imposed tuition fees and ended free higher education. We say abolish tuition fees and student loans. We call for free education and a living grant for all further and higher education students, funded from taxation on the high-paid and on big business, which wants skilled workers but is getting them on the cheap;
- People of all ages should be entitled to free education and training facilities; and,
- For the return to local democratic control of education at all levels, to include representatives of education workers, students and the wider community (Socialist Alliance, 2001, p. 9)

Radical Left Principles for Initial Teacher Education

The similarity between the Radical Right and New Labour in the UK is remarkable.[17] The lack of congruence between the Radical Left and the Radical Right/New Labour axis is less remarkable, since both the Radical Right Conservative and New Labour have identified themselves substantially in terms of their anti-socialism.[18]

Now I want to detail principles for economic and social justice within teacher education. These, I suggest, should form the basis of the review and development of current policy, theory and—not least—practice in initial teacher education. In the table below, I set out those principles, together with New Labour, social democratic (e.g., much of "Old Labour"—the Labour Party prior to Tony Blair's assumption of leadership in 1994) and Radical Right positions on these principles.

Table 4: Fifteen Radical Left Principles for the Initial Teacher Education Curriculum

	Radical Left	New Labour	Social Democratic	Radical Right
(1) the development of classroom skills and competencies	√√	√√	√√	√√
(2) the development of subject knowledge	√√	√√	√√	√√
(3) the development of intellectual critical skills	√√	√√	√	XX
(4) commitment to ethical/moral "critical reflection" and its egalitarianism	√√	XX	√	XX
(5) inclusion of data on equality issues organized both as core units and as permeation	√√	XX	√	XX
(6) a holistic approach to economic and social justice in the curriculum	√√	XX	X	XX
(7) skills in dealing with discrimination, harassment and labeling within classrooms and institutions	√√	√?	√	XX
(8) the development within institutions of open fora on social justice and equality, where students and staff in institutions can meet in a supportive environment	√√	XX?	√?	XX

(9) development of critiques of competing social and economic theories and ideologies in schooling and society	√√	XX	?	XX
(10) development of knowledge and skills to examine critically the ideological nature of teaching and the nature of teachers' work	√√	XX	?	XX
(11) knowledge and skills to critically examine the ideological nature and effects of education policy and its relationship to broader economic, social and political developments	√√	XX	?	XX
(12) the concurrent development of critical reflection, throughout and from the beginning of the ITE course	√√	XX	?	XX
(13) primarily, but not totally predetermined rather than primarily negotiated, curriculum objectives	√√	XX	?	√
(14) support for a major role for higher education institutions in ITE. Opposition to totally/primarily school-based routes	√√	√X	√√	XX
(15) acceptance of different routes into teaching concordant with graduate teacher status and the above principles	√√	XX	?	XX

Key

√√	strong agreement
√	agreement
X	disagreement
XX	strong disagreement
?	not clear/arguably so
??	not at all clear/very arguably so

Radical Left Proposals for a Core Curriculum for ITE

These proposals do more than return to the status quo ante the Thatcherite election victory of 1979, or Labour Prime Minister James Callaghan Ruskin's speech of 1976 that presaged the end of both liberal-progressive and social democratic ends in teacher education and schooling. Instead, the proposals below pursue the four overarching principles for education as a whole by requiring a core curriculum for teacher education.

Table 5: List of Radical Left Proposals for the ITE Core Curriculum

- Include macro- and micro-theory regarding teaching and learning, in which the sociopolitical and economic contexts of schooling and education are made explicit. This refers not only to classroom skills and competencies, but also to the theoretical understanding of children, schooling and society, their interrelationships and alternative views and methods of, for example, classroom organization, schooling and the economic and political relationship to society.
- Embrace and develop equal opportunities so that children do not suffer from labeling, underexpectation, stereotyping or prejudice from their teachers, or indeed, from their peers.
- Enable student teachers to develop as critical, reflective teachers; to be able, for example, to decode media, ministerial (and indeed Radical Left) distortion, bias and propaganda on falling standards in schools and institutions of teacher education. This encourages the development of effective classroom-skilled teachers, able to interrelate and critique theory and practice (their own and that of others).
- Include not only technical and situational reflection, but also critical reflection, so as to question a particular policy, a particular theory, or a particular level of reflection, or such critical questions as: Whose interests are served? Who wins? (If only by legitimating the status quo.) Who loses? (Who has to deny identity in order to join the winners, if this is at all possible?) Who is likely to have to continue accepting a subordinate and exploited position in society (by virtue of their membership in oppressed groups)?

Of the following fifteen more detailed proposals, nos. 1-3 are common across different ideological positions, and because of their near-universality in Britain, I do not develop them here. Nos. 4 and 5 are also widely shared, although they assume different degrees of salience within different rhetorics. The final ten propositions—nos. 6-15—are more specifically Radical Left.

The ITE curriculum should include:

1. *Classroom skills and competencies.* In addition to a deep knowledge of core subjects, student teachers need to develop reflective skills on pupil/student learning and on teaching and classroom management and on stimulating all the children in their classes to learn. They also need to develop skills in monitoring standards and demanding/facilitating the best from all their pupils/students (as set out in current TTA circulars).

   Considerable attention must be paid to student teacher, newly qualified teacher (NQT), Headteacher and HMI/Ofsted evaluation of the adequacy of the various aspects of the ITE curriculum. While these student teacher and NQT data refer to courses validated under and designed to meet the 1989 government criteria for teacher education courses, more permissive than the current criteria, there are serious problems registered through levels of dissatisfaction with the preparation of students for such aspects of diversity as teaching children with special educational needs likely to be met in ordinary schools (Blake and Hill, 1995). More recent data shows a general dissatisfaction with teaching working class and ethnically diverse/ minority ethnic group students (Hill, 2005a).

2. *Subject knowledge.* Clearly, teachers need to know what they are talking about and what they wish students/pupils to learn.

3. *The development of higher education-level analytical and intellectual skills.* This demands that teachers are capable of acting and thinking at graduate level.

4. *Support for a major role for higher education institutions in ITE and opposition to totally/primarily school-based routes.* Higher education institutions are better able to develop the theoretical perspectives outlined above, to enable student teachers to interrelate theory and practice so that they inform each other.

5. *Welcoming of different routes into teaching concordant with graduate teacher status and the above principles.* As long as the above principles are upheld—including the requirement of graduate status for teachers—then there is room for a variety of routes into teaching. The routes into teaching are tactical matters, subject to these principled considerations.

6. *A commitment to the development of the ethic/moral dimension of critical reflection and the Radical Left egalitarian concern with working for economic and social justice and recognition of the interconnection between the two.* If equal opportunity policies stop at celebrating subcultural diversity and establishing positive and nonstereotypical role models, and do not see themselves as a development of a metanarrative of social egalitarianism and justice, then they can be viewed as, in essence, conservative, for failing to challenge the economic, political and social status quo, based as it is on social class, "racial" and sexual and disability stratifications and exploitation. Hence, a Radical Left perspective calls for teacher education (and schooling) to be socially egalitarian, anti-racist and anti-sexist, and also to challenge other forms of structural inequality and discrimination, such as those based on sexuality and disability.[19] It also highlights the partial and therefore illusory nature of economic and social justice within the anti-egalitarian capitalist economic system. Economic justice, of course, is scarcely referred to within capitalist systems, it being one of the desiderata and a sine qua non of capitalism.

7. *Data on equality issues: on racism, sexism, social class inequality, homophobia and discrimination/prejudice regarding disability and special needs.* Many teachers and ITE students are simply not aware of the existence of such data in education and society or the impact of individual labeling, and of structural discriminations on the lives and education and life-opportunities of the children in their classes, schools and society. This is particularly true of teachers trained/educated under the Conservative Party regulations of 1992 and 1993 and also (to an extent only slightly diminished) by the current New Labour regulations.

   Core units/modules on equality and equal opportunities are required.[20] Weaknesses of the permeation model limit effectiveness and, as Gaine (1995) notes, such issues must be put firmly on the agenda, not just slipped into myriad spaces within other sessions. Equality and equal opportunities need to be dealt with holistically in two senses. First, they must be approached conceptually, as part of an holistic and egalitarian program interlinking different forms of oppression; and second, organizationally, as part of teacher education/training courses with units of study focusing on data, theory and policy in general. As Kincheloe et al. (2000) note, radical teachers move beyond white, Anglo-Saxon, middle-class and heterosexual educational norms and explore the subjugated knowledges of women, minority groups and indigenous groups.

8. *An holistic and social class-based approach to social and economic justice in the curriculum.* "Race," gender, social class, sexuality and disability and special needs should be considered as part of an overall understanding of economic and social justice within teacher education courses. Inequalities in practice can be multi-dimensional, and their effects impact one upon the other. The desirability of maintaining their separateness needs to be questioned. However, this is not to ignore the fact that inequalities and forms of oppression can clearly be unidimensional—as, for example, with what was termed in the 1980s in particular, "gay-bashing" or "Paki-bashing." While this terminology is no longer so widely used, it is clear that people can and are attacked, and killed, because of one of their presenting characteristics such as women in sex crimes, and gays and minority ethnic groups in other "hate-crimes."

   However, links should be drawn between, for example, anti-racism and anti-working-class discrimination, so that anti-racism and multiculturalism can lead to, and be informed by, "anti-classism" and anti-sexism. Many teachers can, and more could, substitute the word and concept "class" (or "sex") for "race" in checklists for stereotyping, in policies concerning equal opportunities, appointments policies, classroom-activity choices or subject-option choices/routes in secondary schools. At the classroom level, in an anti-racist checklist for stereotyping in books, the word/concept "race" can be replaced by "sex" or "class."

   Similarly, just as it is possible to look at the different amount of time and types of response given by teachers to boys and girls in the same class, the same observation techniques can be applied to "race," social class, disability and youth sexuality. This is not to declare, *ab initio*, that all children should receive equal amounts of teacher time. Equality of treatment ignores the greater resources required by children with greater needs. Equality of treatment is antithetical to policies of equal opportunities and to a policy for equality.

   Within this developing awareness of inequalities, the essentially and pre-eminently class-based nature of exploitation within the capitalist economic system and its educational, legal and other apparatuses needs to be understood. Social class is the salient form of structural oppression within capitalist society, as various chapters in this volume emphasizes. It is the inevitable and defining feature of capitalist exploitation, whereas the various other forms of oppression are not essential to its nature and continuation, however much they are commonly functional to this. Thus, within the ITE curriculum (and, indeed, where teachers can find spaces within the school, further education, adult education and prison education and other curricula), the existence of various and multiple forms of oppression and the similarity of their effects on individuals and communities should neither disguise nor weaken an analysis (and consequent political and social action) that recognizes the structural centrality of social class exploitation and conflict.[21]

As McLaren (2001) notes, "the key here is not to privilege class oppression over other forms of oppression, but to see how capitalist relations of production provide the ground from which other forms of oppression are produced" (p. 31). For example, referring to a rally supporting affirmative action, McLaren notes that:

> All the speakers decrying the repeal of affirmative action emphasized race but didn't mention social class. Most speakers structured their position from an anti-racist and anti-sexist perspective but failed to connect these to intrinsic features of capitalism.... [R]elations of class were displaced to questions of identity politics. A better analysis would have been to identify the crucial link between the ban on affirmative action and the current intensification of capitalist exploitation and attacks on the working class. (quoted in Rikowski & McLaren, 2001, p. 34)

McLaren and Farahmandpur note that "recognizing the 'class character' of education in capitalist schooling, and advocating a 'socialist re-organization of capitalist society'" are two fundamental principles of a revolutionary critical pedagogy (McLaren & Farahmandpur, 2001a, p. 299).

I am aware here of the different levels of truth (without lapsing into a disabling and uncritical modernist or postmodernist liberal ultra-pluralist relativism). As Allman (1999) notes, there are, first, meta-transhistorical truths. These "seem to hold across the entirety of human history" (p. 136) Second, there are transhistorical truths, which have held well to date but could possibly be invalidated in the future. Third, there are truths historically specific to a particular historical formation, such as capitalism. These were the sort of truths Marx was primarily interested in when analyzing capitalist society. Finally, there are conjuncturally specific truths—propositions that attain validity within specific developmental phases of a social formation, such as current data and specific issues, which are transient to a greater or lesser degree, even though the mode of their analysis may not be so. Clearly, a dialogical and dialectical relationship between critical educators and teachers would result in a degree of negotiated curriculum detail.

9. *Skills in dealing with the incidence of classist, homophobic, racist and sexist remarks and harassment at various levels, such as within the classroom and throughout the institution.* It is important here to address other types of harassment, such as labeling and bullying based on body shape, and their corrosive effects on children's learning, lives and happiness. (There is, however, a danger that generic anti-bullying policies can individualize the problem and deny any structural aspects such as racism, sexism, social class and sexuality.)

10. *The development within institutions of open fora on social justice where students and staff in institutions can meet in a supportive environment.* This is an additional form of learning, where individual self-development comes through sharing experience and ideas. Teachers contribute their knowledge not only by transmission (though this frequently might be part of a teacher's repertoire of teaching methods), but also through interlocution where individual contributions are valued and respected. The culture of such a forum can foster a climate where individual "voices," levels of consciousness and experiences are legitimated. Such "voices," however, should be subject to critical interrogation, not accepted uncritically.[22]

11. *Critiques of competing approaches and ideologies of schooling, teacher education and social and economic organization.* This should include skills to examine critically the nature of the curricula, hidden curricula and pedagogy, schooling, education and society. This enables student teachers to consider and challenge the ideologies that underpin the selection of knowledge that they are being asked to acquire and teach through the whole curriculum, as well as challenges the prioritized model of the teacher and critical mode of reflection. Ultimately, as McLaren and Baltodano (2000) observe, ITE courses should "locate the schooling process in both local and global socio-economic and political contexts, while exploring the relations between them" (p. 43).

    This should include a consideration of the different current major ideologies of education (socialism/Marxism, social democracy, liberal-progressivism, neo-conservatism, neo-liberalism, New Labourism, "Third Way" ideology and their policy expression). In relation to these it should also include understanding and evaluation of anti-racism as well as multiculturalism and assimilationism; Marxist analysis of social class and the concept of a classless society, as well as meritocratic social mobility or elitist stratification and reproduction; anti-sexism as well as non-sexism, and, indeed, sexism. In addition, different models of disability and gay/lesbian/bisexual issues should be addressed.[23]

12. *The development of knowledge and skills to examine critically the ideological nature of teaching and the nature of teachers' work.* Here, student teachers should develop an understanding of the potential role of teachers in transforming society. This is, as Harris (1994) suggests, so that while teachers retain some critical agency in the area of the transmission of knowledge:

> It remains possible for teachers to adopt the function of intellectuals…and…to resist becoming mere managers of day-to-day activities imposed from beyond the school, and to redefine their role within counter hegemonic practice. They can, through their discourse and interventionary practice in the ideological and political determinants of schooling, promote empowerment, autonomy and democracy. (p. 115)

13. *The concurrent rather than the consecutive development of critical reflection, throughout and from the beginning of the ITE course.* Teacher educators differ in their views of which levels, or "arenas" of reflection, make an appropriate starting point for reflection in the learning-to-teach process. Commentators as diverse as Calderhead and Gates (1993), and the British government's DFE *Circular 9/92* (DFE, 1992) all assume or argue that the three levels of reflection need to be developed in sequential order, i.e., that contextual-situational, and indeed critical reflection are more appropriate for teachers who have attained technical and practical skills and skills of reflection.

My own view is that a three- or four-year undergraduate teacher education course provides a sufficient period of time. Furthermore, with appropriate support (as set out in the next proposal) school-centered and school-based components of undergraduate student-teacher courses may well provide a more appropriate immersion into the practices of teaching, learning and schooling and facilitate, organize and encourage the application of theory to practice and practice to theory.

If "learning theory," "critical theory" or issues of the social context of schooling are left until "post-initial training," many Newly Qualified Teachers will not actually get any post-initial training other than "Baker days"—the school-based, in-service education for teachers (INSET). And the in-service training days appear to be overwhelmingly instrumental and technical—in particular, to be concerned with how to "deliver" and to assess the National Curriculum. If contextual, theoretical and social/economic justice and equality issues are not studied during Initial Teacher Education, they may never be.

There are different phases in the induction of beginning teachers. As Stronach and Maclure (1996) point out, beginning teachers go through a phase of being inculcated with the values and ideals of their ITE courses (the idealized competence phase). This is followed by a phase of "coping competencies," of "fitting in" to a school culture, of preoccupation with discipline and of negotiating an identity with school students and teachers. The third phase, when a new teacher has "settled in" and disciplinary/control issues have receded, is the phase of "realized competence" with "quite often the emergence of a surprisingly firm set of beliefs about the nature of teaching, what kids are like, and why standards are as they are" (p. 81).

Whitty (1996), reporting in the Department of Education in Northern Ireland's working group on competencies in ITE, also addresses questions of the phasing (and indeed the location) of competence development. His conclusion is that "awareness of contemporary debates about education," "understanding of schools as institutions and their place within the community" and "awareness of the importance of informed critical reflection in evaluating his or her professional practice" should all be given most attention during initial teacher training, but should also be developed during Further Professional Training, and (for the last competence) during induction, too (pp. 91–92).

14. *Substantially predetermined rather than primarily negotiated curriculum objectives.* Calderhead and Gates (1993) raise the key questions of whether "a truly reflective teaching program" should have "predefined content or…be negotiated," and how to "reconcile the aim of developing particular areas of knowledge, skill and attitudes with the aim of encouraging autonomy and professional responsibility" (p. 3). These are crucial issues in various postmodernist, postmodern feminist and liberal pluralist critiques of the concept of teachers as critical transformative intellectuals. They are also key elements of postmodernist critiques of Marxist class-based transformativist solidaristic analysis and policy proposals in education. They refer to the tension between developing student teacher autonomy on the one hand, and seeking to develop a particular ideology on the other. Liston and Zeichner (1991) observe the significant historical shift of emphasis within the Radical Left:

> At various times the focus has been on the content of programs, the skill of critical analysis and curriculum development, the nature of the pedagogic relationships between teachers and pupils, and between teacher educators and their students, or on the connections between teacher educators and other political projects which seek to address the many instances of suffering and injustice in our society. (p. 33)

The debate centers on whether "democratic participative pedagogy" should typify a course. Arguably, a heavy use of discussion-based and "own experience"-based, small-group collaborative work, typical of much "student-centred/child-centred" Primary schooling and Primary Teacher education in Britain in the 1970s and 1980s, hinders the development of the broad span of critical theoretical insights argued for in this chapter. In accordance with the Radical Left principles outlined here, course objectives, if not the content-based means to their attainment, should—following national debate and taking into account particular student needs at any particular historical juncture—be substantially pre-determined.

This proposal is for the organic intellectual, not the didactic. As Rikowski (2001e) notes, for

> organic intellectuals, the goal is not "to tell the people what to think," but to enable them to think clearly—to provide them with the tools (critical literacy in the first instance) to engage in cultural action incorporating the exercise of critical (dialectical) consciousness aimed at social transformation. (p. 63)

Moreover, transformative intellectuals must engage in self-criticism. This is so especially in relation to forming a dialectical unity with the student groups/teachers that is non-antagonistic, in order to assist in moving people from their "concrete conceptions of the world (their limited praxis)...[toward]...a critical, scientific or, in other words, dialectical conceptualization" (Allman, 1999, p. 115).

15. *The application of critical evaluation to school-based practice and experience.* Theory can provide the analytic and conceptual apparatus for thinking about practice in schools and classrooms, within the formal and within the hidden curriculum, while practice can provide the opportunity for the testing and assimilation of theory.

    Since the British Conservative government's 1992/1993 regulations for teacher training and education (DFE, 1992, 1993) demanded more school basing in ITE-based courses and the continued development of school-based ITE programs, the detheorization of teacher education through an emphasis on untheorized practice is a major problem in the development of effective teaching, in the development of critical transformatory skills, awareness and teaching, and in the development of a revolutionary transformative critical pedagogy.

Conclusion: The Politics of Educational Transformation

Arguments that we live in a postcapitalist, postindustrial, or postmodern era can be contested, as can the Radical Right argument set out in only slightly different ways by Conservative and New Labour governments, that the only future for humankind is the application of free-market economics to the societies of the world. Yet a Radical Left reorganization of global and national societies, and of their educational apparatuses, committed to egalitarianism and economic and social justice, remains viable (see, e.g., McLaren, 2000, 2001).

Radical Right models, even with the social democrat gloss applied by New Labour, are of little relevance in this endeavor. Practices in schooling and in teacher education and training need to be changed rather than accepted and reproduced. Therefore the emphasis should be on challenging and replacing the dominant neo-liberal and neo-conservative cultures rather than reproducing and reinforcing them. Radical Right and Centrist ideology on schooling, training and ITE serves a society aiming only for the hegemony of the few and the entrenchment of privilege, not the promotion of equality and economic and social justice.

On this, Paula Allman (2001) notes:

> The approach to critical education that I advocate in my publications is an approach that is aimed at enabling people to engage in an abbreviated experience of pro-alternative, counter-hegemonic, social relations. These are social relations within which people can learn to "read" the world critically and glimpse humanity's possible future beyond the horizon of capitalism. (p. 13; see also Allman, 1999)

Teacher educators and cultural workers from various other ideological and political perspectives may well agree with a number of the recommendations I make. They may not agree with the explicit emancipatory, critical and transformatory role of teacher educators, education and schooling in the interests of economic and social justice and egalitarianism. Yet this role, and the role of teacher educators and teachers as intellectuals instead of mechanics or technicians, are necessary for the development of a critical, active, interrogative, citizenry—thoughtful, questioning, perceptive as well as skilled—pursuing a democratic, anti-authoritarian, socially responsible and economically and socially just society.

Much of the Left has vacated the ideological battlefield during neo-liberal media and policy offensives and the attempts by governments nationally and internationally at strengthening control and hegemony over the schooling and teacher education ideological state apparatuses. As McLaren (2001) notes, "part of the problem faced by the educational Left today is that even among progressive educators there exists an ominous resignation produced by the seeming inevitability of capital" (p. 28). This is true of the caution of erstwhile Left writers, educationalists and ideologues in Britain and the USA in their retreat from the cultural and educational advances of the 1970s and 1980s. It is a feature of education policy and analysis and other policy areas (typified by the rightward Labour Party shift since Blair became leader in 1994) that has culminated in the New Labour Party of Tony Blair.

I recognize and do not underestimate the limitations on the agency and autonomy of teachers, teacher educators, cultural workers and their sites, and indeed, the very limited autonomy of the education policy/political region of the state from the economic. McLaren and Baltodano (2000) note (with respect to California in particular, but with a wider global resonance) the "greater restrictions on the ability of teachers to use their pedagogical spaces for emancipatory purposes" (p. 34). Hence, I give rather less credence than Ball (1994a, 1994b) and Smyth and Shatlock (1998) to the notion that teachers, and teacher educators, are able to "co-write" texts such as curriculum and assessment circulars (see Hill, 2001a; Evans, Davies & Penney, 1994).

The repressive cards within the ideological state apparatuses are stacked against the possibilities of transformative change through initial teacher education and through schooling. But historically and internationally, this has often been the case. Spaces do exist for counter-hegemonic struggle—sometimes (as in the 1980s and 1990s) narrower, sometimes (as in the 1960s and 1970s) broader.

Having recognized the limitations, though, and having recognized that there is at least some potential for transformative change, whatever space does exist should be exploited…and others, other arenas for contestation, created—forced open.

By itself, divorced from other arenas of progressive struggle, the success of organizational and ideological movements for socialist transformative change will be limited. This necessitates the development of pro-active debate both by, and within, the Radical Left more broadly than within the structures and processes of formal education, the ideological state apparatus of education. But it necessitates more than that. It calls for direct engagement with liberal pluralist (modernist or postmodernist) and Radical Right ideologies and programs, in all the areas of the state and of civil society, in and through all the ideological and repressive state apparatuses. It involves civic courage.

As intellectual workers educating teachers, the ideological intervention of teacher educators is likely to have more impact than that of sections of the workforce less saliently engaged in ideological production and reproduction. But by itself, the activity of transformative intellectual teacher educators, however skilful and committed, can have only an extremely limited impact on an egalitarian transformation of society. Unless linked to a grammar of resistance (Cole, 2004c), such resistant and counter-hegemonic activity is likely to fall on relatively stony ground. As McLaren and Baltodano (2000) suggest:

> Reclaiming schools and teacher education as arenas of cultural struggle and education in general as a vehicle for social transformation in conservative/capitalist times is premised upon a clear commitment to organize parents, students and communities. It stipulates that society needs to develop critical educators, community activists, organic intellectuals and teachers whose advocacy of social justice will illuminate their pedagogical practices. (p. 41; see also Rikowski, 2001e; McLaren & Farahmandpur, 2002a; Rikowski & McLaren, 2001; Cole, 2004c)

In keeping aloft ideals of plurality of thought, of economic and social justice and of dissent, teachers, teacher educators and the community must resist the ideological hijacking of our past, present and future. Teachers and teacher educators are too strategically valuable in children's/students' education to have slick media panaceas and slanted ministerial programs attempt to dragoon them into being uncritical functionaries of a conservative state and of the fundamentally and essentially inegalitarian and immoral society and education system reproduced by the capitalist state and its apparatuses.

The particular perspectives defined in this chapter, from a Radical Left position, are based on a belief that teachers must not only be skilled, competent, classroom technicians, but that they must also be critical and reflective and transformative and intellectual; that is to say, they should operate at the critical level of reflection.

They/we should enable and encourage their/our pupils/students, whether in Britain, the USA, Brazil, India, wherever, not only to gain basic and advanced knowledge and skills, but also to question, critique, judge and evaluate "what is," "what effects it has" and "why?"; and to be concerned and informed about equality and economic and social justice—in life beyond the classroom door and within the classroom walls. Rikowski (2002c) describes such radical educators as those "advocating education as an aspect of anti-capitalist social transformation."

As McLaren (2001) puts it:

> Do we, as radical educators, help capital find its way out of crisis, or do we help students find their way out of capital? The success of the former challenge will only buy further time for the capitalists to adapt both its victims and its critics, the success of the latter will determine the future of civilization, or whether or not we have one. (p. 31)

Notes

1. Together with others, I have advanced Radical Left principles and policy for schooling and/or for Initial Teacher Education in Hill, 1989, 1990, 1991a, 1994a, 1994b, 1997b, 2000d, 2001d; Hill, Cole & Williams, 1997; Cole, Hill, Soudien & Pease, 1997; Hillcole Group, 1991, 1997.
2. I set this out in Hill, 2001a, 2004f, Cole, Hill, McLaren and Rikowski, 2001.
3. I had joined the Labour Party in 1961 at the age of sixteen, organized and led my first demonstration. It was against the U.S. action over the Cuban missile crisis of that year. I went on to organize both smaller and larger demonstrations against the public expenditure "cuts" of the 1970s and 1980s, against fascists, racism and against apartheid in the 1970s and 1980s, and for better and more comprehensive education services. I believed then and still believe in street activity—organized direct action—as well as parliamentarist fora. In the latter connection, I stood twice for Parliament as a Labour Party candidate and was a city councilor and the leader of the Labour Party on a County Council for a number of years in the 1980s—sometimes (if infrequently) with policy power. I was also active as a local secretary or chair of my my local labor union branches for most of the next twenty years, sometimes as a regional representative.

   I stood down from representative Labour Party politics in 1989 but remained active in my union (NATFHE, the lecturers' labor union) as a local official and regional Chair (for South-Eastern England) for a period after that.
4. The Labour Party in the UK, since its foundation in 1901, has always been an amalgam of social democrats, socialists/Marxists and trade union (i.e., labor union) organizations and members, who/which are organically/organisationally part of the party. The fortunes of the socialist Left have waxed and waned. They reached their modern apex in 1981 when the leader of the "Hard Left," Tony Benn, narrowly missed being elected deputy leader of the Labour Party. In the 1980s, what the Conservative press loathingly called "the Loony Left," but what the Left called "good socialists," controlled numerous sections of the Labour Party and numerous inner-city councils, such as Liverpool, the Greater London Council and various London Boroughs, and education authorities such as the Inner London Education Authority.

   With the victory of Tony Blair as "New Labour" leader in the Labour Party in 1994, the Left was, for the ensuing years, arguably at its weakest since the formation of the Party. This has changed since the turn of the century/millennium, with the re-emergence of socialist voices within the Party and with the election of a number of new left-wing trade union leaders and national executives, elected by union members fed up with the pro-business, pro-privatisation, war on Iraq agenda of Tony Blair and New Labour (Murray, 2003).

5 For detail of the Hillcole Group of Radical left Educators, see http://www.tufnellpress.com and http://www.ieps.org.uk.

6 See http://www.ieps.org.uk.

7 See, e.g., Cole & Hill, 1995, 1999, 2002; Cole, Hill & Rikowski, 1997; Hill & Cole, 1993, 1995, 1996a, b; Cole, 2003, 2004a, and Mike Cole's chapter in this book.

8 See McLaren, 1998a, 1998b, 1999a, 1999b, 2000; McLaren & Baltodano, 2000; McLaren & Farahmandpur, 2001a, 2002c; McLaren, Martin, Farahmandpur & Jaramillo (2004). In this phase, Peter and Glenn Rikowski are engaging in e-conversations and e-publications, developing aspects of Marxist educational theory (e.g., McLaren & Rikowski, 2001, 2002; Rikowski & McLaren, 2001).

9 My own experiences are not at all unusual for radical educators. I have been "moved on" from nearly all the jobs I have had because of my political and labor union/trade union activities. It's not legal to do that (to non-promote, to harass, to sideline) labor union officials and activists but it happens. I was "moved on" (i.e., told that if I wanted promotion I would have to move on) from my first teaching job at Stockwell Manor Comprehensive School in the Inner London Education Authority because of my activities as a "flying picket" during the Inner London teachers' strikes of the late 1960s.

At my second post, Forest Girls' Secondary Modern School in Depot Rd. Horsham, I was called in and admonished by the Head Teacher for being pictured in the local press on a construction workers' picket line, being told "we do not expect our staff to be pictured on picket lines. Make sure it doesn't happen again!" I was encouraged to move on after securing the replacement of the (very moderate) local teachers' union (National Union of teachers) representative by a socialist. At my third job, as a lecturer in teacher education at Bognor College, I organized joint industrial action by academic, administrative and manual workers, following which I was "invited" to meet the Director of Education for the Local Education Authority; an almost unheard of "privilege." After a lecture on democracy and education, where I talked about Marx and Tony Benn instead of Plato and Aristotle, I was moved off teaching on teacher-education courses and was periodically sent into exile, teaching off-campus.

It did, in fact, lead to some very enjoyable learning experiences! I taught prisoners, adult education teachers, youth workers, Vietnamese refugees and their teachers in Thorney island Refugee Camp, and at an outpost in England of the United States university, New England College. At that time, I was told by my Head of School of Education, Kate Jacques, that the Principal of my College had told her that "Dave Hill will never get promotion because everyone up and down the country knows he is 'Loony-Left.'" (That was remarkable enough to diarise!) With changes in personnel I was periodically reinstated—and indeed promoted—and I developed and led a Marxist critical reflective course in teacher education, the Crawley four-year, full-time B.Ed. (Bachelor of Education) course for mature (i.e., over 21 years old) students. This Course was avowedly aimed at developing "critical reflection," deliberately used/selected Marxist/socialist lecturers, and tried to deliberately choose schools (for the school-based experience/teaching practice part of the degree) that were radical, anti-racist, anti-sexist, and had awareness of social class inequality. (There weren't too many schools like that, but there were some.) (Hill, 2005a).

I was ultimately dismissed ("made redundant") following the virtual abolition of critical teaching, sociology and politics from teacher education courses in the UK in the mid-1990s.

I have written about this set of experiences in "Brief Autobiography of a Bolshie Dismissed" (1997e), "Critical Research and the Dismissal of Dissent" (1997c) and "White Chalk…on a White Board: The Writing's on the Wall for Radicals in British Education" (1997d). "Brief Autobiography of a Bolshie Dismissed" is on the www.ieps.org.uk website. In the UK, CAFAS (the Council for Academic Freedom and Academic Standards) and NATFHE radical left group "Rank and File" both document political/job victimization of Left (and other) lecturers. (NATFHE is one of the two lecturers' labor unions in England and Wales, the National Association of Teachers in Further and Higher Education.)

Following a year when I worked part-time as a painter and decorator with one of my brothers, and taught part-time at Tower Hamlets College in the East End of London (where my family comes from) I was then appointed to my current post at University College Northampton. There I have been promoted to Professor. It is the first full-time post I have held where I have not been an elected labor union representative and activist/organizer. It's just too far, 140 miles from my home town, for me to be available to get that involved, at branch meetings, organizing, negotiating with management. Perhaps it's no coincidence that the first time I get a major promotion is the first time I have not been able to be active in the Union. Incidentally, one of my leitmotif records/discs is "Power in the Union" by Billy Bragg.

10 The two books produced/co-written by the members of the Hillcole Group of Radical Left Educators are *Changing the Future: Redprint for Education* (1991), and *Rethinking Education and Democracy: A Socialist Alternative for the Twenty-first Century* (1997), both published by the small left-wing publisher Tufnell Press (London).

11 See, e.g., Cole, 1998, 2004b, 2004c, 2005; Hill 2001b, 2001c, 2002a; Rikowski, 2001a, 2001b, 2001c, 2002b; 2003, 2004b, c, d, e; McLaren, 2000; Rees, 2001; McLaren & Farahmandpur, 2002c.

12 See also Cole, 1998, 2004b, 2004c, 2005; Smyth & Shatlock, 1998; Ainley, 1999, 2000; McMurtry, 1999; McLaren 2000; Rikowski, 2000, 2001a, 2001b, 2002a, 2002b; Hatcher & Hirtt, 1999; Hatcher, 2001.

13 Hatcher, 2001; Molnar, 1999, 2001; Hill, 2001b, 2003, 2004b, c; Rikowski, 2001a, 2001b, 2001c, 2002a.

14 Hill, 1994a, 1994b, 1997a, 1997b.

15 See also McMurtry, 1998; Winch, 1998.

16 For Radical Left discussion of these principles, see the citations in note 1 (above) together with Cole, Hill & Shan, 1997; Hill & Cole, 1999; Cole, Hill, McLaren & Rikowski, 2001; McLaren, Cole, Hill & Rikowski, 2001 Cole, 2004d. In Australia this tradition is exemplified in the work of Kevin Harris (1979, 1982, 1984, 1994), and in the United States most recently by Peter McLaren and his associates (e.g., Aguirre, 2001; McLaren, 2000, 2001; McLaren & Farahmandpur, 2001a, 2001b; McLaren & Rikowski, 2001, 2002).

17 Hill, 1999a, 2000, 2001c, 2001d.

18 See Cliff & Gluckstein, 1996; Driver & Martell, 1998; Giddens, 1998, 2000; Cole, Hill, McLaren & Rikowski, 2001; McLaren, Cole, Hill & Rikowski, 2001.

19 See Hill 1991b, 1994a, 1997b; see also Cole, 2004d.

20 See Hill, 1989, which sets out two such courses of the late 1990s from two different institutions. These were West Sussex Institute of Higher Education, where the courses were (co-)

developed by Dave Hill, and Brighton Polytechnic, where the course was developed by Mike Cole. The latter was subsequently criticized by Margaret Thatcher (Thatcher, 1993).

21 See, e.g., Hill, 1999b, 2001a, 2001e, 2002a; Sanders, Hill & Hankin, 1999; Aguirre, 2001; Hill & Cole, 2001; Cole, Hill, McLaren & Rikowski, 2001; Rikowski, 2001a, 2001b, 2001d; Hill, Sanders & Hankin, 2002; McLaren & Farahmandpur, 2002a, 2002b; McLaren & Rikowski, 2001; Rikowski & McLaren, 2001.

22 See Cole, Clay & Hill, 1990; Cole & Hill, 1999, 2002; Sanders, Hill & Hankin, 1999; Kincheloe, Slattery & Steinberg, 2000; McLaren & Farahmandpur, 2001a, 2002a; Hill, Sanders & Hankin, 2002, Cole, 2003, 2004a.

23 See the Institute for Education Policy Studies website <www.ieps.org.uk> for details of undergraduate (BA Education Studies) and graduate modules (MA in Education) with a potential for developing critical education. These were (co-)developed by Dave Hill and/or Glenn Rikowski at University College, Northampton, UK. The modules' aims, content, assessment procedures and bibliographies are set out.

References

Aguirre, L.C. (2001). The role of critical pedagogy in the globalisation era and the aftermath of September 11, 2001. Interview with Peter McLaren. *Revista electronica de investigacion educativa,* 3(2). Online at http://www.redie.ens.uabc.mx/vol3no2/contenido-coral.html.

Ainley, P. (1999). Left in a right state: Towards a new alternative. *Education and Social Justice*, 2(1) 74–78.

———. (2000). *From earning to learning: What is happening to education and the welfare state?* London: Tufnell Press.

Allman, P. (1999). *Revolutionary social transformation: Democratic hopes, political possibilities and critical education.* Westport, CT, & London: Bergin and Garvey.

———. (2000). *Critical education against global capital: Karl Marx and revolutionary critical education.* Westport, CT, & London: Bergin and Garvey.

———. (2001) Foreword. In M. Cole et al. *Red Chalk: On Schooling, Capitalism and Politics.* Brighton: Institute for Education Policy Studies.

Ball, S. (1994a). *Education reform: A critical and post-structural approach.* London: Open University Press.

———. (1994b). Some reflections on policy theory: A brief response to Hatcher and Troyna. *Journal of Education Policy*, 9(2), 171–182.

Blake, D. & Hill, D. (1995). The Newly Qualified Teacher in School. *Research Papers in Education*, 10 (3) pp.309-339.

Calderhead, J. & Gates, P. (1993). *Conceptualising reflection in teacher development.* London: Falmer Press.

Cliff, T. & Gluckstein, D. (1996). *The Labour Party: A Marxist history.* London: Bookmarks.

Cole, M. (1998). Globalisation, modernisation and competitiveness: A critique of the New Labour project in education. *International Studies in the Sociology of Education*, 8(3), 315–332.

———. (2003). Might it be in the practice that it fails to succeed?: A Marxist critique of claims for postmodernism as a force for social change and social justice. *British Journal of Sociology of Education*, 24 (4), 487-500.

———. (2004a). Fun, amusing, full of insights, but ultimately a reflection of anxious times: A critique of postmodernism as a force for resistance, social change and social justice. In J. Satterthwaite, E. Atkinson & W. Martin (Eds.), *Educational counter-cultures: confrontations, images, vision* (pp. 19-34). Stoke on Trent, UK & Sterling, USA: Trentham Books.

———. (2004b). "Rule Britannia" and the new American Empire: A Marxist analysis of the teaching of imperialism, actual and potential, in the English school curriculum. *Policy Futures in Education,* 2 (3).

———. (2004c). Rethinking the future: The commodification of knowledge and the grammar of resistance. In M. Benn & C. Chitty (Eds.). *For Caroline Benn: Essays in education and democracy*. London: Continuum.

———. (Ed.). (2004d). *Education, equality and human rights: Issues of gender, "race," sexuality, special needs, and social class.* 2nd Edition, London: Routledge/Falmer.

———. (2005). New Labour, globalization and social justice: the role of education. In G. Fischman, P. McLaren, H. Sunker & C. Lankshear (Eds.), *Critical theories, radical pedagogies and global conflicts.* Lanham, Maryland: Rowman and Littlefield.

Cole, M., Clay, J. & Hill, D. (1990/91). The citizen as individual and nationalist or as social and internationalist? What is the role of education? *Critical Social Policy*, 30, 10(3), 68–87.

Cole, M. & Hill, D. (1995). Games of despair and rhetorics of resistance: Postmodernism, education and reaction. *British Journal of Sociology of Education*, 16(2), 165–182.

———. (1999). Into the hands of capital: The deluge of postmodernism and the delusions of resistance postmodernism. In D. Hill, P. McLaren, M. Cole & G. Rikowski (Eds.), *Postmodernism and educational theory: Education and the politics of human resistance* (pp. 31–49). London: Tufnell Press.

———. (2002). Resistance postmodernism: Progressive politics or rhetorical left posturing? In D. Hill, P. McLaren, M. Cole & G. Rikowski (Eds.), *Marxism against postmodernism in educational theory* (pp. 91–111). Lanham, MD: Lexington Press.

Cole, M., Hill, D., McLaren, P. & Rikowski, G. (2001). *Red chalk: On schooling, capitalism and politics.* Brighton: Institute for Education Policy Studies.

Cole, M., Hill, D. & Rikowski, G. (1997). Between postmodernism and nowhere: The predicament of the postmodernist. *British Journal of Education Studies*, 45(2), 187–200.

Cole, M., Hill, D. & Shan, S. (1997) *Promoting Equality in Primary Schools.* London: Cassell.

Cole, M., Hill, D., Soudien, C. & Pease, J. (1997). Critical transformative teacher education: A model for the new South Africa. In J. Lynch, S. Modgil & C. Modgil (Eds.), *Education and development: Tradition and innovation*, Vol. 3: *Innovations in developing primary education* (pp. 97–121). London: Cassell.

Department for Education (DFE). (1992). *Circular 9/92. Initial teacher training (secondary phase).* London: DFE.

———. (1993). *Circular 14/93: The initial training of primary school teachers.* London: DFE.

Department for Education and Employment (DfEE). (1998). *DfEE circular 4/98: Teaching: High status, high standards—requirements for courses of initial teacher training.* London: DfEE.

Driver, S. & Martell, L. (1998). *New Labour: Politics after Thatcherism.* Cambridge: Polity Press.

Evans, J., Davies, B. & Penney, D. (1994). Whatever happened to the subject and the state? *Discourse*, 14(2), 57–65.

Gaine, C. (1995). *Still no problem here.* Stoke-on-Trent: Trentham Books.

Giddens, A. (1998). *The third way: The renewal of social democracy.* Cambridge: Polity Press.

———. (2000). *The third way and its critics.* Cambridge: Polity Press.

Giroux, H. & McLaren, P. (1986). Teacher education and the politics of engagement: The case for democratic schooling. *Harvard Education Review*, 56(3), 213–238.

———. (1989). *Critical pedagogy, the state and cultural struggle.* Albany: State University of New York Press.

Harris, K. (1979). *Education and knowledge.* London: RKP.

———. (1982). *Teachers and classes: A Marxist analysis.* London: Routledge & Kegan Paul.

———. (1984). Two contrasting theories. *Education with Production*, 3(1), 13–33.

———. (1994). *Teachers: Constructing the future.* London: Falmer Press.

Hatcher, R. (2001). Getting down to the business: Schooling in the globalised economy. *Education and Social Justice*, 3(2), 45–59.

Hatcher, R. & Hirtt, N. (1999). The business agenda behind Labour's education policy. In M. Allen et al. (Eds.), *New Labour's education policy* (pp. 12–23). London: Tufnell Press.

Hill, D. (1989). *Charge of the right brigade: The radical right's assault on teacher education.* Brighton: Institute for Education Policy Studies, 1 Cumberland Road, Brighton, BN1 6SL. Online at http://www.ieps.org.uk.

———. (1990). *Something old, something new, something borrowed, something blue: Teacher education, schooling and the radical right in Britain and the USA.* London: Tufnell Press.

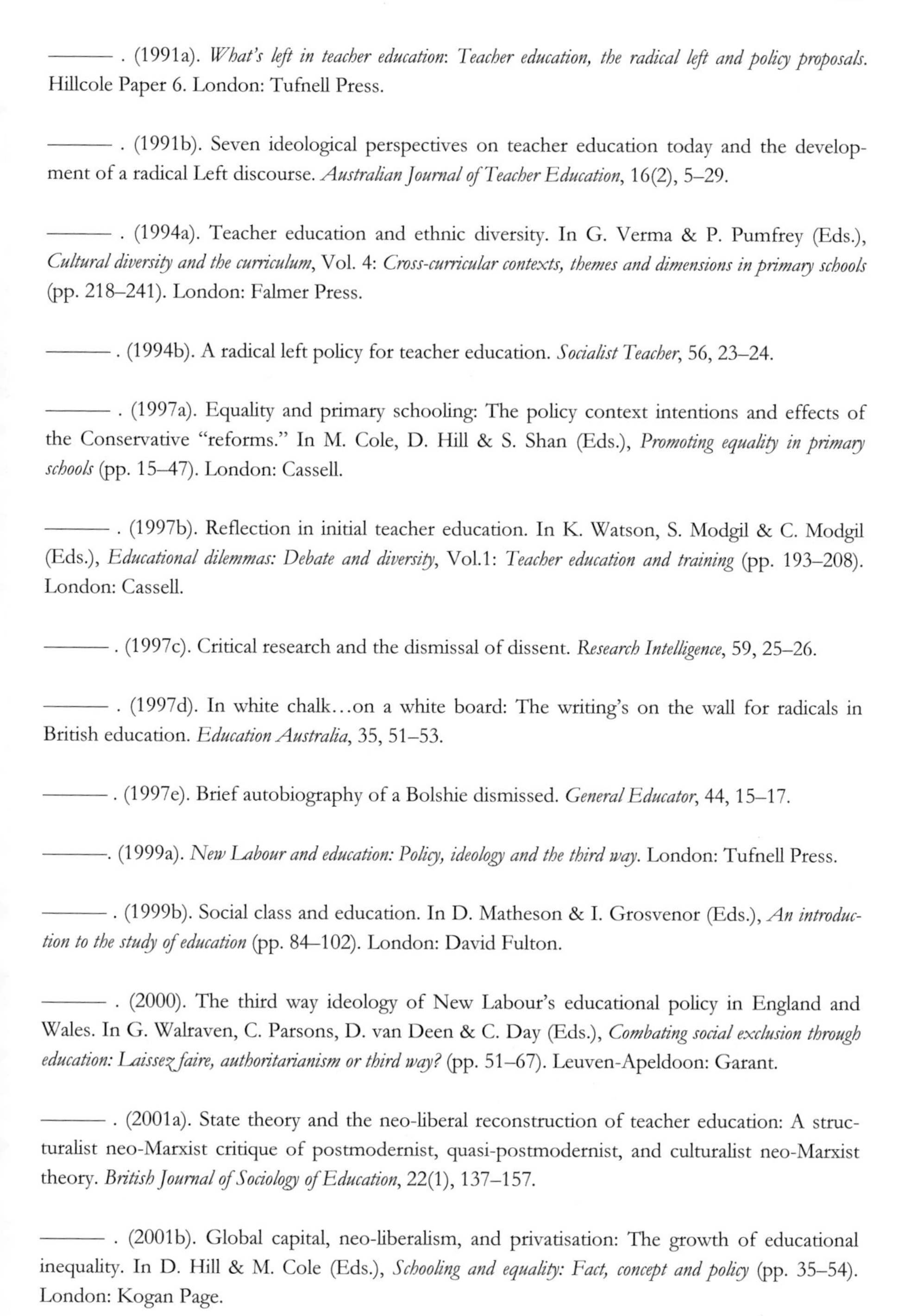

———. (1991a). *What's left in teacher education: Teacher education, the radical left and policy proposals.* Hillcole Paper 6. London: Tufnell Press.

———. (1991b). Seven ideological perspectives on teacher education today and the development of a radical Left discourse. *Australian Journal of Teacher Education*, 16(2), 5–29.

———. (1994a). Teacher education and ethnic diversity. In G. Verma & P. Pumfrey (Eds.), *Cultural diversity and the curriculum*, Vol. 4: *Cross-curricular contexts, themes and dimensions in primary schools* (pp. 218–241). London: Falmer Press.

———. (1994b). A radical left policy for teacher education. *Socialist Teacher*, 56, 23–24.

———. (1997a). Equality and primary schooling: The policy context intentions and effects of the Conservative "reforms." In M. Cole, D. Hill & S. Shan (Eds.), *Promoting equality in primary schools* (pp. 15–47). London: Cassell.

———. (1997b). Reflection in initial teacher education. In K. Watson, S. Modgil & C. Modgil (Eds.), *Educational dilemmas: Debate and diversity*, Vol.1: *Teacher education and training* (pp. 193–208). London: Cassell.

———. (1997c). Critical research and the dismissal of dissent. *Research Intelligence*, 59, 25–26.

———. (1997d). In white chalk…on a white board: The writing's on the wall for radicals in British education. *Education Australia*, 35, 51–53.

———. (1997e). Brief autobiography of a Bolshie dismissed. *General Educator*, 44, 15–17.

———. (1999a). *New Labour and education: Policy, ideology and the third way.* London: Tufnell Press.

———. (1999b). Social class and education. In D. Matheson & I. Grosvenor (Eds.), *An introduction to the study of education* (pp. 84–102). London: David Fulton.

———. (2000). The third way ideology of New Labour's educational policy in England and Wales. In G. Walraven, C. Parsons, D. van Deen & C. Day (Eds.), *Combating social exclusion through education: Laissez faire, authoritarianism or third way?* (pp. 51–67). Leuven-Apeldoon: Garant.

———. (2001a). State theory and the neo-liberal reconstruction of teacher education: A structuralist neo-Marxist critique of postmodernist, quasi-postmodernist, and culturalist neo-Marxist theory. *British Journal of Sociology of Education*, 22(1), 137–157.

———. (2001b). Global capital, neo-liberalism, and privatisation: The growth of educational inequality. In D. Hill & M. Cole (Eds.), *Schooling and equality: Fact, concept and policy* (pp. 35–54). London: Kogan Page.

———. (2001c). *The third way in Britain: New Labour's neo-liberal education policy*. Paper presented at the Conference Marx 111, Paris, September 2001, Université de Sorbonne/Nanterre, Paris. On-line at http://www.ieps.org.uk.

———. (2001d). Equality, ideology and education policy. In D. Hill & M. Cole (Eds.), *Schooling and equality: Fact, concept and policy* (pp. 7–34). London: Kogan Page.

———. (2001e). The national curriculum, the hidden curriculum and equality. In D. Hill & M. Cole (Eds.), *Schooling and equality: Fact, concept and policy* (pp. 95–116). London: Kogan Page.

———. 2002a) Globalisation, Education and Critical Action. *Educate: A Quarterly on Education and Development* (The Sindh Education Foundation, Pakistan), 2, (1) pp 42-45.

———. (2002b). Global capital, neo-liberalism and the growth of educational inequality. *The School Field: International Journal of Theory and Research in Education*, 13(1/2), 81–107.

———. (2003). Global neo-liberalism, the deformation of education and resistance, *Journal for Critical Education Policy Studies,* 1 (1). On-line at http://www/jcps.com.

———. (2004a). Critical transformative action for economic and social justice. *Development Education Journal,* 10 (2).

———. (2004b). Educational perversion and global neo-liberalism: A Marxist critique. *Cultural Logic: An electronic journal of Marxist Theory and Practice.* Online at http://eserver.org.

———. (2004c). Books, banks and bullets: Controlling our minds—the global project of Imperialistic and militaristic neo-liberalism and its effect on education policy. *Policy Futures,* 2, 3 (Theme: Marxist Futures in Education). Online at http://www.triangle.co.uk/pfie.

———. (2004d). O neoliberalismo global, a resistência e a deformação da educação. *Curriculo sem Frontieras* 3, 3 (Brazil) 2004) On-line at http://www.curriculosemfronteiras.org.

———. (2004e). Enforcing capitalist education: Force-feeding capital through/in the repressive and ideological educational apparatuses of the state. In E. Wayne Ross & D. Gabbard (Eds.) *Education and the Rise of the Security State.* New York: Praeger.

———. (2004f). The state and education: Structuralist neo-Marxism, theory and education policy. In G. Fischman, P. McLaren, H. Sünker & C. Lankshear (Eds.). *Critical theories, radical pedagogies and global conflicts.* Boulder, Colorado: Rowman and Littlefield.

———. (2005a forthcoming). *New Labour and education: Ideology, (in)equality and capital* (sole author). London: Tufnell Press.

———. (2005b forthcoming). *Charge of the right brigade: The radical right restructuring of schooling and initial teacher education in England and Wales under the Conservative and New Labour governments 1979-2004.* (sole author). Lampeter, Wales: Edwin Mellen Press.

Hill, D. & Cole, M. (1993). *Postmodernism, education and the road to nowhere: A materialist critique.* Paper presented at the Annual Association for Teacher Education in Europe (ATEE). Lisbon University.

———. (1995). Marxist theory and state autonomy theory: The case of "race"-education in initial teacher education. *Journal of Education Policy*, 10(2), 221–232.

———. (1996a). Materialism and the postmodern fallacy: The case of education. In J.V. Fernandes (Ed.), *Proceedings of the Second International Conference of Sociology of Education* (pp. 475–594). Faro, Portugal: Escola Superior de Educacão da Universidade do Algarve.

———. (1996b). Postmodernism, educational contemporary capitalism: A materialist critique. In M.O. Valente, A. Barrios, A. Gaspar & V. Teodoro (Eds.), *Teacher training and values education* (pp. 27–89). Lisbon: Association for Teacher Education in Europe in association with Departamento de Educacão da Faculdade de Ciencias da Universidade de Lisboa.

———. (2001). Social class. In D. Hill & M. Cole (Eds.), *Schooling and equality: Fact, concept and policy* (pp. 137-159). London: Kogan Page.

———. (Eds.). (1999). *Promoting equality in secondary schools.* London and New York: Cassell.

Hill, D., Cole, M. & Williams, C. (1997). Teacher education and equality in the primary school. In M. Cole, D. Hill & S. Shan (Eds.), *Promoting equality in primary schools* (pp. 91–114). London: Cassell.

Hill, D., McLaren, P., Cole, M. & Rikowski, G. (Eds.). (1999). *Postmodernism in educational theory: Education and the politics of human resistance.* London: Tufnell Press.

———. (Eds.). (2002). *Marxism against postmodernism in educational theory.* Lanham, MD: Lexington Press.

Hill, D., Sanders, M. & Hankin, T. (2002). Marxism, class analysis and postmodernism. In D. Hill, P. McLaren, M. Cole & G. Rikowski (Eds.), *Marxism against postmodernism in educational theory* (pp. 167–206). Lanham, MD: Lexington Press.

Hillcole Group. (1991). *Changing the future: Redprint for education.* London: Tufnell Press.

———. (1997). *Rethinking education and democracy: A socialist alternative for the twenty-first century.* London: Tufnell Press.

Kincheloe, J., Slattery, P. & Steinberg, S. (2000). *Contextualising teaching: Introduction to education and educational foundations.* Boulder, CO: Westview Press.

Krupskaya, N. (1985). *On labour-oriented education and instruction.* Moscow: Progressive Publishers.

Liston, D. & Zeichner, K. (1987). Critical pedagogy and teacher education. *Journal of Education*, 169(3), 117–137.

Liston, D. & Zeichner, K. (1991) *Teacher education and the social conditions of schooling.* London: Routledge.

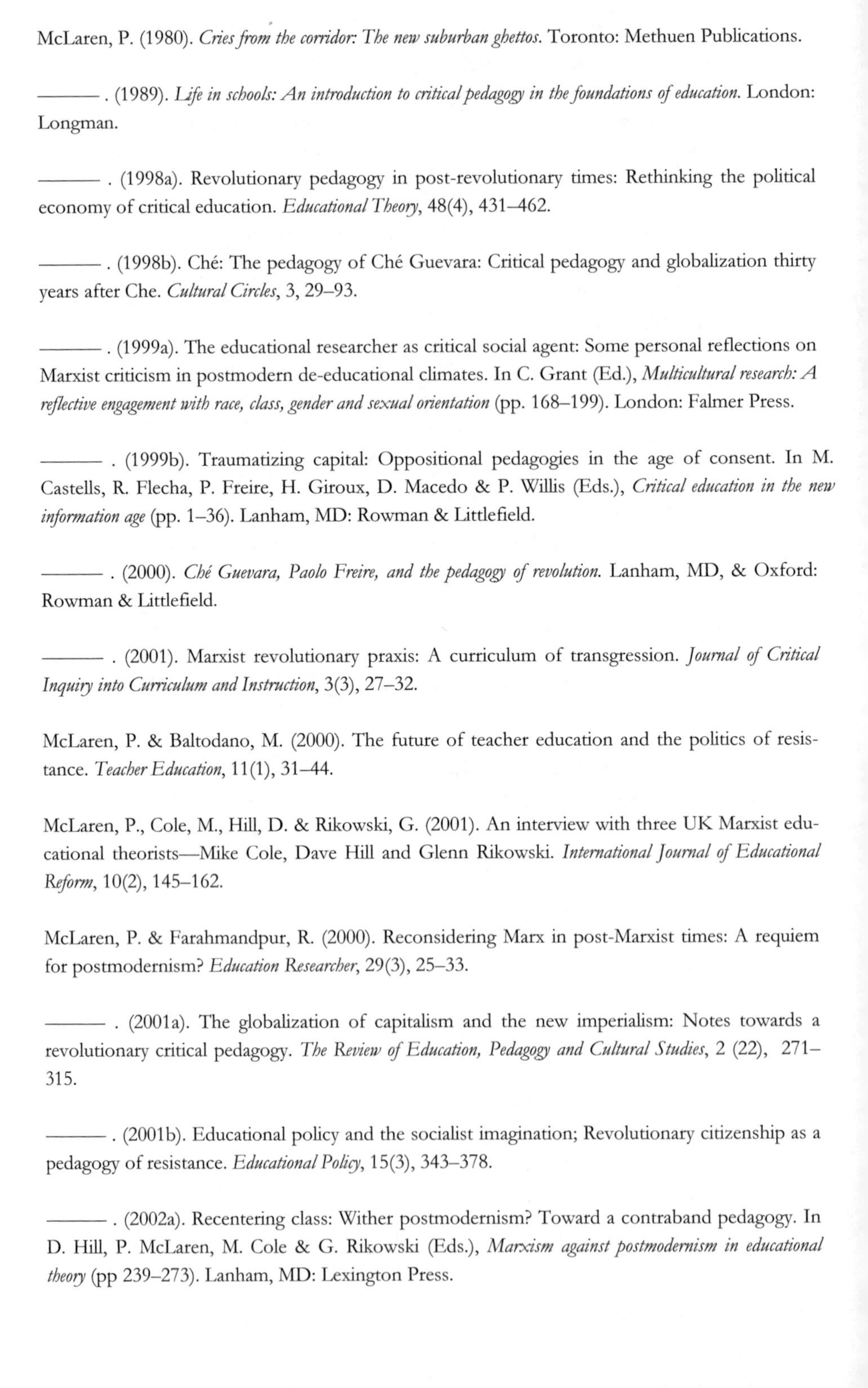

McLaren, P. (1980). *Cries from the corridor: The new suburban ghettos.* Toronto: Methuen Publications.

———. (1989). *Life in schools: An introduction to critical pedagogy in the foundations of education.* London: Longman.

———. (1998a). Revolutionary pedagogy in post-revolutionary times: Rethinking the political economy of critical education. *Educational Theory*, 48(4), 431–462.

———. (1998b). Ché: The pedagogy of Ché Guevara: Critical pedagogy and globalization thirty years after Che. *Cultural Circles*, 3, 29–93.

———. (1999a). The educational researcher as critical social agent: Some personal reflections on Marxist criticism in postmodern de-educational climates. In C. Grant (Ed.), *Multicultural research: A reflective engagement with race, class, gender and sexual orientation* (pp. 168–199). London: Falmer Press.

———. (1999b). Traumatizing capital: Oppositional pedagogies in the age of consent. In M. Castells, R. Flecha, P. Freire, H. Giroux, D. Macedo & P. Willis (Eds.), *Critical education in the new information age* (pp. 1–36). Lanham, MD: Rowman & Littlefield.

———. (2000). *Ché Guevara, Paolo Freire, and the pedagogy of revolution.* Lanham, MD, & Oxford: Rowman & Littlefield.

———. (2001). Marxist revolutionary praxis: A curriculum of transgression. *Journal of Critical Inquiry into Curriculum and Instruction*, 3(3), 27–32.

McLaren, P. & Baltodano, M. (2000). The future of teacher education and the politics of resistance. *Teacher Education*, 11(1), 31–44.

McLaren, P., Cole, M., Hill, D. & Rikowski, G. (2001). An interview with three UK Marxist educational theorists—Mike Cole, Dave Hill and Glenn Rikowski. *International Journal of Educational Reform*, 10(2), 145–162.

McLaren, P. & Farahmandpur, R. (2000). Reconsidering Marx in post-Marxist times: A requiem for postmodernism? *Education Researcher*, 29(3), 25–33.

———. (2001a). The globalization of capitalism and the new imperialism: Notes towards a revolutionary critical pedagogy. *The Review of Education, Pedagogy and Cultural Studies*, 2 (22), 271–315.

———. (2001b). Educational policy and the socialist imagination; Revolutionary citizenship as a pedagogy of resistance. *Educational Policy*, 15(3), 343–378.

———. (2002a). Recentering class: Wither postmodernism? Toward a contraband pedagogy. In D. Hill, P. McLaren, M. Cole & G. Rikowski (Eds.), *Marxism against postmodernism in educational theory* (pp 239–273). Lanham, MD: Lexington Press.

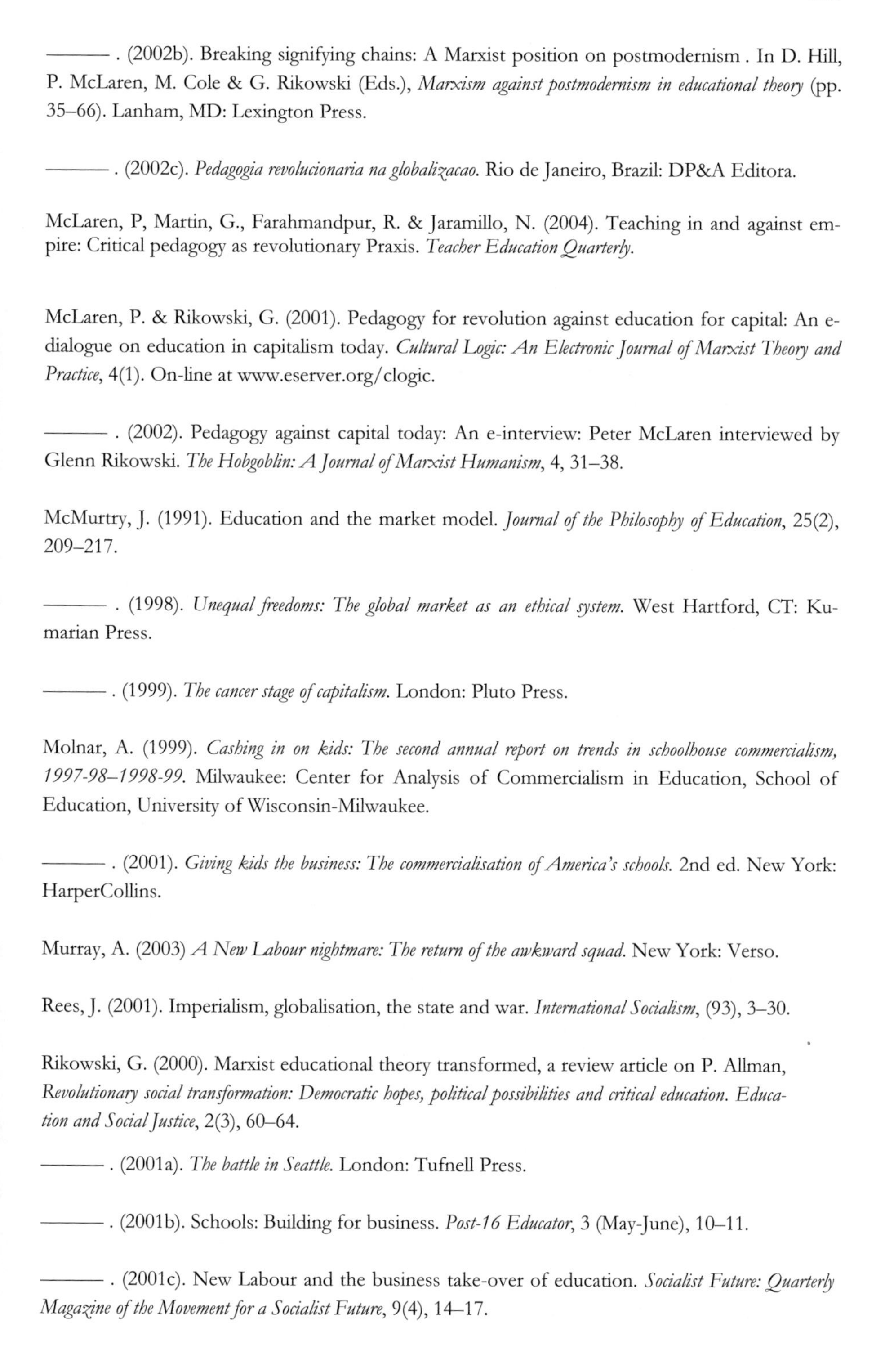

——— . (2002b). Breaking signifying chains: A Marxist position on postmodernism . In D. Hill, P. McLaren, M. Cole & G. Rikowski (Eds.), *Marxism against postmodernism in educational theory* (pp. 35–66). Lanham, MD: Lexington Press.

——— . (2002c). *Pedagogia revolucionaria na globalizacao.* Rio de Janeiro, Brazil: DP&A Editora.

McLaren, P, Martin, G., Farahmandpur, R. & Jaramillo, N. (2004). Teaching in and against empire: Critical pedagogy as revolutionary Praxis. *Teacher Education Quarterly.*

McLaren, P. & Rikowski, G. (2001). Pedagogy for revolution against education for capital: An e-dialogue on education in capitalism today. *Cultural Logic: An Electronic Journal of Marxist Theory and Practice*, 4(1). On-line at www.eserver.org/clogic.

——— . (2002). Pedagogy against capital today: An e-interview: Peter McLaren interviewed by Glenn Rikowski. *The Hobgoblin: A Journal of Marxist Humanism*, 4, 31–38.

McMurtry, J. (1991). Education and the market model. *Journal of the Philosophy of Education*, 25(2), 209–217.

——— . (1998). *Unequal freedoms: The global market as an ethical system.* West Hartford, CT: Kumarian Press.

——— . (1999). *The cancer stage of capitalism.* London: Pluto Press.

Molnar, A. (1999). *Cashing in on kids: The second annual report on trends in schoolhouse commercialism, 1997-98–1998-99.* Milwaukee: Center for Analysis of Commercialism in Education, School of Education, University of Wisconsin-Milwaukee.

——— . (2001). *Giving kids the business: The commercialisation of America's schools.* 2nd ed. New York: HarperCollins.

Murray, A. (2003) *A New Labour nightmare: The return of the awkward squad.* New York: Verso.

Rees, J. (2001). Imperialism, globalisation, the state and war. *International Socialism*, (93), 3–30.

Rikowski, G. (2000). Marxist educational theory transformed, a review article on P. Allman, *Revolutionary social transformation: Democratic hopes, political possibilities and critical education. Education and Social Justice*, 2(3), 60–64.

——— . (2001a). *The battle in Seattle.* London: Tufnell Press.

——— . (2001b). Schools: Building for business. *Post-16 Educator*, 3 (May-June), 10–11.

——— . (2001c). New Labour and the business take-over of education. *Socialist Future: Quarterly Magazine of the Movement for a Socialist Future*, 9(4), 14–17.

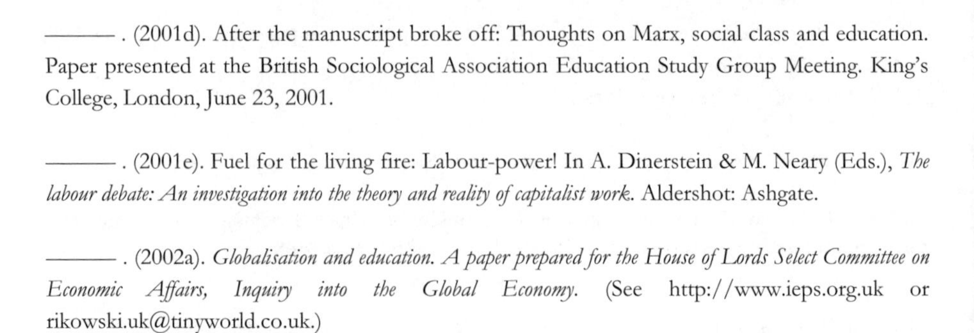

———. (2001d). After the manuscript broke off: Thoughts on Marx, social class and education. Paper presented at the British Sociological Association Education Study Group Meeting. King's College, London, June 23, 2001.

———. (2001e). Fuel for the living fire: Labour-power! In A. Dinerstein & M. Neary (Eds.), *The labour debate: An investigation into the theory and reality of capitalist work*. Aldershot: Ashgate.

———. (2002a). *Globalisation and education. A paper prepared for the House of Lords Select Committee on Economic Affairs, Inquiry into the Global Economy*. (See http://www.ieps.org.uk or rikowski.uk@tinyworld.co.uk.)

———. (2002b). Transfiguration: Globalisation, the World Trade Organisation and the national faces of the GATS. *Information for Social Change*, (14), 8–17.

———. (2002c). *The importance of being a radical educator in capitalism today*. Paper presented at Wawrick University Education research seminar, 7 June, 2002.

Rikowski, G. & McLaren, P. (2001). Pedagogy against capital today: An e-interview with Peter McLaren (Peter McLaren interviewed by Glenn Rikowski). *The Hobgoblin: Journal of Marxist-Humanism*, 4. On-line at http://www.members.aol.com/thehobgoblin/index.html.

Robertson, L. (2000). Early literacy and young emergent bilingual pupils: The exclusive nature of the National Curriculum and the National Literacy Strategy. In G. Walraven, C. Parsons, D. van Deen & C. Day (Eds.), *Combating social exclusion through education: Laissez faire, authoritarianism or third way?* (pp. 189–206). Leuven-Apeldoon, Belgium: Garant.

Robertson, L.H. & Hill, R. (2001). Excluded voices: Educational exclusion and inclusion. In D. Hill & M. Cole (Eds.), *Schooling and equality: Fact, concept and policy* (pp. 73–93). London: Kogan Page.

Sanders, M., Hill, D. & Hankin, T. (1999). Education theory and the return to class analysis. In D. Hill, P. McLaren, M. Cole & G. Rikowski (Eds.), *Postmodernism in educational theory: Education and the politics of human resistance* (pp. 98–130). London: Tufnell Press.

Smyth, J. & Shatlock, G. (1998). *Re-making teaching: Ideology, policy and practice*. London: Routledge.

The Socialist. (2004). Education manifesto for the June 2004 elections. 14 May.

Socialist Alliance. (2001). *People before profit: The Socialist Alliance manifesto for the general election*. London: Socialist Alliance. On-line at http://www.socialistalliance.net.

Stronach, I. & Maclure, M. (Eds.). (1996). *Educational research undone: The postmodern embrace*. Buckingham: Open University Press.

Taaffe, P. & Mulhearn, T. (1988). *Liverpool: City that dared to fight*. Liverpool: Fortress Books.

Thatcher, M. (1993). *The Downing Street years*. London: Harper Collins.

Whitty, G. (1996). Professional competencies and professional characteristics: The Northern Ireland approach to the reform of teacher education. In D. Hustler & D. McIntyre (Eds.), *Developing competent teachers* (pp. 86–97). London: David Fulton.

Winch, C. (1998). Markets, educational opportunities and education: Reply to Tooley. *Journal of Philosophy of Education*, 32(3), 429–436.

Chapter 10

Karl Marx, Radical Education and Peter McLaren: Implications for the Social Studies

Curry Malott

As radical educators counter popular postmodern critiques of Marxist theory while simultaneously resurrecting the life-work of Karl Marx as a response to the intensification of the globalization of capital, which is marked by unprecedented inequality and human suffering (see McLaren, 2000; Chomsky, 1999), the debate over educational theory rages on (McLaren & Rikowski, 2001). For example, Marxist educator Glenn Rikowski, in a discussion piece with Peter McLaren (McLaren & Rikowski, 2001), highlights the importance of the current Marxist resurrection in educational theory, arguing that "…educational postmodernism was on the road to totally eclipsing Marxist educational theory by absorbing any form of potential radicalism and spitting it out as a fashion statement" (p. 7).

Although acknowledging the importance of critiquing postmodernism, Rikowski (McLaren & Rikowski, 2001) argues that "we need to move on. The development of Marxist science (a negative critique of capitalist society) and a politics of human resistance are just more important…" (p. 9). Following Rikowski, and because of the focus on that important debate in this volume, I will not engage with postmodern critiques in detail here. Rather, this chapter focuses on the role education plays "…in the perpetuation of the capital relation" as argued by Allman, McLaren and Rikowski (2002). Specifically, I will apply what these and other authors are saying about how education is situated within the process of creating capitalist relations of exploitation to the social studies, thus underscoring McLaren and others' implied impact on my work as a Marxist educator-in-process.

I focus on the social studies because it is the area of formal education in the United States that is explicitly dedicated to the process of citizen formation, which, in short, determines the relationships governing society's useful labor, thus giving way to the particular form that society takes. Introduced by the Committee on Social Studies in 1913, the social studies was from the beginning a contested terrain between progressives, such as John Dewey and George Counts, and the conservatives, such as scientific efficiency proponents like David Snedden, whose corporate-sponsored campaign successfully defined the official purpose of the social studies (Hursh & Ross, 2000).

The century-long class struggle within the social studies has been over what type of citizens the social studies officially seeks to engender (Hursh & Ross, 2000; Kincheloe, 2001). That is, does the social studies perpetuate status quo inequalities, or does it actively work to transgress the dominant social order for a society based on the free association of humans in the reproduction of their world?

The social studies emerged during a high point in progressive thought in the United States as a response to a history curriculum that was designed to mold people to be industrious and thrifty using the banking method of education, which assumed that students were devoid of "valuable" knowledge (Saxe, 1991). Conservatives were interested in reducing the cost of educational assimilation in order to increase the pool of surplus workers needed to fill the growing industrial economy (Kincheloe, Slattery & Steinberg, 2000). Progressives such as John Dewey, on the other hand, sought a more civics-oriented, democratic alternative to replace and combat the conservative educational curriculum (Dewey, 1916; Hursh & Ross, 2000; Kincheloe, Slattery & Steinberg, 2000; Saxe, 1991), which again was part of the larger social struggle for equality and justice.

More recent educational theorists/activists, such as Peter McLaren and Paula Allman, in continuing the progressive legacy of resistance and struggle, argue that a dialectical understanding of self and society is necessary for knowing how one is situated within the process of value production, which is key for engendering democratic citizens ready to liberate themselves, and in the process, humanity, from the labor/capital relation. Marx's dialectic, according to Allman (2001):

> pertains to the movement and development of the material reality of capitalism, movements and developments that result from human beings actively producing their material world and with it their consciousness as well....Marx's dialectic...is open and allows for reciprocity wherein that which determines is also mutually determined or shaped at the same time; and thus there is no outcome that is inevitable or irreversible. (pp. 4–5)

Traditionally and even today, however, social studies instruction, rather than embracing a dialectical perspective, tends to be devoid of even the most basic elements of dialectics (Loewen, 1995; Ross, 2000; Kincheloe, 2001), which, I will argue, is a trend that must be reversed. Rather, social studies is too often geared toward fostering obedience to authority through the memorization of disconnected facts in the preparation of standardized tests based on the values and beliefs of the dominant, white-supremacist capitalist society (Loewen, 1995; Ross, 2000; Kincheloe, 2001). Ultimately, "Traditional Social Studies Instruction" (TSSI) (Ross, 2000) serves to create citizens who are willing to sell their labor as a commodity in the market for a wage, thus producing surplus value, which represents the great tragedy of labor because it is surplus value, that is, capital that is used as a form of social control to oppress the working class (discussed below).

This chapter outlines the focal drive of capital, the creation of value through the commodification of human labor-power, a specific aspect of today's Marxist rejuvenation in educational theory and possible implications these ideas could have for the social studies. First, I provide a brief description of my first encounter with McLaren's early Marxist work in *Life in Schools* (1989), focusing on how it is different from his current Marxism. In my discussion of McLaren's and others' recent Marxist scholarship, I highlight some of the authors outside of the field of education on whom they currently draw. Then I outline the theory of value that many Marxist educators, such as McLaren, Allman, Farahmandpur and Rikowski, advocate, which is based on Marx's *Capital*, Volume 1 (1967). Finally, I make an argument for possible implications—as articulated by McLaren and others—that Marx's theory of value could potentially have for the social studies.

First Encounters and Beyond

I first came across McLaren's work as a punk-rocking sociology Master's student at New Mexico State University (NMSU) between 1996 and 1998. My thesis work, which dealt with the accommodative and resistive elements of punk rock counter-culture, led me to the section in McLaren's *Life in Schools* (1989) on resistance theory. That is, I was interested in the dialectics of working-class culture as it both penetrates and accommodates the dominant, capitalist society. Summarizing Willis' (1977) work, McLaren notes how the working-class student resistors documented in *Learning to Labour* paradoxically glorified "manual labor" while simultaneously challenging the reproduction of themselves as workers by creating a counter-culture through which they refused to engage in "mental labor." Thus, in the end, they sabotaged any opportunities they may have had to achieve upward social mobility.

The effect that student resistance has on reproducing the working class represents a focus on the "consequences" or "symptoms" of capitalism. That is, student resistance is most notably a "consequence" of the alienating nature of capitalist education. Allman (2001) argues that only if the left focuses on the contradictions (i.e., the dialectical commodification of human labor) from which the "consequences" of capitalism emerge (i.e., student resistance and labor movements), will they be able to challenge capitalism as a social relation. Similarly, Glenn Rikowski (1997), calling for a complete restructuring of Marxist educational theory, argues that "...an analysis of labour-power is the most appropriate starting point for rebuilding Marxist educational theory" (p. 13). Rikowski criticizes the Marxism of Bowles and Gintis (1976) and Willis (1977) for focusing on systems and institutions, which are the consequences of the historical materialization of process and processes. Rikowski, Allman, McLaren and other "labor-power" educational Marxists take as the ultimate goal of their revolutionary pedagogies the complete uprooting of the labor/capital relation rather than the reformation of capital. That is, as Peter Hudis (2000) notes in "Can Capital Be Controlled?":

> Any effort to control capital without uprooting the basis of value production is ultimately self-defeating. So long as value and surplus-value persist, capital will strive to self-expand; any external boundaries established for it, whether by state intervention or regulation, can and will eventually be overcome. (p. 2)

Part of the process of "uprooting the basis of value production," as underscored by Harry Cleaver (2000) in summarizing Chapter 1 of Volume 1 of Marx's *Capital* (1967), is not merely to liberate work from capitalism, therefore creating "non-alienating" work, but rather to destroy work as a social relation within capitalism. Workers then cease to be workers because work itself is a form of social control and domination. That is, the goal is "…not to make a religion of work" (Cleaver, 2000, p. 69). For example, "the lads" in Willis' (1977) Marxist study on working-class student resistance glorified manual labor as students, and thus supported the capital-labor relation by making "a religion of work" through affirming their status as creators of value, and thus capital. Allman et al. (2002), drawing on Marx (1867/1967), also hold that the working-class goal of anti-capitalist struggle should not be to become workers for a socialist "state capitalism." Rather, the goal should be to "…implode the social universe of capital out of which the labor/capital antagonism is constituted" (p. 14), thereby increasing one's potential to become more fully human in the Freirean sense (1998) through liberation from the constraints of an oppressive relationship.

McLaren's recent work, although far from fashionable (McLaren, 2002), deals more with the "causes" or "roots," rather than the "consequences," of capitalism. For example, McLaren argues that "the key question that drives much of my work can be captured in the following question: How is labor constituted as a social relation within capitalism?" (McLaren & Rikowski, 2001, p. 3). Taking this focus, rather than simply describing the inequalities that emerge in a capitalist society, unveils and challenges the historical process from which injustices emerge. I will now turn to a discussion of today's Marxist educational theory, focusing on how McLaren and others are answering the above-stated question, that is, How is labor constituted as a social relation within capitalism? This examination will take us to the production of value, but first I will begin with a very brief discussion of today's Marxist/postmodern debate.

Today's Marxism in Educational Theory: A Brief Overview of Value

In declaring the death of Marxism, those on both the left and the right have used the 1989 fall of Soviet communism as "evidence." For example, in supporting arguments made by progressive educator Stanley Aronowitz, Pinar, Reynolds, Slattery and Taubman (2000) argue that the failure of Marxist-oriented class struggle has led to "history itself…undermin[ing] class analysis as a primary category of social and educational analysis" (p. 295). Allman et al. (2002), on the other hand, stress the relevance of Marx's dialectical theory of class because of the global proliferation of those entering the ranks of the working class, and thus the commodification of human labor-power. These authors stress that they have become skeptical of those on the left who

"...blame history or specific political conditions pertaining at specific historical conjunctures..." (p. 4) for their rejection of Marxism. In another recent article, McLaren (2002) argues that "these days it is far from fashionable to be a radical educator. To identify your politics as Marxist is to invite derision and ridicule from many quarters, including some on the left" (p. 36).

Supporting their Marxist analysis, McLaren and Farahmandpur (2001) look to the objective conditions of today's global reality, such as the fact that the income of "...the 225 richest people [is] roughly equal to the annual income of the poorest 47% of the world's population" (p. 345). They argue that Marxism, rather than being irrelevant, is perhaps more important now than ever. Citing Parenti's (2001) work, McLaren notes how the fall of Soviet communism has eliminated socialist competition, allowing U.S. corporations to wage class war on the people of the world more ruthlessly than ever before. The result is major reductions in social spending, such as money on education, and more people being forced to sell their labor-power for more hours in today's U.S. service economy in order to survive. For example, between 1973 and 1994 the income of the richest 5% of the U.S. population increased 5%, whereas the income of the poorest 5% decreased by almost 2%, resulting in the top 5% receiving 46.9% of income and the bottom 5% receiving 4.2% (Kloby, 1999, p. 37).

However, Allman et al. (2002), promoting today's Marxist rejuvenation despite rampant postmodern criticism, argue that analyses that focus exclusively on describing the consequences of capitalism, such as social inequalities, can only take us so far. What is more, a focus on the consequences of capital run the risk of blurring the fact that social class is not a natural and inevitable category, but a contested social relationship based on the commodification and appropriation of human labor in the abstracted form of surplus-value. What is needed, the authors contend, is not just a description of the rampant injustices inherent in capitalist society, but a dialectical understanding of capitalism, which takes us to its heart: that is, to the use and exchange value of commodities.

Marx begins Volume 1 of *Capital* (1867/1967) with a discussion of commodities, because "the wealth of those societies in which the capitalist mode of production prevails, presents itself as 'an immense accumulation of commodities'" (p. 35). For products of human labor such as food or human labor itself to become commodities, they must first have a "use-value." That is, they must be of some use in terms of maintaining or reproducing humanity. Because most of what humans need to survive, such as clothing, food and shelter, requires human labor to produce them, human labor itself has "use-value" and is in fact the source of all value (Marx, 1967). Use-values, such as food, become "exchange-values" when they are exchanged for another product, such as medicine. Products become commodities when they are made for others and transferred to others through an exchange (Marx, 1967; Allman, 2001). However, products do not become commodities until they enter into the dialectical capital relation. That is, the working class, the source of all wealth, is the opposite of the capitalist class, whose wealth is dependent on the existence of an able and willing labor force. In other words, labor and capital define each other. Capitalism could not exist without a working class. The working class, on the other hand, is not dependent on capital, and would cease to exist as the working class without capital, the goal of their historic struggle (Marx, 1967; Cleaver, 2000; Allman et al., 2002). The basis of this relationship is the value inherent in the ability of humans to labor.

Human labor has a use-value to capital because it can be used to produce value and "surplus-value" (created by the human labor that exceeds what Marx called "necessary labour," that which is needed for survival). From the capitalist perspective, labor-power only has a use-value to capital, because only capital owns the means of production, which is why people are forced to exchange their ability to labor for a wage (Cleaver, 2000; Allman, 2001). Work therefore not only produces value, but it is also a form of social control (Cleaver, 2000). According to the capitalist view, the working class only finds an exchange value in its labor in the form of a wage. From the working class's perspective, on the other hand, its own labor-power has a use-value in terms of its ability to work for critical consciousness and to organize against the capital/labor relation, that is, to smash all useful labor within capital and replace it with the free association of people in the creation and recreation of our collective world (Cleaver, 2000; Hudis, 2000; Allman, 2001; McLaren, 2002). This difference in views underscores the contradictions embedded within the internal relations between capital and labor.

Allman et al. (2002) argue that the concept of internal relation "…is the key that unlocks the purported difficulty of Marx's thought" (p. 5). In Volume 1 of *Capital* (1967), Marx's analysis of the material reality of capitalist society led him to notice that the capital-labor dialectic represents the internal relation of opposites, where the positive element (capital) benefits from the relation, and the negative side (labor) is severely limited and often devastated by the relation (Allman et al., 2002). As a result, capitalism is based on the antagonistic relationship between two opposing forces, capitalists and those relegated to the status of worker. In other words, because capitalism becomes possible when people, out of necessity, are forced to sell their own labor as a commodity in the market, capitalism is defined by the existence of a capitalist class which purchases people's capacity to create more value than the minimum amount that is needed for them to survive. The further down wages are pushed and the more people are relegated to the working class, the more unpaid labor hours will be accumulated in the hands of the capitalist class (Allman et al., 2002, p. 15). The fact that labor is purchased for a wage hides the profit that is actually accumulated through this process (Marx, 1967; Allman, 2001; Merryfield, 2001).

What is more, capitalist education seeks to create larger pools of skilled workers than there are jobs for in order to weaken the working class through the creation of competition and division. This drives down the value of human labor-power and thus generates increasingly large sums of surplus-value, that is, capital, or what Marx called "dead labor" (McLaren & Baltodano, 2000; Allman et al., 2002).

However, as previously suggested, the history of the development of capital is a contested terrain. This is demonstrated, for example, by some of the consequences of capitalism, such as labor movements vying for a larger share of the value they create through their labor-power. The non-dialectical way "the lads" in Willis' (1977) study understood capitalism and their status as workers (described above) is also a consequence of capitalism. The role of revolutionary education is therefore to assist students to better understand how capitalism works through a multitude of pedagogical practices, such as "problem posing" (see Freire, 1970/1998). These practices are intended to enhance the liberatory tendencies among those relegated to the working class through critically reflecting on one's own experiences and assumptions about self, Other and the world.

McLaren's (2000) work on "revolutionary pedagogy" and Allman's (2001) work on "revolutionary education," for example, offer a framework to understand the role the working class plays in reproducing itself through education. That is, Allman et al. (2002) argue that the tension that exists between teachers and students (see Willis, 1977, for example) is representative of how capitalists divide and conquer the working class. Because the work of teachers, reproducing future labor-power through socializing their students into the capitalist system of production, is necessary labor for the creation of surplus-value, Allman et al. (2002) consider teachers to be part of the working class. To redress this dilemma, the authors argue that teachers need to better understand their own role in reproducing the working class as their own labor-power is increasingly commodified (i.e., used to produce value for others) as education is privatized (i.e., formerly public schools now for-profit under the management of private firms; see McLaren & Farahmandpur, 2001), which is central to the process of globalization (Rikowski, 2002). Similarly, Marxist social studies educator Rich Gibson (2000), describing what he considers to be the role of a radical educator, argues that workers such as teachers earning $45,000 are not capitalists, and are thus part of the working class. What is more, like Allman et al. (2002), Gibson (2000) argues that educators need to learn to ask important questions such as "where [does] value come from, and [what are] the social relations that rise from struggles over value[?]" (p. 14). These questions, Gibson contends, will facilitate the much-needed development, in students and teachers, of a critical understanding of capitalist society with the potential of challenging its internal relations.

Marxist educator Glenn Rikowski argues that McLaren's recent work on revolutionary pedagogy and its connection to teacher education has "...momentous implications and consequences for the anti-capitalist struggles ahead" (McLaren & Rikowski, 2001, p. 17) because it demands that teachers have a well-developed understanding of the "inner dynamics" of capitalism in order to understand what is happening to their students and themselves. McLaren argues that education is central to the perpetuation of capitalism, because teachers play a pivotal role in either developing or hindering students' understanding of capitalism and their relationship to it (McLaren & Rikowski, 2001; Allman et al., 2002). A revolutionary pedagogy can therefore assist students in uncovering and challenging the root causes of capitalism such as the commodification of labor (McLaren, 2000; Allman, 2001). I will now provide an outline of current social studies instruction and possibilities for the development of a Marxist social studies.

Preliminary Suggestions for a Marxist Social Studies

Based on the preceding discussion of how today's Marxist educators, as exemplified by McLaren, are talking about the "essence" of capitalism, that is, the social production of value and commodities, a Marxist social studies must go beyond describing the consequences of capitalism and join the struggle against the labor-capital relation. In other words, it must also go beyond arguing for a simple redistribution of wealth and the freeing of work from the constraints of capital, and instead work against the commodification of human labor-power. That is, it must work to completely destroy the capital relation (Hudis, 2000). A description of today's social studies instruction is, nevertheless, a useful place of departure for the outlining of a possible Marxist social studies.

In a discussion of today's social studies, Marc Pruyn (in press) quotes the official "primary purpose" of the social studies offered by the National Council for the Social Studies (NCSS), which is to "help…young people develop the ability to make informed and reasoned decisions for the public good as citizens of a culturally diverse, democratic society in an interdependent world." Pruyn argues that "…many in the criticalist tradition of social education [such as McLaren]…would consider [this definition] traditional, even 'conservative'" (p. 5, from original manuscript). A self-identified criticalist/Marxist, Pruyn makes the case that the social studies should not just develop "informed citizens" but should also foster the development of "…cultural/political social activists who are encouraged to manifest their beliefs with the ultimate goal of fighting oppression and furthering social justice" (p. 5, ibid).

Wayne Ross (2000) describes the social studies taught today throughout the U.S. public school system as dominated by "Traditional Social Studies Instruction" (TSSI), which he argues is based on such characteristics as memorizing disconnected facts, preparing students for standardized tests, treating learners as passive, normalizing white, middle-class culture and putting teachers at the center of learning. As a result, Ross argues that because of conservative teacher education programs, the institutional pressures schools place on teachers, and the traditional curriculum, the social studies tend to teach a spectator-oriented conception of democracy that helps to create spectator citizens unequipped to participate actively in a democracy (p. 55). This description of traditional social studies does not even foster the development of "informed citizens" as put forth by the NCSS.

Similarly, in *Getting Beyond the Facts* (2001), Joe Kincheloe argues that the current body of research on the social studies suggests that classroom instruction is more geared toward controlling student actions than engaging them in real learning (p. 17). Both students and teachers of the social studies thus tend to demonstrate a lack of interest in the topic. In his influential text *Lies My Teacher Told Me* (1995), James Loewen reports that the social studies has consistently been identified by students as the most boring subject in school, despite the fact that students tend to do better in it than other subjects. It is unique, argues Loewen, in that college and university professors agree that the more high school classes students have in social studies, the more misinformed they become about history, economics and the like. Because social studies is often presented from the distorted perspective of the ruling class, which commonly discounts the struggles of the poor, more oppressed students thus tend to do worse than less oppressed students. For example, students "of color" tend to do worse than "white" students in the social studies (Loewen, 1995). Moreover, based on Loewen's analysis of U.S. high-school history textbooks, the social studies tends to present social problems as already solved or about to be solved. Those problems are thus predictable; they are flooded with blind, over-optimistic patriotism; and they are anything but dialectical. In sum, U.S. history textbooks tend to keep students blind to the dialectical nature of history, and their main message is to be good and to not question authority, because capitalism, although slightly imperfect, is the only viable economic system the world always has and will ever have to offer.

The notion that capitalism is our only option is the perspective of capitalists themselves, not the perspective of the working class. What is more, today's TSSI serves the interests of maintaining the labor-capital relation by striving to engender a citizenry not only able, but also willing, to work as wage laborers, therefore producing that which oppresses us: capital. Where, then, can we, the educational left, as community workers, turn for ideas about how to combat the root causes of capitalism? The critical social studies educators cited herein argue for an equal distribution of wealth and the development of an informed citizenry capable of actively participating in a democracy. For example, Wayne Ross (2000), arguing against the development of passive citizens through TSSI, holds that "...citizens should have the opportunity to inform themselves; take part in inquiry, discussion and policy formation; and advance their ideas through political action" (p. 55).

A Marxist social studies, on the other hand, would work to foster the development of a citizenry not only able to engage in debate and inquiry for social justice, but against the labor-capital relation in particular. That is, it would work to engender a citizenry aware of the intricate workings of capitalism and their particular location within the production process of value. To reiterate, Gibson (2000), for example, argues that a Marxist social studies should ask questions such as "...where [does] value come from (labor), and [what are] the social relations that rise from struggles over value?" (p. 14). Gibson states that these are "key" economic questions that have been "erased" by capital's influence over the social studies. These and other questions would play a fundamental role in the development of a Marxist social studies.

Conclusion

Finally, through the contested terrain of the "social universe of capital," which is everywhere all the time, the relation between labor and capital must be successfully challenged if humanity is to have a future at all (Rikowski, 2002; Allman, 2001). The social studies, and education in general, could play an increasingly important role in this process by radicalizing teacher education programs through the reintroduction of Marxist theory. Central to a Marxist social studies should be an acknowledgment of the partial autonomy of working-class culture (Cleaver, 2000) as demonstrated by Willis' (1977) study of student resistance. That is, a Marxist social studies should choose as a point of departure the working class's various levels of consciousness, challenging student resistors, for example, to extend their views and actions to more revolutionary levels through an active engagement with Marxism. McLaren's (2000) work on revolutionary and Marxist pedagogy, I believe, should play a pivotal role in this process.

References

Allman, P. (2001). *Critical education against global capitalism: Karl Marx and revolutionary critical education.* London: Bergin & Garvey.

Allman, P., McLaren, P. & Rikowski, G. (2002). After the box people: The labour-capital relation as class constitution—and its consequences for Marxist education theory and human resistance. On-line at http://www.ieps.org.uk.

Bowles, S. & Gintis, H. (1976). *Schooling in capitalist America: Educational reform and the contradictions of economic life.* New York: Basic.

Chomsky, N. (1999). *Profit over people: Neoliberalism and global order.* New York: Seven Stories.

Cleaver, H. (2000). *Reading capital politically.* San Francisco: AK Press.

Dewey, J. (1916). *Democracy and education.* New York: The Free Press.

Freire, P. (1998). *Pedagogy of the oppressed.* New York: Continuum. (Original work published 1970)

Gibson, R. (2000). Methods for social studies: How do I keep my ideals and still teach? Online at http://www-rohan.sdsu.edu/~rgibson/Methods.htm.

Hudis, P. (2000). Can capital be controlled? *The Journal of Marxist-Humanism.* On-line at http://www.newsandletters.org.

Hursh, D. & Ross, W. (Eds.). (2000). *Democratic social education: Social studies for social change.* New York: Falmer Press.

Kincheloe, J. (2001). *Getting beyond the facts: Teaching social studies/social sciences in the twenty-first century.* New York: Peter Lang.

Kincheloe, J., Slattery, P. & Steinberg, S. (2000). *Contextualizing teaching.* New York: Longman.

Kloby, J. (1999). *Inequality, power and development: The task of political sociology.* New York: Humanity Books.

Loewen, J. (1995). *Lies my teacher told me: Everything your American History textbook got wrong.* New York: Simon & Schuster.

Marx, K. (1967). *Capital: A critical analysis of capitalist production.* New York: International Publishers. (Original work published 1867)

McLaren, P. (1989). *Life in schools: An introduction to critical pedagogy in the foundations of education.* New York: Longman.

———. (2000). *Ché Guevara, Paulo Freire, and the pedagogy of revolution.* New York: Rowman & Littlefield.

———. (2002). Marxist revolutionary praxis: A curriculum of transgression. *Journal of Critical Inquiry into Curriculum and Instruction*, 3(3), 36–41.

McLaren, P. & Baltodano, M. (2000). The future of teacher education and the politics of resistance. *Teaching Education*, 11(1), 47–58.

———. (2001). Educational policy and the socialist imagination: Revolutionary citizenship as a pedagogy of resistance. *Educational Policy*, 15(3), 343–378.

McLaren, P. & Rikowski, G. (2001). Pedagogy for revolution against education for capital: An e-dialogue on education in capitalism today. Available on-line at http://eserver.org/clogic/4-1/mclaren%26rikowski.html.

Merryfield, A. (2001). Metro Marxism, or old and young Marx in the city. *Socialism and Democracy*, 15(2), 63–84.

Parenti, M. (2001). Rollback: Aftermath of the overthrow of communism. In G. Katsafanas (Ed.), *After the fall: 1989 and the future of freedom* (pp. 153–158). New York: Routledge.

Pinar, W., Reynolds, W., Slattery, P. & Taubman, P. (2000). *Understanding curriculum: An introduction to the study of historical and contemporary curriculum discourses.* New York: Peter Lang.

Pruyn, M. (in press). Paulo Freire and critical multicultural social studies: One case from the teacher education borderlands. *Taboo: The Journal of Culture and Education.*

Rikowski, G. (1997). Scorched earth: Prelude to rebuilding Marxist educational theory. *British Journal of Sociology of Education*, 18(4), 551–574.

———. (2002). Transfiguration: Globalization, the World Trade Organization and the national faces of the GATS. On-line at http://www.ieps.org.uk.

Ross, W. (2000). Diverting democracy: The curriculum standards movement and social studies education. In D. Hursh & W. Ross (Eds.), *Democratic social education: Social studies for social change* (pp. 43–63). New York: Falmer Press.

Saxe, D. (1991). *Social studies in schools: A history of the early years.* Albany: State University of New York Press.

Willis, P. (1977). *Learning to labour: How working-class kids get working-class jobs.* Westmead, England: Saxon House.

Contributors

Roberto E. Bahruth
roberto@mac.boisestate.edu

Roberto Bahruth is a fluent speaker of Spanish who learned the language while living and working for eight years in Latin America. He has taught English as a Second Language since 1974. While teaching in a bilingual fifth grade in Texas, he employed a whole language approach with his students. *Literacy con Cariño* is their success story (Heinemann Educational Books, 1991). A new edition of *Literacy con Cariño* was released in 1998 and includes a foreword by Paulo Freire & Donaldo Macedo. Roberto holds a Ph.D. in Applied Linguistics and Bilingual Education from The University of Texas at Austin. While at UT, he received the George I. Sánchez Endowed Presidential Scholarship for significant contributions to the field of minority education. He has also been honored as an invited guest lecturer at Harvard University during the spring semester of 1996; guest lecturer at Sun Yat sen National University in Kaohsiung, Taiwan; at Seminar Kibbutzim Teachers' College in Tel Aviv, Israel; Hebrew University, Jerusalem; with the Ministry of Education, State of Israel, Jerusalem; and San Carlos National University in Guatemala. Presently, he is Professor of Teacher Education at Boise State University, specializing in Literacy, Bilingual Education and Applied Linguistics. He was honored with the "Outstanding Faculty Award 1997-98" by the Associated Students of Boise State University. Most recently he received the Top Ten Scholars Award 2002 at Boise State University.

Alípio Casali
a.casali@uol.com.br

Alípio Casali is a philosopher and an educator. He is a professor at the Pontifícia Universidade Católica de São Paulo, where he worked closely with Paulo

Freire (1990-1997). Additionally, he worked within the Government of the city of São Paulo (1989-1992).

Mike Cole
mike.cole2@ntlworld.com

Mike Cole is Senior Lecturer in Education at the University of Brighton, England. He has written extensively on equality issues. Recent publications include *Red Chalk: On Schooling, Capitalism and Politics,* Brighton: Institute for Education Policy Studies (2001); *Schooling and Equality: Fact Concept and Policy,* London: Kogan Page (2001); *Education Equality and Human Rights*, London: Routledge/Falmer (2002); *Marxism Against Postmodernism in Educational Theory,* Lanham, MD: Lexington Press (2002) and *Professional Values and Practice for Teachers and Student Teachers,* London: David Fulton (2003). A second, completely revised edition of *Education Equality and Human Rights,* with a foreword by Peter McLaren, will be published by Routledge/Falmer in 2005. He is the author of *Marxism, Postmodernism and Education: Pasts, Presents and Futures*, London: Routledge/Falmer (forthcoming 2005).

Antonia Darder
adarder@uiuc.edu

Antonia Darder is professor of Educational Policy Studies and Latino Studies at University of Illinois, Urbana Champaign. Her teaching and research focus on questions of racism and class inequality, as these relate to issues of culture, class, language and pedagogy. Her books include *Culture and Power in the Classroom, Reinventing Paulo Freire: A Pedagogy of Love*, and *After Race: Racism after Multiculturalism.*

Alicia de Alba
postupv@xal.megared.net.mx

Alicia de Alba is a full-time researcher with the National Autonomous University of Mexico and the National System for Research in Mexico. She conducted her postgraduate research with Ernesto Laclau at the Centre for Theoretical Studies in the Humanities and the Social Sciences at the University of Essex, in England. She has been invited to deliver papers and seminars by universities in Mexico, Argentina, Costa Rica, Cuba, Ecuador, Great Britain, Spain, the United

States, Canada and Australia. Since 1988, she has had an intense intellectual relationship with Peter McLaren. Her specialty fields include curriculum and the pedagogy of cultural contact.

Ramin Farahmandpur
farahmandpur@hotmail.com

Ramin Farahmandpur is an assistant professor in the Department of Educational Policy, Foundations and Administrative Studies at Portland State University. He completed his Ph.D. with an emphasis in Curriculum Theory and Teaching Studies from the Graduate School of Education and Informational Studies at UCLA. Farahmandpur has authored and co-authored a number of essays on a wide range of topics including globalization, Imperialism, neoliberalism, Marxism, and Critical Pedagogy. His forthcoming book (with Peter McLaren) entitled *Teaching against Globalization and the New Imperialism: Essays on Critical Pedagogy* will soon be published by Rowman & Littlefield.

Ana Maria Araújo Freire
nitafreire@uol.com.br

Ana Maria Araújo Freire holds a Ph.D. in education from São Paulo Catholic University. She wrote the afterword and the clarifying notes for Paulo Freire's *Pedagogy of Hope* (1996). She is co-editor of *The Paulo Freire Reader* (1998) with Donaldo Macedo and the author of *Literacy in Brazil.* She has presented internationally at conferences and as a guest speaker on such themes as educational reform, social justice and emancipation. Much of her current work also involves publishing the final texts of her late husband, Paulo Freire, as well as continuing his legacy—in theory and practice—of promoting emancipatory, loving, revolutionary pedagogy.

María Marcela González Arenas
postupv@xal.megared.net.mx

María Marcela González Arenas cuenta con la Maestría en Educación (U.P.V.), el Diplomado en Historia de México y el Diplomado en Informática Aplicada a la Educación, es Candidata a Doctor en Historia y Estudios Regionales (Instituto de Investigaciones Histórico Sociales de la U.V.). Autora de diversos ensayos y traducciones de artículos y libros publicados por instituciones educativas y la UNAM en editoriales como Siglo XXI, Editores, Miguel Ángel Porrúa y Ediciones Pomares de España, así como la traducción del libro: *Life in Schools* del Peter McLaren y de varios libros de Colin Lankshear. Actualmente es Coordinadora General de la Maestría en Educación y la Especialidad en Investigación Educativa de la misma universidad y participa en la Integración del Estado de Conocimiento de Filosofía, Teoría y Campo de la Educación con el Consejo Mexicano de Investigación Educativa y en otros proyectos interinstitucionales nacionales e internacionales de investigación educativa y educación ambiental con el CESU de la UNAM.

María Marcela González Arenas holds an MA in education, a specialization in Mexican history, and is a doctoral candidate in history and regional studies. She has authored various essyas and tranlated numerous articles and books into Spanish, including *Life in Schools* by Peter McLaren and various books by Colin Lankshear. She is also an activist and leader in Mexico in the area of educational research.

Dave Hill
dave.hill@northampton.ac.uk

Dave Hill is Professor of Education Policy at University College Northampton, UK. He has been an elected labor movement activist and representative since the 1960s. In 1989 he co-founded the Hillcole Group of Radical Left Educators (with Mike Cole) and the independent Radical Left policy unit the Institute for Education Policy Studies (www.ieps.org.uk). In 2003 he founded (and is currently chief editor of) the *Journal for Critical Education Policy Studies* (www.jceps.com). He writes in the area of Marxist analysis of education policy, neo-liberalism, capital, economic and social equality and justice. His most recent books, with Mike Cole, Peter McLaren and Glenn Rikowski, are *Red Chalk: On Schooling, Capitalism and Politics* (Brighton: Institute for Education Policy Studies, 2001) and *Marxism Against Postmodernism in Educational Theory* (Lexington Books, 2002). His next books are *New Labour and Education: Policy, (In)Equality and Capital* (Tufnell Press, 2004) and *Charge of the Right Brigade: The Radical Right Restructuring of Schooling and Initial Teacher Education in England and Wales under the Conservative and New Labour Governments 1979-2004* (Lampeter, Wales: Edwin Mellen Press, 2005). He describes himself as "a deaf, working class, democratic socialist/Marxist activist."

Luis Huerta-Charles
lhuertac@nmsu.edu

Luis Huerta-Charles is an Assistant Professor from Mexico who teaches Early Childhood/Bilingual Education at New Mexico State University. His experiences as a bilingual learner have been invaluable to him in exploring issues of early childhood education, teacher education, and bilingual education related to socially just practices in the Borderlands.

Pepi Leistyna
pleistyna@hotmail.com

Pepi Leistyna is an Assistant Professor in the Applied Linguistics Graduate Studies Program at the University of Massachusetts Boston, where he coordinates the research program and teaches courses in cultural studies, media analysis, and language acquisition. Speaking internationally on issues of democracy and education, a Fellow of the Education Policy Research Unit, and Associate Editor of the *Journal of English Linguistics*, Leistyna's books include *Breaking Free: The Transformative Power of Critical Pedagogy*, *Presence of Mind: Education and the Politics of Deception*, *Defining and Designing Multiculturalism*, *Corpus Analysis: Language Structure and Language Use* and *Cultural Studies: From Theory to Action.*

Zeus Leonardo
zleonard@csulb.edu

Zeus Leonardo has published articles and book chapters on critical education and social theory with special attention to issues of race, class, and gender. He is the author of *Ideology, Discourse, and School Reform* (2003, Praeger). His recent work can best be described as the political integration of ideology critique and discourse analysis. Zeus is currently an Assistant Professor in the College of Education at California State University, Long Beach.

Curry Malott
currymalott@hotmail.com

Curry Malott has taught sociology and social studies at New México State University, multicultural education at Oregon State University and is now an Assistant Professor of education at Brooklyn College. Dr. Malott also continues to participate in local sk8boarding and music scenes, not only through skateboarding and playing music, but by recording musical artists who skate. He is the founder of Punk Army Sk8boards & Records. He is the author of numerous articles and book chapters dealing with revolutionary, and potentially revolutionary, movements within popular culture. His most recent book, with Milagros Peña, *Punk Rockers' Revolution*, has just been published through Peter Lang.

Marcia Moraes
msmoraes@gbl.com.br

Marcia Moraes is a Professor at Universidade do Estado do Rio de Janeiro (UERJ-Brazil). During her first years in the field of education, she was an elementary, secondary and high school teacher. She is also a former Associate Professor at the University of St. Thomas-Minnesota. Her publications include diverse articles in education and the books *Bilingual Education: A Dialogue with the Bakhtin Circle* (U.S.: SUNY) and *Ser Humana: Quando a mulher está em discussão* (Brazil: DP&A).

Marc Pruyn
profefronterizo@yahoo.com

Marc is an Associate Professor of social studies education and as the Director of Elementary Education at New México State University. His research interests include exploring the connections between education for social justice, multiculturalism, critical pedagogy and theory, and the social studies in the Chihuahuan Borderlands and beyond. Turn-ons: Marxism; anarchism; zombie movies; and, playing the drums. Turn-offs: W; empire; sexism; and, capitalism.

Shirley R. Steinberg
msgramsci@aol.com

Shirley Steinberg is the head of the graduate Program of Literacy at Brooklyn College and the author many books, chapters and articles, including *Kinderculture*, *13 Questions* and *Changing Multiculturalism*. She is a leading figure in the fields of critical pedagogy, cultural studies and educational foundations.

TEACHING CONTEMPORARY SCHOLARS

Joe L. Kincheloe & Shirley R. Steinberg
General Editors

This innovative series addresses the pedagogies and thoughts of influential contemporary scholars in diverse fields. Focusing on scholars who have challenged the "normal science," the dominant frameworks of particular disciplines, *Teaching Contemporary Scholars* highlights the work of those who have profoundly influenced the direction of academic work. In a era of great change, this series focuses on the bold thinkers who provide not only insight into the nature of the change but where we should be going in light of the new conditions. Not a festschrift, not a re-interpretation of past work, these books allow the reader a deeper, yet accessible conceptual framework in which to negotiate and expand the work of important thinkers.

For additional information about this series or for the submission of manuscripts, please contact:

Joe L. Kincheloe & Shirley R. Steinberg
c/o Peter Lang Publishing, Inc.
275 Seventh Avenue, 28th floor
New York, New York 10001

To order other books in this series, please contact our Customer Service Department:

(800) 770-LANG (within the U.S.)
(212) 647-7706 (outside the U.S.)
(212) 647-7707 FAX

Or browse online by series:

WWW.PETERLANGUSA.COM